THE POLITICS OF JUSTICE

THE
POLITICS OF JUSTICE

Lower Federal
Judicial Selection
and the
Second Party System,
1829–61

KERMIT L. HALL

UNIVERSITY OF NEBRASKA PRESS
LINCOLN AND LONDON

Portions of chapters 1 and 10 previously appeared in somewhat
different form in, respectively, *Michigan History* 59 (Fall 1975) and
the *Vanderbilt Law Review* 29 (October 1976), © 1976 by the Vanderbilt School of Law.

The publication of this book was assisted by a grant from The
Andrew W. Mellon Foundation.

Publishers on the Plains

UNP

Manufactured in the United States of America

Library of Congress Cataloging in Publication Data

Hall, Kermit.
  The politics of justice.

  Bibliography: p. 233
  Includes index.
  1. Judges—United States—Appointment, qualifications, tenure, etc.—
History. 2. Political parties—United States—History. 3. United States—Politics and
government—1815–1861. I. Title.
KF8776.H34   347'.73'14   79–9238
ISBN 0–8032–2302–1

For Phyllis and Katherine

CONTENTS

LIST OF TABLES

PREFACE

This book attempts to construct a bridge between generations of American historians while integrating the interests of constitutional, legal, and political scholars in a long-neglected topic—the selection of lower federal court judges. In assessing the contradictory currents in that process during the second party system, I have avoided trying to reconstruct every nomination. I have chosen, instead, in each administration, nominations that illuminate unique problems and that allow for comparison over time. Of course, the past reveals itself only grudgingly; many of the most valuable records and personal correspondence relating to judicial appointments are lost or destroyed. The central figures in the selection process—the presidents—usually did not commit to writing their precise reasons for making specific nominations. In a compensatory effort, I have cast a wide net for sources, emphasized those nominations about which abundant material exists in the National Archives, and constructed a collective portrait of the nominees. Although the collective portrait does not fit neatly with a chronologically organized text, the detailed information about the nominees themselves helps to clarify the process by which they were selected.

In researching and writing this book, I have accumulated many institutional, professional, and personal debts. There are more persons than I could possibly acknowledge, but I am especially grateful to Donald Mossholder and Charles Stovall of the Legislative, Judicial, and Diplomatic Records Division of the National Archives and R. Michael McReynolds, Assistant to the Archivist of the United States. The staffs of the Library of Congress and the Genealogical Society Library of the Church of Jesus Christ of Latter-Day-Saints in Salt Lake City, Utah, were especially generous with their time and resources. The American Council of Learned Societies, the American Philosophical Society, the Vanderbilt University Research Council, and Wayne State University extended financial assistance.

I am grateful to the Michigan History Division, Michigan Department of State, for permission to use portions of my essay "Andrew Jackson and the Judiciary: The Michigan Territorial Judiciary as a Test Case, 1828–1832," which originally appeared in *Michigan History*, in chapter 1, and to the editor of the *Vanderbilt Law Review* for permission to reprint in chapter 10 material which originally appeared under the title "240 Men: The Antebellum Lower Federal Judiciary, 1829–61," © 1976 by the Vanderbilt School of Law.

Over the past four years several colleagues provided aid, comfort, and criticism. Maxwell Bloomfield, Don H. Doyle, Richard E. Ellis, James W. Ely, Jr., John W. Johnson, Robert J. Kaczorowski, Richard Latner, Melvyn P. Leffler, Samuel T. McSeveney, R. Kent Newmyer, James Rawley, John R. Schmidhauser, George D. Sussman, and Mary K. B. Tachau read and commented on part or all of the manuscript. Paul L. Murphy and William J. Brazill, Jr., displayed the confidence in and patience with this project that prove once again that open minds and compassionate souls still thrive within the history profession. Finally, I owe a special debt to my wife, Phyllis, who typed and proofed the manuscript more times than either of us wish to remember. Together they saved me from many egregious errors, but the shortcomings that remain are my own.

INTRODUCTION

American historical writing proceeds on the whole on a generational basis, but even within the context of this process the shift in emphasis in the study of the pre–Civil War years has been particularly dramatic. An earlier generation treated these years as a prelude to Fort Sumter; the study of antebellum politics was an exercise in Civil War causality, with slavery and sectionalism the most important ingredients. A recent generation of scholars—the so-called new political historians—have taken exception to this "Civil War synthesis"; they insist on appreciating the political culture of the era on its own terms in order to illuminate the historical process of political development and the antecedents of contemporary political institutions.

Methodological differences further widen the generational gap. Through quantitative methods, case studies, and behavioralist theory the new political historians have systematically tested and found wanting many earlier assumptions about antebellum politics. Ethnocultural conflict, for example, appears to them to explain more about popular voting habits on the local and state level than did slavery and sectionalism. They have also shifted attention to the historical role of antebellum parties, and this emphasis has lent a sense of developmental coherence to the study of politics; the party system of the pre–Civil War era has emerged not as an isolated entity but as one of a series of two-party systems that have risen, stabilized, and collapsed since 1789.

The second party system, so called to distinguish it from earlier party competition between Federalists and Jeffersonians, began with the election of Andrew Jackson in 1828 and ended with the election of Abraham Lincoln in 1860.[1] The second party system was the product of a distinctive political culture in which popular participation and partisanship replaced social deference and disdain of party.

The new political historians know little about the impact of the new mass political parties on practices other than voting and legislative behavior. The advent of the new party system surely touched other aspects of political life. Did, for example, the traditional forms of political organization, such as friendship and kinship alliances, disappear? If so, was this development coincidental with the inauguration of Andrew Jackson? Or, did it occur later? The concept of party system and its corollary notion of political modernization accentuate abrupt change by obscuring the persistence of traditional forms of political activity. The new political history has deflated the more excessive claims about the impact of slavery, sectionalism, and territorial expansion, but other dimensions of antebellum politics require attention before the insights of both generations can be forged into a meaningful synthesis.

Historians interested in antebellum politics might profitably turn to topics other than voting and legislative behavior. They have alternately cast the Democratic and Whig parties as either "electoral machines" consumed by the practical problems of winning elections or engines of ideology run by like-minded men of distinct socioeconomic positions committed to the maintenance of certain critical beliefs. These conflicting views of the nature of the party system have been tested most frequently against the actions of voters and legislators. Parties, however, fulfill functions other than those of selecting candidates, contesting elections, and organizing legislative bodies. They have also participated in the recruitment of nonelected governmental decision-makers, such as federal district and territorial judges.

Except in the case of Supreme Court justices, the politics of federal judicial selection during the second party system has never received serious historical attention. Traditionally, constitutional historians have analyzed the evolution of public law through Supreme Court decisions, while legal historians have examined the evolution of statutes, legal procedures, and the careers of such luminaries as Chancellor James Kent. While both constitutional and legal historians have in recent years demonstrated an increasing sensitivity to the work of social and political historians, they have not thought it necessary to investigate the social bases of the judiciary or the way in which judges received their posts. Political historians, for the most part, have almost totally ignored what President James K. Polk called the "secret history of the federal government"—the distribution of the federal patronage.[2]

Political scientists, on the other hand, have paid close attention to the judicial selection process, judicial backgrounds, and the politics of court administration. While concentrating on the twentieth century, such scholars as Joel Grossman, John Schmidhauser, and Harold Chase have plumbed the rich interaction of legal and partisan values in the selection process. Their studies suggest that historians can enhance their understanding of the interconnectedness of law, society, and politics by devoting more attention to the lower federal courts and the distribution of the judicial patronage.

Patronage denotes the reciprocal relations between persons with power to bestow favors and persons anxious to receive favors. Like voting and legislative behavior, the distribution of political influence through the judicial patronage during the era of the second party system can be viewed in the context of political modernization. Indeed, such a perspective offers a useful heuristic tool by which to integrate this study with much of the recent literature on political parties.

The argument that the judicial selection process mirrors political modernization involves two issues—the extent to which the process became institutionalized and the degree to which a functional elite replaced a traditional elite. In a modernizing political culture, critical political activities become institutionalized—that is, the decision-making process tends to become formal, impersonal, automatic, and bureaucratic—and nominees for appointment to public office are usually selected on the basis of special training and experience.[3] The first question, then, has to do with how the judges were brought to the bench; the second, with who the judges were.

In a developing political culture party politicians distribute public offices in exchange for support. In this sense patronage is formal; the allocation of offices is a calculated activity in which party interests take precedence over personal wishes. This party-directed mode of patronage has two purposes. First, parties rely on the patronage to reward or discipline followers or to lure new adherents. Second, parties fulfill the administrative task of organizing the government through the allocation of appointive offices. However, in attempting to satisfy partisan and public demands, parties contend with the often frustrating practical realities of public service. Low pay, uncertain tenure, and indifferent working conditions may dissuade the best and most politically acceptable candidates from accepting public office.

In a traditional political culture patronage involves an informal hierarchy of kinship and friendship relations in which persons possessed of influence bring it to bear in behalf of their clients (kinsmen and friends). Kinship ties may be of two kinds: consanguineal or affinal.

In the former, two persons are kin if one is descended from the other or if both are descended from a common ancestor. In the latter, the kinship relations are created by marriage. The term friendship also has two meanings. It may refer to an expressive or emotional psychological relationship, or it may denote an instrumental relationship, in which persons join in a mutual agreement to strive cooperatively after certain goals. Kinship and instrumental friendship do not necessarily displace institutional relations; however, their existence suggests that generalizations about a political culture which stress modernizing qualities (i.e., a shared party membership) must take account of these informal subterranean connections.

During the period from 1829 to 1861 parties imposed institutional coherence on the judicial selection process. With the exceptions of the Tyler and Fillmore administrations, presidents from Jackson through Buchanan shared the partisan affiliation of their judicial nominees. In this broad sense parties fulfilled the administrative task of recruiting lower court judges—an activity that paralleled the better-known purpose of the second party system, the organizing of the electorate. Through control of the White House, Democrats dominated the selection process; they constituted 80 percent of all judicial nominees.[4]

Understanding the selection process and the development of the antebellum political culture begins, but does not end, with this discovery of partisan consistency. The aberrations in party uniformity during the Tyler and Fillmore administrations require explanation. Further, the dynamic process of distribution of political influence can best be understood by discerning who controlled the allocation of these offices and how they did so. A chief purpose of this book is to identify the principal mediators who influenced the outcome of the selection process. Only by identifying these principal mediators is it possible to speculate with confidence about the extent to which the selection process kept pace with the modernization of the political culture. Senators, representatives, territorial party leaders, sitting lower court judges, and Supreme Court justices all had an opportunity in the constitutionally open selection process to mediate the selection of lower court judges. Of these, senators of the president's party are usually assumed, through the extra constitutional practice of senatorial courtesy, to have exercised a decisive influence over appointments to the district court bench. This practice means that if a senator of the president's party objects to a court nomination in his state, the full Senate will vote against the nominee. It also implies that when vacancies occur, the president will defer to the opinions of the senators in his party who represent the involved states. The practice of senatorial courtesy and the executive branch's internal organization of the selection process are the two most critical elements in the institutionalization of the selection process. Most scholars have agreed that senatorial courtesy emerged full-blown with the advent of competitive Whig and Democratic parties in 1840. This was not so.

Traditional personal connections bound mediators to successful judicial candidates. Thirty percent of all judicial nominees during the era of the second party system had consanguineal or affinal ties to principal mediators. The frequency of these connections varied: Jackson, for example, made 47 percent of his nominations from candidates with these family connections.[5] In the midst of this supposedly modern mass two-party system, significant vestiges of a traditional political order persisted.

THE POLITICS OF JUSTICE

I

THE KING OF ENGLAND

James G. Bryce nominated to the Senate for the appointment of Judge in the United States Court!! Good God sir is
it possible??? Have the President and his advisors become so
hardened so *reckless* so *indifferent* to their reputations and
standing in this state? —Andrew W. McDonald to William
Armstrong, February 19, 1832[1]

Contradictory evidence has fostered disagreement about Andrew
Jackson, his presidency, and the early Democratic party. Increasingly,
however, Old Hickory and the Democracy have appeared as the pro-
totypes of modern party politics. Jackson, it has been argued, was the
"first modern President," who enhanced the powers of the chief
executive through resort to the veto, insistence on separation of powers, and systematic distribution of public offices to the party faithful.
The Democratic party succumbed to this political revolution; a new
breed of party politician devised "specialized, large scale organizations, flexible, functional and impersonal," to supplant the political
rule of traditional oligarchical elites.[2]

Jackson's presence in the White House altered the political scene,
but too frequently historians have emphasized terms such as "revolutionary" and "modern" to the neglect of historical continuity. Voter
turnout in Jackson's two successful presidential campaigns revealed
heightened popular interest in national affairs; however, until 1840
even more voters participated in state elections, an indication of the
continued primacy of state politics. A national two-party system
emerged only gradually; National Republicans, Anti-Masons, Nullifiers, and Bank Democrats coalesced in the Whig party in 1836, but
not until 1840 did that party offer a single presidential candidate. In
the 1830s leaders such as Martin Van Buren gradually surmounted
suspicion of parties, but Whigs claimed rhetorically to be a no-party
party. Furthermore, like the city from which he governed, Jackson
was isolated and vulnerable, the captive of slow transportation and
rudimentary communications. Old Hickory had to span the administrative and political distance separating the capital of the nation from
the states, and he had to conquer the inertia of a generation of presidential subservience to Congress.[3]

The president understood that he might foster national cohesion and instill new respect for the presidency by mustering the decentralized and loosely organized Democratic party. Distribution of the federal offices was one means of furthering these mutually reinforcing goals. He confided to Martin Van Buren in 1832 that he sought "to administer the government in such a way as will strengthen the Democratic party, unite the whole and provide the greatest prosperity to our beloved country."[4] He vowed to impose an impersonal efficiency on government by rotation-in-office, replacing officeholders appointed by earlier administrations with loyal Democrats. Jackson also insisted on an end to nepotism; the selection of kinsmen for office abetted political corruption and inefficiency and allowed a few men to control the administrative machinery of government. This scheme of rotation-in-office stressed rational efficiency, but Jackson was less concerned with expertise than with the moral and political fitness of his nominees. When critics charged that his policies deprived the public of experienced servants, the president replied that the duties of "all public officials" were "so plain" that "men of intelligence" could qualify.[5] Intelligence alone would not suffice. "In a free government," he concluded, "the demand for moral qualities should be made superior to that of talents."[6] These were hardly the sentiments of a modern bureaucrat.

Jackson proceeded with restraint and even ambivalence in distributing federal offices. National Republicans, and later Whigs, portrayed Old Hickory as a true spoilsman; they denounced him for undermining "the integrity of government" by abusing the "most delicate and important branch of executive power."[7] Jackson, however, viewed politicians generally and party men especially with suspicion; he refused to conceive of his efforts to restore virtuous government as a strictly partisan enterprise. While proclaiming a policy of rotation-in-office that brought roars of protest from his opponents, he made relatively few removals; indeed, during eight years he removed slightly more than one-third of all officers requiring Senate confirmation.[8]

Lower federal judgeships were amongst the most important offices Jackson filled. As with other matters of public policy, the president held contradictory views of the federal judiciary. Like vocal state rights Democrats in Congress, Jackson distrusted the federal courts. He believed in the sovereignty of the states and he claimed the prerogative to interpret the Constitution without regard to the judiciary. Yet, like conservative and moderate congressional Democrats, Jackson respected the concept of separation of powers; he recognized the responsibility of the federal judiciary to settle a host of constitutional issues. He complained, for example, that South Carolina Nullifiers threatened the Union because they refused to submit their grievances to the federal courts. He resisted pleas by radical congressional Democrats who wanted to "reform" the lower federal courts by restricting their jurisdiction, and he refused to endorse repeal of the Judiciary Act of 1789. To the contrary, he urged extension of the federal circuit court system and requested Congress to strengthen the office of attorney general.[9]

The historical development of the lower federal courts and constitutional and legal provisions governing the judicial selection process limited Jackson's independence in making judicial nominations. Diversity and administrative decentralization characterized the lower federal courts. Jackson and his successors during the era of the second party system had to fill vacancies in two kinds of lower federal courts, one constitutional, the other legislative. Under Article III, section 1, of the Constitution, the first Congress created a three-tiered structure of constitutional courts. Beneath the Supreme Court of the United States, the court of final review which alone was specified in Article III, the Judiciary Act of 1789 established two levels of inferior federal tribunals, the district and circuit courts. The former were courts of first instance presided over by a single judge. The most important jurisdiction granted these courts was over admiralty and maritime causes. Each district court was made responsive to local interests by being established wholly within the boundaries of a particular state and by being required to adopt the procedures and fees followed in the courts of that state. The circuit courts encompassed several states and exercised important original, as well as some appellat, jurisdiction. With the brief exception of the years from 1801 to 1802, the circuit courts were not permanently staffed; instead, justices of the Supreme Court sat with a district judge from the state in which the circuit was held to try cases.[10]

Congress also established legislative courts in the territories under the power of Article IV, section 3, of the Constitution. These courts were not established by the Judiciary Act of 1789 but by the legislative acts organizing each territory. Territorial courts did not exercise the "judicial power of the United States," but they formed an integral part of the federal judicial system by bringing to the distant and sparsely settled territories the authority of the central government. They heard not only cases arising under federal law but controversies involving the common law and acts of the territorial legislature; simultaneously, they fulfilled the roles of both state and federal courts. The organization of these courts varied, but Congress typically provided a three-man bench; the judges sat *en banc* as a court of appeals and presided over jury trials in separate districts within the territory.[11]

Different constitutional and legal provisions affected the selection of judges for the constitutional and legislative courts. Article II, section 2, of the Constitution required the Senate to advise and consent to nominations made by the president "of Judges of the Supreme Court and all other officers of the United States." District court judges were considered "superior" officers subject to Senate approval.[12] By requiring the consent of the Senate, the Constitution insured that local interests would have an important role in the selection process. The Judiciary Act of 1789 reinforced the importance of localism by requiring that each district judge "reside in the district . . . for which he was appointed."[13] By the time of Jackson's administration, the policy of nominating state residents was thoroughly established. Once appointed, district judges enjoyed significant independence: their salaries could not be diminished, and they held office during good behavior subject only to removal through the impeachment process.

Jackson had greater discretion to mold the territorial than the district court judiciary. In organizing every territory, Congress specified that the Senate advise and consent to judicial nominations, but inasmuch as the territories had only a single delegate to Congress without a vote in the Senate, the president could exercise greater discretion in making selections unimpeded by members of the upper house who might claim the right to designate a nominee. Furthermore, after 1789 territorial judges gradually lost their independence. At first Congress granted these judges tenure during good behavior, but by the mid-1820s this practice changed; a limited term of four years replaced good behavior. Not only could a president be certain that the territorial judiciary would turn over once every four years, but the Supreme Court in *American Insurance Company* v. *Canter* in 1828 decided that territorial judges were not protected under Article III; therefore, the president, if he wished, might ignore the impeachment process and summarily remove territorial judges before the expiration of their terms.[14]

In filling vacancies in the constitutional and legislative courts, Jackson had little administrative assistance. The secretary of state was the most important cabinet officer. Jackson's four secretaries of state monitored requests for judicial patronage—receiving, organizing, and keeping on file letters sent from applicants and their supporters. Frequently members of Congress addressed the president, but the bulk of this correspondence ultimately went into the files of the secretary of state.

Jackson actively participated in the selection process. He viewed all of the correspondence, often scribbling on the letters specific instructions about how the administration should proceed to fill a particular vacancy. Sensitive to the discretionary powers of the federal judiciary, Jackson appreciated that judicial decision making often reflected a judge's values. If possible, Old Hickory expected to know these before he submitted a nomination. He vowed to nominate a candidate only "if his principles of the Constitution are sound, and well fixed." Although he did not demand personal interviews, at least one observer concluded that they could be "advantageous"; in making judicial nominations Jackson did "not act upon the number of certificates furnished . . . but upon knowing the fitness and qualifications of the applicants," deciding upon nominees "without much advice."[15] While Jackson strove to maintain the independence of the president in the selection process, this ostensible modernizer of American politics frequently heeded the wishes of political cronies to nominate their friends and kinsmen to the federal bench.

II

During eight years in office, Jackson nominated seventeen district court judges, all of them Democrats. Immediately on entering the White House he filled vacancies in Ohio and Louisiana. Outgoing President John Quincy Adams had issued temporary direct commissions to two judges, but when the Senate convened in December, 1828, it refused to confirm regular nominations for these recess appointees, leaving Jackson to dispose of the offices. In selecting judges for Ohio and Louisiana, Jackson followed a pattern that persisted throughout his administration: he relied on state party leaders, rather than the congressional wing of the Democratic party, and he demonstrated a personal interest in and knowledge of his nominees.

The Ohio Democracy exercised an uneasy domination over state politics. Jackson in 1828 narrowly won the presidential vote, but National Republicans captured the governorship and, before relinquishing control of the state legislature, elected Jacob Burnett as the second United States senator of the party from Ohio. In view of the close division between the parties, Caleb Atwater, an enthusiastic Jacksonian, cautioned the president that "one single bad appointment . . . and Ohio is lost."[16]

The absence of Senate representation and a state party organization forced Ohio Democratic leaders to clamor individually for the attention of the president. Jackson responded to these conflicting demands by trusting established political friends. Elijah Hayward of Cincinnati, an original organizer of the Ohio Democracy and editor of the leading Democratic newspaper, journeyed to Washington and intervened successfully with the president on behalf of John W. Campbell. The Adams county lawyer had no previous judicial experience, but he had faithfully served the party, losing the 1828 race for governor and subsequently finishing second to Burnett for the Senate seat. Campbell was an early Jacksonian; as a member of Congress in 1825 he had cast one of the two votes by Ohio for Old Hickory in the disputed presidential election. Jackson rewarded both Hayward and Campbell for past loyalty, but in doing so he ignored other Democratic candidates with more distinguished records of judicial service.[17]

The vacant Louisiana judgeship tested the president's injunction against nepotism and his willingness to cooperate with Democratic senators. Limited suffrage and conflict between American and French resident had stunted the development of a state-wide Democratic organization; instead, a handful of prominent spokesmen vied to dominate local politics, in part through recognition of their conflicting claims on the federal patronage. Martin Gordon, president of the Orleans Steam Navigation Company, led the American faction; Sen. Edward Livingston claimed support among French residents.[18]

Both Livingston and Gordon attempted to mediate the selection process. The former had a personal interest in the appointment; he had pending before the court litigation involving ownership of extensive properties along the waterfront of New Orleans. Whether out of self-interest, family loyalty, political aggrandizement, or all three, Livingston urged the nomination of his brother-in-law, Henry Carleton, a bilingual New Orleans attorney with an established federal court practice.[19] Political rather than personal gain motivated Gordon; as collector of the port of New Orleans, he expected to control the distribution of federal patronage. Coincidentally, an able and sympathetic federal judge well versed in admiralty and commercial law would benefit his extensive shipping business. Gordon recommended Samuel H. Harper, clerk of the court and prominent spokesman for the American faction in the New Orleans city council and the Louisiana legislature. Members of the New Orleans bar practicing in the federal court also endorsed Harper, emphasizing that his experience in the clerkship would facilitate the transition of judicial power.[20]

Harper furthered his candidacy by traveling to Washington and securing a personal interview with the president. When questioned by

Jackson, Harper stressed his state rights beliefs and his willingness to preside impartially over the Livingston litigation. Apparently persuaded by these guarantees, the president on March 6 elevated the clerk of the court to the bench, rejecting Carleton because of his family connection to Livingston and the specter of conflict of interest that would be raised by such a nomination.[21]

Jackson respected the role of state party leaders in organizing the selection process, but his injunction against nepotism loosened. In August, 1829, the death of Judge John Samuel Sherburne created a vacancy in the New Hampshire district. Admiralty and maritime suits were the most important litigation on the docket of this otherwise inactive court. During the preceding three years, Justice Joseph Story had disposed of these causes while on circuit without the assistance of the chronically ill Sherburne.[22]

The death of the judge coincided with a period of crucial political development in New Hampshire. The state Democratic party was an island of Jacksonian strength in the otherwise National Republican sea of New England. Jackson in 1828 lost the state, but, under the leadership of Isaac Hill, the party captured the legislature and governorship. A member of Jackson's "Kitchen Cabinet," Hill was the most prominent Democrat in New England and the undisputed ruler of the New Hampshire Democracy. Nonetheless, Hill and the party were vulnerable. In early 1830 the emerging anti-Jackson coalition in the Senate rejected three New Hampshire nominees to federal posts, including Hill as second comptroller of the treasury. Further, the gubernatorial election would occur in November, and a demonstration of Democratic strength in filling the district court post promised to renew the stature of the party, which had been badly undermined by the Senate rejections. Andrew Dunlap of Boston reminded the president that the successful appointment of the New Hampshire district judge was "of the greatest importance to our cause throughout *the whole part of the Country.*"[23]

The president considered two candidates: Sen. Levi Woodbury and Gov. Matthew Harvey. Woodbury was the lone Democratic senator from New Hampshire, a distinguished former state supreme court judge, and a devoted Jacksonian. He refused an informal offer made by the president through Attorney General John McPherson Berrien; the responsibilities of the judgeship were "too small" to cause him to relinquish his Senate seat.[24]

Attention then turned to Governor Harvey. Isaac Hill believed Harvey to be a deficient campaigner whose deferential style clashed with the image of popular democracy cultivated by the New Hampshire party leader. Hill persuaded the president to offer the governor the district court post, freeing Harvey's younger brother, Congressman John Harvey, to become the Democratic nominee for governor. The younger Harvey endorsed the scheme, but Matthew Harvey pondered the ethical and political wisdom of the arrangement for several weeks, deciding only reluctantly to accept the recess commission offered by the president.[25] Traditional and modern patronage practices converged when Jackson filled the New Hampshire post; he accepted nepotism in order to solidify Democratic hegemony over the state.

Kinship and instrumental friendship connections also influenced the selection of district judges for Tennessee and Maryland.[26] The president in January, 1834, nominated Morgan W. Brown of Nashville to the federal bench for Tennessee. In doing so he dismissed the recommendations of both Tennessee senators—Felix Grundy and Hugh Lawson White—and a host of Tennessee Democrats who condemned Brown as politically unacceptable because he had edited an anti-Jackson newspaper during the Nullification Crisis. The president, however, set aside these criticisms in favor of recommendations by Brown's brother, William Little Brown, and brother-in-law, John Catron, both Democratic state supreme court justices. These intimate personal and political friends of the president successfully argued that their kinsman's behavior was an unfortunate but excusable temporary aberration.[27]

Two years later, in April, 1836, Jackson nominated Upton Scott Heath of Baltimore as district judge for Maryland. Heath was an early supporter of the president, a member of the 1832 national Democratic convention, director in 1835 of the Second Bank of the United States, and a Jackson presidential elector. As in New Hampshire, partisan commitment and family ties converged; the candidate's brother, recently defeated Congressman James P. Heath, and a distant relative and long time political associate, Roger B. Taney, secretary of the treasury and future Supreme Court chief justice, successfully mediated Heath's selection.[28]

Kinship and friendship connections shaped the district court selection process, but so too did Jackson's desire to appoint judges with proper political and constitutional views. The president assessed the ideological predispositions of potential nominees through personal knowledge, the assurances of trusted party leaders, and interviews. He welcomed, for example, the state rights and anti-Bank beliefs of both his appointees to the Eastern District of Virginia, Phillip P. Barbour and Peter V. Daniel.[29]

Jackson during his second term forged an appointment strategy sensitive to the constitutional and political views of district court nominees. This was undoubtedly a reaction to the crises that engulfed the administration. The president's veto in 1832 of the bill rechartering the Second Bank of the United States precipitated a major constitutional debate over presidential powers; Jackson intended to bring to the federal courts judges amenable to the concept of presidential independence. The Nullification Crisis heightened agitation over the constitutional position of slavery. Although a staunch defender of the Union, the president believed masters entitled to constitutional protection of their peculiar property; thus, the chief executive endorsed strict enforcement of the Fugitive Slave Act of 1793. The practical limitations posed by the decentralized and loosely knit Democratic party impeded any presidential quest for ideological purity on the federal bench. These practical restraints on the selection process and the issues of presidential powers and maintenance of the Fugitive Slave Act of 1793 united in the selection of judges for Ohio in 1833 and Indiana in 1835, the most controversial of Jackson's second term district court nominations.

The president's Bank policy spurred the evolution of a new two-party system in Ohio. Following the removal of the deposits of the federal government from the Bank in September of 1833, National Republicans and dissident Democrats, unhappy with the Bank veto and the prospect of Martin Van Buren's succession to the White House, coalesced in the Whig party under the leadership of Sen. Thomas Ewing.[30]

The death in September, 1833, of Judge John W. Campbell coincided with this partisan realignment. Of the eight serious aspirants to the post, two Steubenville lawyers—Humphrey Howe Leavitt and Benjamin Tappan—emerged as the strongest contenders. The former was anxious to trade the uncertainty of his seat in Congress for the security of a district judgeship. In the House of Representatives Leavitt had steadfastly backed the administration; he was one of three members of the Ohio delegation to vote against rechartering the Bank. His candidacy posed a dilemma for the administration, however; if Jackson nominated Leavitt, a Whig or Bank-Democrat might gain the House seat. Ultimately, the will of Vice-President Martin Van Buren prevailed over the recommendations of the Ohio Democratic congressional delegation. Van Buren applauded Leavitt as an "upright man" of sound constitutional principles, but he persuaded the president that the Ohio Democrat could best serve the party by remaining in the House.[31]

Much of the anti–Van Buren leadership of the Ohio Democracy believed Benjamin Tappan too controversial to hold the federal post. Like his New England brothers, Arthur and Lewis Tappan, Benjamin condemned the peculiar institution and the Fugitive Slave Act of 1793 with such persistence that he angered moderate Democrats anxious to facilitate cooperation with the South. His avowed atheism fueled further hostility. As a result, the Democratic governor, Robert Lucas, and John A. Bryan, chairman of the recently organized state Democratic committee, refused to endorse Tappan.[32]

Elijah Hayward once again mediated the selection process. With Leavitt's candidacy dead, Democratic members of the Ohio congressional delegation, including Leavitt and the antislavery senator, Thomas D. Morris, recommended Tappan, but it was Hayward, in a personal interview, who convinced a skeptical Jackson of the candidate's constitutional soundness. The Cincinnati editor assured the president that Tappan was a "Democrat of the Jeffersonian school": he opposed the Bank; and he was safe, despite regrettable outbursts, on the slavery issue. He was also favorable to Van Buren's presidential aspirations. With the hope of diminishing the expected opposition, the chief executive did not wait for the Senate to reconvene; instead, on October 12, 1833, he granted Tappan a recess commission.[33]

Jackson responded in much the same way when in July, 1835, the death of Judge Benjamin Parke created a vacancy on the district bench for Indiana. As he had done in Ohio, the president considered the candidates' beliefs and relied on the recess appointment power to defuse potential opposition.

Rival factions of the Indiana Democratic congressional delegation clashed over Parke's successor. Senators William Hendricks and John Tipton endorsed a state supreme court judge, Stephen C. Stevens. House Democrat Amos Lane, on the other hand, recommended Jesse Lynch Holman, a resident of his congressional district, a former National Republican, and in 1824 a presidential elector for John Quincy Adams. Holman had read law with Henry Clay in Kentucky before moving to Indiana, where he freed his slaves and joined the antislavery opposition to William Henry Harrison. A strong religious commitment complemented his disdain of the peculiar institution; he was a lay Baptist minister and a proponent of colonization. His friend and political ally Lane in August, 1835, went to Washington to plead personally for Holman's appointment.[34]

The Indiana vacancy also attracted attention among Democratic slaveholders in northern Kentucky. They claimed a proprietary interest in the judgeship; a small but important portion of the docket of the federal court in Indiana included cases of escaped slaves from Kentucky. In urging the selection of Samuel Todd of Frankfort, Kentucky, Democrat Landon F. Sharp cautioned Jackson that "the residents of Kentucky" felt "a peculiar interest in having a Judge from a slave state to fill that office." Proper enforcement of the Fugitive Slave Act of 1793 required, he concluded, the appointment of a judge "who had not been educated with prejudices against slave property."[35]

Initially, Jackson was more interested in which candidate—Stevens or Holman—would sustain the presidential prerogative rather than in which would more effectively implement the Fugitive Slave Act. He directed both applicants to submit statements about the constitutional powers of Congress to charter a national bank and of the president to veto such a bank and to remove the federal deposits. Despite his National Republican antecedents, Holman sympathized with Jackson. "It has always been my settled conviction," the Indiana lawyer replied, "that the expansion of the powers of Congress, by implication, is extremely dangerous and I am well convinced that the framers of the Constitution had no thought of a Bank such as the present one." Stevens pleaded that it was "extremely painful to write on such subjects for the express purpose of influencing my own appointment." He was "decidedly and unequivocally hostile" to rechartering the Bank, but he also concluded that removal of the federal deposits was of "questionable constitutionality"; an "entirely unnecessary" act that created "disagreeable conflict of opinions." Jackson settled on Holman, granting him a recess commission dated September 16.[36]

Some Indiana Democrats bitterly protested. V. P. Van Antwerp, a Terre Haute lawyer and supporter of Van Buren for president, complained that the appointment gave "great dissatisfaction" on two counts. First, by selecting Holman the administration had endorsed his views of religion and slavery, making difficult the task of unifying the state party and attracting adherents of William Henry Harrison. Second, Lane, Van Antwerp contended, had placed personal friendship above party interest. The new judge should not have come from Lane's congressional district but from Indianapolis, where his continued involvement in state politics "might have aided the cause of the country and the party."[37]

The divisiveness of the Holman nomination reappeared when the first session of the Twenty-fourth Congress convened in December, 1835. Democratic members of the Indiana House delegation, with the exception of Lane, petitioned Jackson to nominate another candidate. Congressman Ratliff Boon claimed that Holman "disgusted" the president's friends, lacked the proper qualifications for office, and possessed the attitude of "a fanatic on the subject of slavery . . . and religion." Senators Hendricks and Tipton, however, decided that Senate debate over Holman would only produce further party division. Thus, they joined Lane in stressing that while the judge was a "friend and efficient advocate of colonization," he was also "opposed to the madness and folly of abolitionists."[38]

Jackson responded cautiously. He delayed submission of a regular nomination for Holman until he could personally interview the judge. Holman responded to questions about his willingness to enforce the Fugitive Slave Act with a copy of his first decision, in which he returned a fugitive to Kentucky with a ringing endorsement of the constitutionality of the 1793 act. Jackson, Holman observed after the interview, "was particularly pleased." The chief executive silenced Boon by agreeing to appoint his leading candidate for the judgeship, James Whitcomb, to head the United States Land Office. When submitted to the Senate, Holman's nomination was promptly confirmed.[39]

In selecting district court judges Jackson groped toward the future, clinging to the vestiges of traditional personal politics while responding to the pressures of an emerging party system. He was sensitive to the political priorities confronting state Democratic leaders; he responded more uniformly to their demands than to the recommendations of Democratic senators. As a strong chief executive he projected his Democratic political and constitutional faith onto the district courts. Frequently, however, he sought these partisan and ideological goals through traditional political means. The impersonal efficiency typical of a modern bureaucratic state, sometimes ascribed to Jackson's presidency, did not characterize the process by which the administration selected district court judges. The judges frequently attained office as much through kinship or instrumental friendship connections as through proper political and constitutional views. Instead of allowing party organization and cabinet subordinates to structure the selection process, Jackson frequently assumed direct control. These informal personal connections fulfilled an important function; they bridged the distance between the national government and the states that the decentralized and loosely knit Democratic party did not span.

III

The distribution of territorial judgeships entailed administrative and political variables different from those present in the selection of district court judges. First, party development in the territories lagged behind the states. Denied the organizational stimulus of contested presidential elections, the territories developed factional alignments dominated by a few personalities whose political goals bore little relationship to the interests of national parties. Second, the territorial judiciary was vulnerable to rotation-in-office. Pre-Jackson presidents stressed the necessity of an independent territorial judiciary; routinely, they renominated judges whose terms of office had expired. John Quincy Adams in 1828 observed that "the necessity of renomination was as much in the spirit of the Constitution as the permanent tenure of judicial office."[40] In the same year, however, the Supreme Court, in the *Canter* decision, decided differently. By finding the judges of the legislative courts unprotected by Article III, the justices seemingly enabled a president to remove or fail to reappoint a territorial judge.[41] Third, vacant territorial judgeships aroused contradictory demands from two different constituencies: territorial residents fearful of carpetbag rule, and state and congressional party leaders intent on exploiting the patronage.

Under these circumstances Jackson was attentive to party interests but sensitive to informal personal pressures. He adopted a moderate policy of rotation-in-office; of twelve Adams appointees, the new Democratic president, by the end of his second term, had reappointed four and replaced five others whose terms had expired. He removed one judge; the remaining two resigned. Clearly, appointment by the previous administration was not reason in and of itself for removal. Jackson did not nominate his kinsmen, but he did select Tennessee friends and candidates with family ties to prominent mediators. The chief executive willingly nominated nonresidents; 60 percent of his nominees did not reside in the territory to which they were nominated.

Of Jackson's forty judicial nominations, the majority—twenty-three—were to the territories. Three territories existed when Jackson took the oath of office: Michigan, Florida, and Arkansas.[42] In the course of their duties, the judges of each of these territories became embroiled in political controversy.

Personal rivalries and factionalism characterized Michigan politics. Until he joined Jackson's cabinet in mid-1831, Gov. Lewis Cass generally remained above factional squabbling through an adroit distribution of local offices. Persistent factionalism stemmed, at least in part, from fundamental differences over the conduct of the territorial judiciary.[43]

The Detroit Junto consisted of most of the territorial officer hol-
ders appointed by John Quincy Adams, including "attorneys, and
other persons connected with the courts of law." Chief Justice William
Woodbridge, the most influential political figure in the territory with
the exception of Cass, led the Junto. He was assisted by his colleague
on the territorial supreme court, Associate Justice Henry L. Chipman.
Through the *Michigan Herald*, which Chipman edited sub rosa after
his appointment to the bench in 1828, the Junto endorsed the National Republicanism of John Quincy Adams.[44]

John P. Sheldon, editor of the *Detroit Gazette*, led frustrated office
seekers and attorneys in opposition to the Junto. Personal animus
partly motivated Sheldon; Woodbridge had repeatedly frustrated his
attempts to win election as territorial delegate. The editor, however,
was a longstanding critic of the territorial judiciary. Beginning in
1824 the *Gazette* had condemned the judges' insistence on technical
common law pleadings and their repeated exercise of judicial review
to overturn legislation passed by the territorial council. The *Gazette* in
1828 endorsed the election of Jackson in the hope a new president
would reconstruct the territorial judiciary.[45]

In early 1829 factional antagonism and latent animosity over the
judiciary burst into a major judicial controversy whose repercussions
extended to the White House. Sheldon, in the *Gazette,* had exhibited
unusual zeal in lampooning the judges for agreeing to review the
conviction of a known thief because the trial judge had committed a
procedural error in trying the case. On the initiative of Chief Justice
Woodbridge the court ordered Sheldon to cease further commentary
until it settled the appeal. When the editor persisted, the judges
unanimously ordered him jailed for contempt of court.[46]

The anti-Junto faction demanded the immediate removal of the
Judges. Sheldon and his followers appealed to constitutional law and
practicality. They argued, on the basis of *Canter,* that impeachment
extended only to judges of the constitutional courts; the president,
they maintained, possessed a summary removal power over territorial
judges. Moreover, they insisted, impeachment was a clumsy weapon
against judicial tyranny; twice in the preceding three years the House
of Representatives had refused to impeach District Judge James
Hawkins Peck of Missouri for abuse of the contempt power.[47]

The fragmented Jacksonian movement in Michigan and the
president's constitutional scruples thwarted these demands. Lewis
Cass approved the application of rotation-in-office to antiadministration officeholders, but he refused to break completely with the Junto,
and he denounced the infusion of "party feeling" into the conduct of

territorial justice. The president adopted the narrowest possible interpretation of his power to remove territorial judges. The *Canter* decision, he concluded, applied only when Congress had explicitly authorized that the judges served only at the pleasure of the president. Although the *Canter* decision applied directly to Florida territory, whose judges served fixed terms without mention of the president's removal power, Jackson rejected the decision as a precedent for action against the Michigan judges, who also served fixed four-year terms without provision of presidential removal. However, when the terms of the judges did expire in 1832, the president acted; he failed to reappoint three of them, and reappointed Solomon Sibley only after Cass testified to his political and constitutional soundness.[48]

Through the selection process the chief executive fused partisan and personal interests. He selected Ross Wilkins of Pennsylvania, David Irvin of Virginia, and George Morell of New York—lawyers with impressive credentials as early Jackson supporters. If confirmed, these nominees would extend the influence of the administration to Michigan by installing a cadre of loyal Democrats on the territorial bench. Beyond establishing an administration presence in the territory, Jackson intended the selections to have an impact on Capitol Hill, even if it meant breaching his edict against nepotism. Ross Wilkins was the nephew of Sen. William Wilkins of Pennsylvania, and David Irvin was the brother of Congressman William Irvin of Ohio. Both legislators sought appointments for their kinsmen at the same time they were questioning Jackson's Bank policy. Apparently, the president used the Michigan judicial patronage to prod wavering members of the congressional wing of the party to sustain the administration. He rewarded Sen. William L. Marcy of New York for his faithful support by nominating Morell.[49]

Both Michigan factions criticized the nominations. Sheldon complained that the president should have selected territorial residents, but he ultimately accepted the nominees as preferable to further Junto control of the courts. William Woodbridge, however, was bitter: the president had dispatched a "new batch of party men" to the territory with the purpose of assuming political control.[50]

Political conflict involving the judiciary also surfaced in Florida and Arkansas. In both territories the election of Jackson unleashed latent hostility toward some of the judges. The president adopted a moderate policy of rotation-in-office and, in selecting new judges, blended partisan interests with instrumental friendship and kinship connections.

In Florida, unlike Michigan, the dominant political faction was identified with the new administration. Gov. William Pope DuVal and Richard K. Call led the Tallahassee Nucleus, a fluid alliance of middle Florida planters and territorial officers bound to one another by a common involvement in land speculation. Territorial delegate Joseph M. White directed the opposition. With support in east and west Florida, the White faction charged that the Nucleus reaped private profit from control of the public offices.[51]

Jackson in 1831 had his first opportunity to nominate a Florida judge when the term of Thomas Randall of the Middle District expired. Although Randall later became a Whig, in the early 1830s he had a nominal commitment to the new administration. Moreover, his judicial career benefited from well-placed family connections within the Adams and Jackson administrations. He was the son-in-law of Adams's attorney general, William Wirt, who had secured his first appointment to Florida territory. Subsequently, his uncle, Commissioner of Pensions Peter Hagner, persuaded Jackson to reappoint him.[52]

The terms of the three other Florida judges expired the following year. Jackson reappointed Judge James Webb to the Southern District, but at the urging of the Nucleus the president replaced Judges Joseph L. Smith of east Florida and Henry M. Brackenridge of west Florida.[53]

Smith was plagued by controversy. Belligerent and truculent in temperament, he nonetheless won the respect of east Florida residents for providing a legal refuge against the land speculation activities of the Nucleus. He first gained attention in 1824 when he exploded in a fit of rage during a billiards game, nearly caning his opponent to death. The following year the territorial delegate, Richard K. Call, unsuccessfully petitioned the House of Representatives to impeach Smith for lack of judicial temperament and acceptance of fees for legal services. The judge in 1829 further provoked the Nucleus when he jailed a prominent land speculator and member of the faction for contempt of court. The Nucleus demanded that Jackson remove him, supporting their position with the same arguments put forth by the anti-Junto forces in Michigan. At the same time, property owners in east Florida pleaded for his retention; they applauded the judge's independence of the Nucleus. Jackson claimed that despite the *Canter* decision he lacked the constitutional authority to remove the judge. However, when Smith's term expired, the president promptly heeded the wishes of the Nucleus.[54]

Henry M. Brackenridge was less controversial than Smith, but he too had earned the enmity of the Nucleus for acting independently in settling land cases in his west Florida district. The judge's former law partner, Gov. William Pope DuVal, spearheaded the attempt to remove him from office. Once again, Jackson refused to remove a sitting territorial judge; instead, in early 1831 he interviewed Brackenridge, seeking assurances of his political compatibility with the administration. Apparently, Jackson was at first satisfied with Brackenridge's answers; he agreed to reappoint him. Under further prodding by Governor DuVal, who claimed the judge was secretly plotting with territorial delegate White against the administration, Jackson reversed his decision. When notified of the appointment of his successor, Brackenridge during the spring of 1832 lashed out against the president in a series of bitter letters published in Florida and Washington newspapers. He derided Jackson as a "despot" and a "liar" who "ignored the wishes of the people of Florida" by sending "total strangers to govern over them."[55]

Sen. Richard M. Johnson of Kentucky and Peter V. Daniel of the Virginia Privy Council in early 1832 mediated the selection of Brackenridge's successor. They persuaded Jackson to nominate James G. Bryce, a twenty-six-year-old state rights enthusiast, member of the Virginia House of Delegates, and editor of the anti-Bank *Winchester Virginian*. Johnson requested the nomination as a favor to his longtime friend, the Reverend John Bryce, the father of the nominee. Daniel, however, urged the selection on political grounds; by nominating the obscure Bryce, the administration could demonstrate to its recalcitrant Virginia critics, such as Sen. John Tyler, the "folly of their opposition."[56]

Jackson was more interested in embarrassing his Senate critics than in finding an able nominee to fill the other Florida vacancy. He nominated Charles Biddle, the brother of Nicholas Biddle, president of the Second Bank of the United States, to replace Smith. Charles Biddle in 1826 immigrated to Nashville, where he combined irregular study and practice of the law with a flourishing social life. In April 1831 he ingratiated himself with the president by acting as master of ceremonies at a welcoming celebration for embattled Secretary of War John H. Eaton. The Democratic congressional delegations from Tennessee and Pennsylvania recommended Biddle, but Jackson surely took rueful delight in asking the Senate opposition to accept both Nicholas Biddle's bank and his Democratic brother.[57]

The president also devoted personal attention to the Arkansas judiciary. In that territory two factions, which reflected the major streams of immigration from Kentucky and Tennessee, divided in their support of the judiciary. During the Adams administration,

Robert Crittenden's Kentucky faction mediated selection of the four-man territorial court. With Jackson's ascendancy the opposition, led by former Tennessean and territorial delegate Ambrose H. Sevier, anticipated that the president would act on their charges that the territorial judges had purposefully delayed settlement of disputed Spanish land titles in order that they and the Crittenden faction might profit.[58]

Sevier urged his old friend in the White House to break the hold of the Crittenden faction over Arkansas politics. As a first step, he recommended the immediate removal of William Trimble, the cousin of Supreme Court Justice Robert Trimble, and James Woodson Bates, a former law partner of Robert Trimble. Sevier accused Judge William Trimble of "interfering in local elections" and bringing "under attack . . . through his decisions in the court room . . . those who differ with him in politics."[59] In the spring of 1830 a congressional investigation rejected allegations of massive court-abetted land fraud in Arkansas, but it did conclude that the judges, especially Trimble, had repeatedly ignored the legal interests of the government. In conjunction with Sevier's charges, this was apparently enough to persuade Jackson to set aside temporarily his constitutional scruples. The act creating Arkansas afforded the president a basis upon which to act; it provided that the judges held office for four-year terms "at the pleasure of the President."[60] Brushing aside charges by the Crittenden faction that he intended to erect a "despotism" through "destruction of our independent judiciary," Jackson removed Trimble. He replaced him with Edward Cross, a Tennessee native and longtime resident of the territory recommended by Sevier and Tennessee's Sen. Felix Grundy.[61]

Sevier also eliminated Bates, although it took longer. Perhaps chastened by the hostile reaction to Trimble's removal or perhaps persuaded that Bates was less culpable than Trimble, the president allowed the judge to serve until the expiration of his term. Then Jackson replaced him with Charles Scott Bibb, the thirty-one-year-old son of Sen. George Mortimer Bibb of Kentucky. The appointment rewarded the elder Bibb for his defense in the Senate of the president's Bank policy and the removal of Trimble.[62]

Kinship and cronyism also figured in Jackson's other Arkansas nominations. While he replaced the other Adams appointees, Jackson in 1832 and 1836 renominated Chief Justice Benjamin Johnson, the father-in-law of territorial delegate Sevier and the brother of Sen. Richard M. Johnson. Cave Johnson, also a brother of Chief Justice Johnson and a Jackson crony, mediated the selection of his law partner and fellow Tennessean, Alexander M. Clayton, to replace Bibb. When vacancies occurred in 1834 and 1835, the president nominated two Tennessee friends and political supporters: Thomas J. Lacy and Archibald Yell. The former was a Jackson protégé and the grandson of John Overton, one of the president's most intimate friends. With the assistance of Congressman James K. Polk, the semiliterate Yell bargained for the judgeship in order that he might "be sure of a safe income for two or three years."[63]

"Conciliation of individuals," observed Martin Van Buren, "formed the smallest, perhaps too small a part of Jackson's patronage policy."[64] The president only sporadically attempted to cultivate influence with wavering congressional Democrats through distribution of territorial judgeships; he imposed strict limitations on his removal powers and adopted only a modest program of replacing Adams appointees as their terms expired. Nonetheless, even his limited application of rotation-in-office to the territorial judiciary was a significant manifestation of executive independence in the selection process. As an activist president, Jackson frequently exploited the territorial judicial patronage to reward partisan loyalists, their kinsmen, and his political cronies from Tennessee. Within the boundaries of a shared Democratic affiliation, Jackson persisted in maintaining a traditional and highly personal scheme of selection.

IV

"At all times," Andrew Jackson explained in 1830, he "regretted in his nominations, to have to differ with Senators of a State." Nonetheless, Old Hickory believed that "duty" often compelled such action.[65] This assertion of independence stirred protest; repeatedly, the emerging Whig opposition in the Senate accused him of "executive usurpation." Sen. Joseph Kent of Maryland claimed that the president manipulated members of Congress by giving either them or their friends lucrative offices. Instead of a tribune of the people, the president, Kent argued, had become a "despot"—a "kind of King of England."[66]

Two conditions accentuated strife between the president and the Senate. First, throughout Jackson's two terms the upper house fluctuated in partisan composition; loyal administration Democrats held only thin majorities. Beginning in 1832, Elijah Hayward observed, the "odds and ends of political factions" coalesced in the Whig party. Hayward characterized this new opposition as "partisans of the *Bank* . . . Federalists, Clay men, Webster men, McLean men, Nullifiers and apostate politicians."[67] Before this partisan realignment, Senate Democrats held at most a four-vote majority. During Jackson's second term parity existed in the Twenty-fourth Congress between Democrats and National Republicans; in the Twenty-fourth Congress Jacksonians claimed only a two-vote majority over the newly formed Whig opposition. These precarious majorities often evaporated as lax party discipline allowed Senate Democrats to drift over to the opposition.[68]

Second, antipartyism persisted on Capitol Hill. The president rarely articulated the benefits of his patronage policy, but Democrats such as Sen. William L. Marcy of New York bluntly asserted the claims of his party to the "spoils." National Republicans and conservative Democrats protested such crass partisanship; officeholders selected on the basis of party affiliation would, once in office, think first of party and second, if at all, of the public interest. This criticism of the baneful effects of party was mostly rhetorical; the opposition rejected legislation intended to emphasize merit and to reduce executive control of the patronage. Nonetheless, even Marcy attempted to reassure the public that the Jacksonians recognized that quality could not be subordinated to partisanship. "In bestowing the patronage," the New Yorker explained in 1833, "I first look to the qualifications of the candidates; if they have these, their political merits and the wishes of political friends are next to be regarded."[69]

These conditions abetted conflict between the president and the Senate over the judicial patronage. During the Twenty-second Congress and the first session of the Twenty-third Congress, from December 5, 1831, to June 30, 1834, the administration nominated twenty judges. The upper house rejected three of these and delayed for more than one month the confirmation of four others. The emerging Whig opposition in the Senate challenged the nominations of judges to district courts in western Pennsylvania and Ohio and to territorial courts in Michigan, Florida, and Arkansas.

The selection of Thomas Irwin of Uniontown as judge for the Western District of Pennsylvania stirred factional disharmony within the Democratic party of that state. Jackson on April 14, 1831, issued a recess commission to the Pennsylvania congressman; the following December he nominated him for a regular appointment. The proadministration "Amalgamator" faction, through Sen. Isaac D. Barnard, endorsed Irwin. The "Family" faction, on the other hand, opposed him. Recently vanquished Secretary of the Treasury Samuel D. Ingham and newly elected Sen. William Wilkins, whom Irwin replaced on the federal bench, aligned the Family faction in national politics with the president's nemesis, Vice-President John C. Calhoun.[70]

Wilkins orchestrated the opposition to Irwin. The senator urged Jackson to appoint his nephew to a judgeship in Michigan territory, while at the same time he sought to undermine the president by securing Senate rejection of Irwin. He encouraged members of the Pittsburgh bar loyal to the Family to protest the selection of a non-Pittsburgh lawyer who had never practiced before the federal courts and whose brief service during the fall of 1831 offered "small expectation of any advantageous enlargement of his judicial capabilities." Wilkins also advised his fellow senators to reject the nominee on three different grounds. He claimed, first, that Jackson had abused his recess appointment power; although there had been sufficient time to make the nomination, the president had purposely delayed action until Congress had adjourned, and only then, free from immediate Senate scrutiny, had he appointed Irwin. Second, Wilkins argued that in any event, Irwin's recess appointment was faulty; Irwin as a member of Congress had voted to increase the salary of the district judge and was, therefore, constitutionally prohibited from holding the office until his term expired upon the convening of a new Congress. Third, the senator asserted that Jackson had acted in bad faith; the president had broken his inaugural pledge not to interfere in local politics by appointing members of Congress to public offices.[71]

Wilkins precipitated a clash in the Senate over the independence of the president in the selection process. By demonstrating that the chief executive had intentionally circumvented immediate Senate scrutiny of Irwin, Wilkins attracted support from a coalition of National Republicans and conservative Democrats. At the same time, William L. Marcy, as chairman of the Democratic-controlled Committee on the Judiciary, rallied to the president's defense. On the constitutional issue, the chairman insisted that with the adjournment of Congress, Irwin's term had expired. Marcy also successfully solicited letters from the Pennsylvania bench and bar praising Irwin's legal talents. In mid-January 1832 Marcy favorably reported the nomination, but he quickly returned it to the committee when Senate rejection seemed imminent. Wilkins on March 21 committed the error of reopening debate in order to present further memorials from the Pittsburgh bar critical of the nominee. With twelve senators absent and over the protests of Wilkins, Marcy quickly moved for confirmation. The upper house by a two-vote majority confirmed Irwin.[72]

The emerging Whig coalition was also unsuccessful in challenging the constitutionality of the president's modest application of rotation-in-office to the territorial judiciary. Jackson, during the first two months of 1832, nominated six judges for Michigan, Florida, and Arkansas. Vacancies had occurred in these territories as the terms of judges appointed by John Quincy Adams expired.

The Whig coalition in the Senate attempted to limit presidential power by extending the protection of Article III to the territorial judiciary. Sen. Samuel A. Foote of Connecticut, on February 14 sponsored a resolution that demanded the president explain his actions and inquired whether the superseded judges "had been found incompetent or have been guilty of malfeasance in office . . . and whether the citizens of those territories have requested that they might not be reappointed." Sen. Thomas Ewing of Ohio on March 21 replaced this mild resolution with a more vigorous indictment of the president. He successfully returned to the judiciary committee the nomination of David Irvin to the Michigan bench with instructions to consider a resolution declaring that the Constitution and the Northwest Ordinance of 1787 protected judges of that territory in their offices during good behavior subject to "impeachment only." The Ohio senator argued that the president could not appoint Irvin in place of the incumbent, James Duane Doty, since the latter had originally been appointed in 1822 to hold office during good behavior. Ewing dismissed as unconstitutional under Article III an 1824 law that reduced the terms of the Michigan judges, including Doty, to four years. He also chose to ignore the *Canter* decision.[73]

The Ewing resolution struck too severe a blow at presidential and congressional control over the territorial judiciary. The full Senate voted thirty to seven against it; only Ewing and a handful of National Republicans were willing to accord to judges of the legislative courts the protection of Article III.[74]

Senate rejection of the Ewing resolution had significant consequences. The upper house immediately confirmed the three Michigan nominees. Further, the majority of the Senate accepted Jackson's program of rotation-in-office as a constitutionally legitimate exercise of presidential power and, in comparison with the clumsy impeachment process, an administratively preferable means of dealing with the territorial judiciary.[75]

The Democratic majority in the House also endorsed presidential power over these judges when it considered impeachment charges against Chief Justice Benjamin Johnson of Arkansas. Jackson, during the second session of the Twenty-second Congress, renominated Johnson. The Crittenden faction, however, led by Little Rock lawyer William Cummins, intended to block confirmation of Johnson as punishment for the role of his son-in-law, territorial delegate Ambrose H. Sevier, in the removal of Judge William Trimble. Cummins warned the president that if the chief justice was reappointed, he would seek the impeachment of Johnson on the basis of "irritability of temper, rudeness on the bench, incapacity, a vacillating and inconsistent course in judical decisions, and habitual intemperance." Johnson was often brusque and heavy-handed as a judge, but he was also the leading territorial authority on land law. The president denounced the charges as "futile, contemptable [*sic*] and without merit." The Senate apparently agreed; it quickly confirmed the chief justice.[76]

The House of Representatives responded to Cummins's allegations by confirming presidential power over the territorial judiciary. The Democratic-dominated House Committee on the Judiciary reported in February, 1833, that "there were not grounds for impeachment." The committee added that "the price of impeaching subordinate officers, and especially such as hold their offices by a tenure not more firm . . . than the judge of a Territorial court, should soon be found highly inconvenient . . . to the public interest."[77] The committee stopped short of directly affirming the president's removal power; instead, it issued an implicit invitation to the chief executive to assume such power in lieu of the unwieldy impeachment process. Jackson did not accept this enticement to greater power; to the contrary, he persisted in the belief that the "President has not power to remove a territorial judge."[78]

Congress accepted an incremental growth of presidential power over the territorial judiciary, but the emerging Whig coalition in the Senate maintained the prerogative of the upper house to advise and consent to judicial nominations. Its members did so by appealing to lingering fears of party, claiming that the president had sacrificed the traditional independence and skill of the judiciary to partisan purposes. Such tactics swayed enough Democratic senators to bring about the rejection of James G. Bryce and Charles Biddle as judges for Florida territory and Benjamin Tappan as district judge for Ohio.

Territorial delegate Joseph M. White in early 1832 campaigned against confirmation of Jackson's Florida nominees. He solicited from within the territory memorials praising Joseph L. Smith and Henry M. Brackenridge as experienced jurists well versed in the complexities of land law. He also received assistance from outside Florida. Congressman William Armstrong of Virginia forwarded allegations that youthful James G. Bryce, a resident of Armstrong's congressional district, had "frequent habits of gambling" and was "a man of ordinary capacity and of less than ordinary attainments in his profession." Sen. John Tyler, a critic of the president's patronage policies, complained that Bryce had more experience as a newspaper editor than as a lawyer.[79] From Tennessee unidentified critics alleged that Charles Biddle was "neither a lawyer nor a sober man," and that Jackson had selected him as reward for establishing a new administration newspaper in Nashville.[80] On the basis of this, White appealed to the Senate to "prevent mere partisans destitute of all proper qualifications from being thrust into Judicial office . . . making it the prize of the Gladiators of the Press" and a "passive instrument of Executive will."[81]

The president failed to muster sufficient Democratic votes to stem White's attack. The disjunction between the professional and partisan qualifications of the nominees persuaded moderate and conservative Democrats to abandon the administration. The Senate on May 17 decisively rejected Biddle by a vote of twelve to twenty-nine. More Democrats accepted Bryce, but his newspaper work and modest legal experience weighed against confirmation; the upper house rejected him on a tie vote, with both senators from Virginia opposed.[82]

Jackson boasted after leaving the White House that "whenever the Senate rejected a good man," he "gave them another hot potato."[83] Whether he decided Bryce and Biddle were not "good men," or whether he wanted to avoid further controversy, Jackson retained his independence without further confrontation. He refused demands to reappoint the old judges or to nominate candidates from within the territory. Instead, he nominated nonresidents with impeccable legal credentials: Robert R. Reid of Augusta, Georgia, and John A. Cameron of Fayetteville, North Carolina. The nominees were prominent Democrats, but they possessed the professional stature Biddle and Bryce sorely lacked. The Senate in late May quickly confirmed them.[84]

The Whig coalition during the first session of the Twenty-third Congress also rejected Benjamin Tappan as district judge for Ohio. The president in October, 1833, issued a recess commission to Tappan, believing that the Senate was less likely to reject a regular nomination for the controversial Tappan if he was already on the bench. Elijah Hayward, in this vein, cautioned the new judge to "be prudent" if he expected to be "permanently fixed on the Bench."[85]

Tappan was his own worst enemy. Moderate and conservative Senate Democrats might have abided his controversial views on slavery and religion if he had withdrawn from party affairs, but he did not. The judge retained nominal editorial control over the *Steubenville Mirror,* a pro-Jackson newspaper, and he presided in December, 1833, over a meeting of the Democratic party of his county. The following January he attended, while holding court, a convention of the state party in Columbus, where he played a crucial behind-the-scenes role in persuading the delegates to endorse Martin Van Buren for president.[86]

Administration critics turned this partisan activism against the judge. Whig Sen. Thomas Ewing of Ohio convinced his colleagues that Jackson had appointed Tappan for "the purpose of engineering and controlling political meetings" rather than "administering justice."[87] Supreme Court Justice John McLean, a staunch Methodist whose judicial circuit included Ohio, also pressed for rejection. Furthermore, Ohio boosters of McLean's presidential ambitions feared that the presence of the flamboyant Tappan might leave McLean to "be seen in the background."[88]

Fear of subordination of the judiciary to partisan expediency exercised a powerful influence over the upper house. The Senate on May 29 voted eleven to twenty-eight to reject. Tappan's slavery views spurred his rejection by the Senate, but they were not the overriding consideration; four slave-state senators voted for the judge. Equally significant was the judge's partisan activism; it lent credence to exaggerated charges that Jackson planned to fashion the federal courts into partisan instruments. Suspicion of the efficacy of a party-directed selection process undermined senatorial courtesy; the Democratic colleagues of Sen. Thomas D. Morris of Ohio, who urged Tappan's confirmation, refused to accept a shared partisan affiliation as a reasonable basis upon which to defer to him in the selection process.[89]

The president avoided further confrontation. In place of Tappan he nominated his second choice, Congressman Humphrey H. Leavitt of Steubenville, Ohio, a staunch Jacksonian and an able lawyer free from controversy. Ewing and McLean approved the new nominee; he "was the best that could be nominated from the Jacksonian ranks."[90]

The chief executive and the Senate groped to define their respective powers within the selection and appointment processes. By the end of his administration, Jackson held the high ground; despite the three rejections, he had successfully asserted his independence of the Senate. This was so because the emerging Whig coalition in the upper house turned the appointment process into an interparty contest by charging the administration with partisanship and executive usurpation. Yet with lingering antipartyism and with small numerical differences in the strength of nascent Whigs and Democrats, the upper house was unable consistently to maintain an independent position.

Furthermore, Congress contributed directly to the growth of presidential power. By refusing to employ the impeachment power

against territorial judges, the legislative branch tacitly approved
Jackson's application of rotation-in-office to the territorial judiciary.
Despite the willingness of Congress to augment his powers, Jackson
maintained a pristine view of the constitutional independence of the
territorial judiciary; he adopted a modest policy of replacing some
judges when their terms expired, but he refused to embark on a
program of wholesale removals. The Congress's reluctance to impeach territorial judges and Jackson's refusal to exploit fully his removal powers created an administrative anomaly: the judges were
"neither impeachable nor amenable before any earthly tribunal for
any corruption."[91]

V

Andrew Jackson was simultaneously a harbinger of change and a
representative of tradition. He frequently pursued in filling lower
court vacancies a party-directed selection process intended to facilitate development of state and territorial Democratic parties and to
reward and woo alternately members of the congressional wing of the
party. In doing so he enhanced the power and the independence of
the presidency by extending the concept of rotation-in-office to the
territorial judiciary, by exploiting the recess appointment power, and
by maintaining the presidential initiative in the selection process.

Nevertheless, this seeming prophet of modern party government
directed a selection process rooted in tradition. The decentralized and
loosely structured Democratic party inadequately bridged the space
separating the president from the distant states and territories. As a
result, the president frequently nominated friends and kinsmen of
principal mediators and his Tennessee cronies. More than administrative necessity compelled such behavior; Jackson was uneasy with
politics and politicians. Instead of imposing an impersonal efficiency
on the selection process, the president endeavored to place his im-
print upon the lower federal judiciary; he sought judges whose views
paralleled his own, frequently conducting personal interviews. In the
context of this personal and informal selection process, Jackson accepted the traditional independence of the judiciary. He applied a
modest policy of rotation-in-office to the territorial judiciary, but he
refused to assume the power to remove territorial judges, even
though Congress and the Supreme Court tacitly approved such a
practice as administratively essential and constitutionally proper.

2

MUFFLED OARS

Union, Harmony, Self-Denial—Everything for the cause,
nothing for men.—*Albany Argus*, August 5, 1836[1]

With the election of Martin Van Buren to the White House, the party professional replaced the charismatic hero. Unlike his predecessor, the leader of the Albany Regency and the architect of the bisectional Democratic coalition believed in subordinating personal goals to partisan success. National Republicans and Whigs seized upon the partisan character of Van Buren, submerging the statesman in the politician, and later historians have adopted their point of view. The New Yorker's contemporary critics derided him as a "subtle and intriguing man"; he was the "little Magician," devoid of principles and "captured by the humbug of party."[2]

This caricature of the eighth president, while neatly illustrating the disruption of traditional political culture associated with the rise of the second party system, obscures the complexity of Van Buren and the difficulties besetting his administration. Through the pragmatic lessons of political success, the New Yorker understood, more fully than Old Hickory, the value of an impersonal, well-organized, and disciplined party. The president, however, never intended to impose on the national party the centralizing organizational techniques associated with the Regency. He complemented his faith in party with a firm philosophical allegiance to the traditional canons of Jeffersonian democracy: state rights, strict construction of the Constitution, and limited national government. The New Yorker conceived of himself not as the architect of a powerful central party but as the overseer of a broad sectional coalition whose success depended upon disciplined state Democratic organizations like the Regency. When the Democracy captured the principal agencies of American government—the state legislatures and governors' mansions—it would also control the national government.[3] The Panic of 1837 revealed the contradictions of this strategy; when Van Buren attempted to act for the nation by supporting a modest centralization of the finances of the federal government through an independent treasury, he alienated conservative state Democrats.

Van Buren was as cautious as he was shrewd. Unlike Jackson, the new chief executive had fashioned his political career in the legislative branch of government; he appreciated the value of an even, restrained temperament. His position within the decentralized, state-centered, and factionally divided Democratic party dictated such prudence. In winning the 1836 election he had less popular support than had his predecessor; indeed, Van Buren's candidacy had prompted some Democrats to join the Whig ranks, further realigning the two-party system. Democratic leaders disgusted with the nomination and freed from personal attachments to Jackson deserted in the key states of Pennsylvania, Georgia, Tennessee, and Indiana. This accretion of strength to the Whig party continued while Van Buren held office.[4]

Van Buren appreciated the need to heal Democratic divisions. He wished to provide a much-needed respite from the quarreling that had plagued Jackson's administration, especially between the chief executive and the Congress. The new president sought to allay the suspicions of southern Democrats by pledging his administration to safeguard the interests of slaveholders. He also formulated a strategy of moderation and conciliation in dealing with federal officeholders; he adopted Jackson's cabinet for his own and allowed Old Hickory's other appointees to retain their posts.[5] Nonetheless, in distributing lower court judgeships, his sense of caution and his need to strengthen his tenuous political position took precedence over his quest for political harmony. Van Buren did not use such valuable posts to lure wavering Democrats to the administration; instead, he consistently gave them to fellow partisans already committed to him.

The president held moderate views about the judiciary. Van Buren in the 1821 New York state constitutional convention argued against proposals to limit judicial tenure and to elect judges; he believed that security in office fostered an independent judiciary. As a senator he voted to improve the administration of the lower federal courts, to extend the circuit court system, and to retain the twenty-fifth section of the Judiciary Act of 1789.[6] He dismissed as "too radical" Thomas Jefferson's proposal that Congress circumvent the impeachment process by limiting the terms of federal judges. During Jackson's administration he also forthrightly argued for the continued independence of the territorial judiciary, urging Old Hickory not to remove the judges. This broad support for the judiciary was tempered by a fear that too powerful federal courts would erode the executive prerogative. Van Buren ridiculed the notion that judges were mere oracles; he believed that, to the contrary, the judicial decision-making process reflected the experiences and beliefs of the judge. In this vein the new president committed his administration to nominees "who will . . . stick to the true principles of the Constitution"; as such, Democrats "were not in so much danger of falling off in the true spirit."[7]

The president's simultaneous quests for party harmony and like-minded judges converged in a selection process more party directed than it had been during Jackson's administration. By retaining Secretary of State John Forsyth, Van Buren facilitated continuity in the disposition of applications and recommendations. The new president, however, pursued judicial nominations with less direct personal involvement than had his predecessor; he expected Forsyth to acquire the sort of personal knowledge of nominees that Jackson had often sought through interviews. Van Buren also relied more fully on the various components of the Democratic party: cabinet members, state party leaders, and the congressional wing. An informal and traditional web of patron-client relations persisted, although less conspicuously than under Jackson; only 24 percent of Van Buren's lower court nominees had kinship connections to principal mediators, compared with nearly one-half of Jackson's.

In making seventeen judicial nominations, Van Buren enjoyed two advantages. First, he had only to protect, not to claim, the independent role of the chief executive in the selection and appointment processes. The battles during the Jackson administration between the president and the Senate had resulted in a decisive victory for the executive branch, which fostered stability. Second, a Democratic majority in the upper house enhanced this constancy. Senate Democrats in the Twenty-fifth Congress held a twelve-vote margin, although this was halved during the following Congress. The selection of federal judges became a distinctly intraparty process, revealing the increasing significance of party in the broader political culture. Much of Van Buren's legislative program stirred controversy, but he fostered harmony between the legislative and executive wings of the party in making judicial selections; the Senate accepted without vote all of his lower court nominees, and only one selection—William Marvin of Florida territory—encountered opposition.[8]

II

The geographic distribution of district court vacancies tested Van Buren's commitment to party harmony; seven of eight openings occurred in the slave states. Van Buren confronted a difficult task in fashioning Democratic unity in the South: he lacked broad popular support there; Democratic leaders balked at accepting his leadership; the Whig party was a growing threat in every state; and moderate and extreme state rights Democrats clamored to control their respective state party organizations. As two-party politics gradually supplanted the oligarchic Democratic factionalism that prevailed during the Jackson administration, southern Democrats expected the national administration to stem the Whig threat and to discipline party recalcitrants through distribution of federal offices.[9] Despite his pledge to foster unity among the rival factions of the party, Van Buren, at least in selecting district court judges, consistently deferred to the wishes of moderate southern Democrats.

During his first two years in office Van Buren had only two opportunities to nominate district court judges. The first came in July, 1837, with the death of Judge Samuel H. Harper of Louisiana. The second resulted from the resignation in September, 1838, of Judge George Adams of Mississippi, a Jackson appointee tired of the extensive travel imposed by district court service.[10] In both instances, the president proceeded cautiously; he filled the judgeships only after receiving the recommendations of proadministration state party leaders.

The transformation in the leadership and organization of the Louisiana Democratic party typified changes occurring throughout most of the South. During the mid-1830s Edward Livingston died and Martin Gordon lost domination of his faction. Into this void stepped John Slidell and William Christy. Under their leadership Democrats had established a tentative state-wide organization, but factional divisions persisted. Slidell objected to the unionist position adopted by Jackson during the Nullification Crisis, feared that the national party was not receptive to the idea of state rights, and complained that Van Buren, as a northerner, could not be trusted. Nonetheless, Slidell, who was a New York native and former confidant of Van Buren, assisted the Democratic candidate in capturing the Louisiana electoral vote because he viewed the leading Whig candidate, Hugh Lawson White, with even greater suspicion. William Christy led the former adherents of Gordon's customhouse faction. They backed Jackson's Nullification policy and during the 1836 election supported Van Buren.[11]

Divisions in the Louisiana Democracy provided Van Buren with some discretion in choosing a new judge, but ultimately he responded to the recommendations of party moderates. The most outspoken state rights advocates, led by Slidell, urged the appointment of his brother, Thomas, a New Orleans attorney and longtime foe of Martin Gordon. The old customhouse faction, led by Christy and Sen. Alexander Mouton, endorsed federal District Attorney Philip K. Lawrence.[12] In addition to the recommendations of Christy and Mouton, Lawrence, a New York City native had two unique qualifications. First, he was personally known to the president through his cousin, Congressman Cornelius Van Wyck Lawrence, the mayor of New York City and a Van Buren presidential elector. He had also actively worked for the new president; when Christy in 1835 established the short-lived *New Orleans Morning Post,* with the intention of boosting Van Buren's presidential stock, Lawrence abandoned his law practice to assume the editorship. Second, Lawrence benefited from the support of much of the legal community of the city, who applauded his familiarity with court operations. Practical politics, administrative efficiency, and personal interests thus prompted Van Buren's decision to appoint Lawrence.[13]

In Mississippi the domination by Samuel and William M. Gwin over the state Democratic party reduced the president's freedom to act. The Jacksonian movement in Mississippi by 1838 had split as a result of the Nullification Crisis, the rechartering of the Bank of the United States, and personal animosity between Jackson and Sen. George Poindexter. The Gwin brothers forged proadministration Democrats into the powerful Mississippi Regency; they exercised power so complete that the Democratic senator, Robert J. Walker, complained that he learned only "second hand" about the distribution of federal offices.[14]

The economic dislocation produced by the Panic of 1837 added a special urgency to the duties of the federal judge for Mississippi. The panic unleashed a torrent of litigation involving foreclosures against land speculators, cotton producers and shippers, and small businessmen in Natchez, Jackson, and Vicksburg. Congress in 1838 responded to demands for quicker federal justice by dividing the state into two districts with a marshal and district attorney assigned exclusively to each. These reforms benefited litigants and witnesses, but they increased the burden on the federal judge. The post of federal district judge for Mississippi was no sinecure; it required the judge to travel extensively, to supervise court operations in two districts, and to hear cases involving commercial, contract, and equity law.[15]

The expectations of the Regency and the interests of the president coincided in the appointment of a recently removed Congressman, Samuel J. Gholson. Gholson had in February, 1838, lost his House seat after a bitter partisan struggle over the composition of the Mississippi congressional delegation. The administration as well as the Regency had wanted Gholson seated, for although they were distinctly a minority in the Senate, Whigs enjoyed near parity with Democrats in the House; seating another Whig would only diminish administration strength and embarrass the Regency. Despite the feverish administration efforts, the House rejected Gholson's claim; instead, it seated Thomas J. Word, a Whig. The subsequent appointment of Gholson to the district judgeship rewarded a loyal Democrat, reasserted the prerogative of the president, and confirmed the influence of the Regency with the national administration.[16]

Van Buren conformed to the wishes of Louisiana and Mississippi Democratic party leaders. Such cooperation underscored the president's determination to forge an alliance between the national administration and moderate southern Democratic leaders. This cooperation was partly imposed upon the chief executive; he lacked the power to ignore the demands of influential state party organizations such as the Mississippi Regency. This cooperation had the practical advantage of solving the administrative problem of locating suitable judges. Nonetheless, the sensitivity displayed by Van Buren to the recommendations of moderate state rights Democrats in the South was not altogether a matter of expediency; rather, it revealed the president's inclination to appoint judges with acceptable beliefs, including an attachment to the Union. This ideological dimension was especially pronounced in the selection in 1839 of a district judge for South Carolina.

The Palmetto State was an aristocratic political anomaly with a divided Democratic party. There were no state-wide elections, and the legislature had sole responsibility for choosing presidential electors. Denied the synthesizing effect of contested presidential elections, beset by persistent antipartyism, and torn by the Nullification Crisis, the Democratic party was split into Nullifier and Unionist factions.[17] The president's old nemesis, Sen. John C. Calhoun, after temporarily leading the Nullifiers into the Whig party, by 1839 had rejoined the Senate wing of the Democracy. He brought his colleague, Sen. William G. Preston, with him. Despite Calhoun's change of allegiance, Van Buren continued to favor the loyal unionist leadership of Joel R. Poinsett, Alfred Huger, and James Pringle. He appointed Poinsett secretary of war, made Huger postmaster of Charleston, and named Pringle collector of customs.[18]

Following the death of Judge Thomas Lee in October, 1839, both factions offered candidates. The Nullifiers, led by Congressman Robert B. Rhett, realized that Van Buren would not accept any

nominee closely identified with the secessionist movement. They recommended William P. Finley, a Charleston lawyer who had adopted a
moderate position during the crisis—he had criticized the excesses of
Nullification and had also denounced Jackson's threatened resort to
military power through the Force Bill.[19] Unionists expected Poinsett
to mediate the selection, but the secretary of war adopted a neutral
position between the two leading contenders, Edward McCrady and
Robert B. Gilchrist.[20] McCrady was endorsed by Dr. Joseph Johnson,
one of Charleston's most influential unionists, but he had no support
among the Charleston bar or the federal officeholders.[21] These two
groups endorsed federal District Attorney Gilchrist, who had demonstrated his loyalty to the Union during the Nullification Crisis by
accepting the post of district attorney when others refused. A prominent Charleston attorney observed that "Gilchrist did not flinch in the
discharge of his duties to the government."[22] Supreme Court Justice
James Moore Wayne, whose circuit included South Carolina, echoed
these sentiments. "Gilchrist," Wayne observed, was "decidedly the
best District Attorney in the United States. I should feel fortunate in
having such an associate in my circuit duties."[23]

Van Buren blended the justice's wishes with administrative neces-
ity and ideological consistency. With the district court still open and
cases remaining on the docket, the president acted quickly; six days
after Lee's death, he issued Gilchrist a recess commission. He
applauded the district attorney's well-known Unionist sympathies;
Gilchrist deserved the post, the president concluded, because of "his
acceptance of the office . . . in South Carolina in difficult times."[24]
Van Buren acted independently of South Carolina's two Democratic
senators; he ignored their endorsements of Finley and exercised his
recess appointment power without subsequent opposition from the
upper house.[25]

Traditional patronage practices predicated on kinship sometimes
appeared in this party-directed selection process. Isaac S. Pennybacker of Virginia, for example, was appointed to the Western
District of that state during the same recess between the Twenty-fifth
and Twenty-sixth Congresses when Gilchrist was appointed. Like the
South Carolina judge, Pennybacker was a unionist aligned with the
proadministration faction of his state party. His brother-in-law, Virginia Democratic Congressman Green B. Samuels, not the state's
senators, mediated the selection process.[26]

Kinship also influenced the selection of a successor for Judge William Rossell of New Jersey, who died in the summer of 1840. Two-
party competition in that state had developed rapidly. Whigs and

Democrats divided over a host of state issues, the most important involving the decision by the Democratic-controlled state legislature to grant a transportation monopoly, known as the Joint Company, to several prominent Democrats. Until the late 1830s Democrats regularly bested the emerging Whig opposition at the polls through a combination of centralized party organization and skillful leadership. Trenton lawyer Stacy G. Potts guided the Democratic State Central Committee, but in 1840 he shared overall direction of the party with Congressman Peter D. Vroom, Sen. Garrett D. Wall, and Van Buren's former secretary of the navy, Mahlon Dickerson.[27]

The selection of Rossell's successor became entangled in the aftermath of the disputed New Jersey congressional election of 1838. Democrats appeared to have captured five of six seats in the House of Representatives, but when the defeated Whig candidates charged election fraud, a sympathetic Whig governor certified their returns as official. The ultimate composition of the New Jersey delegation had national significance; House recognition of the insurgent Whigs would have destroyed the thin Democratic majority in the Twenty-sixth Congress. When the ousted New Jersey Democrats appealed, the Democratic-controlled House, on a close party vote, ordered them seated.[28]

Two of the embattled Democratic congressman—Philemon Dickerson and Peter D. Vroom—applied for the district judgeship. Both were early Jackson supporters and both were former governors. If Van Buren appointed either of them, he ran the risk of reducing the already slender Democratic House majority; the Whigs' recent successes suggested that they would be likely to elect a successor. Moreover, Whigs were certain to charge that in appointing either congressman, the president was tacitly admitting the tenuous nature of Democratic claims to the House seats.[29]

New Jersey Democrats compounded Van Buren's dilemma by refusing to agree on a candidate. Stacy G. Potts urged the president to nominate Mahlon Dickerson's younger brother, who had "sacrificed a lucrative practice to take a seat in Congress" and had been "bitterly persecuted" by Whigs as a result of his legal work for the Joint Company. Potts dismissed all other candidates (including Vroom); they had "never done anything—never made any sacrifice—never become known." Potts discounted arguments that a Whig might succeed Dickerson in the House, but concluded that a Whig would undoubtedly replace Vroom. The state party chairman insisted that the appointment of Vroom would also handicap Van Buren in the forthcoming presidential election by denying him the assistance of an able campaigner.[30]

Sen. Garrett D. Wall pleaded with Van Buren to select a candidate from outside Congress. The senator understood that he could exercise no special prerogative over the president in determining the outcome of the selection process; therefore, Wall enlisted the aid of Silas Wright, the Democratic senator from New York and a member of the Regency, who urged Van Buren to retain Dickerson in Congress. When the chief executive explained that he intended to nominate Dickerson because he possessed the "proper Democratic views," both Wright and Wall countered that, with the disposition of Dickerson's House seat unsettled, his nomination would represent an implicit recognition of the veracity of Whig claims. Both senators feared the disruptive consequences in the upper house of Whig charges that Dickerson had only clung to his House seat as a "steppingstone to a better place."[31]

The president formulated a compromise intended to circumvent senate opposition, to assist his reelection, to sustain the Democratic majority in the House, and to place his first choice, Philemon Dickerson, on the federal bench. Van Buren on July 13, 1840, nominated Mahlon Dickerson instead of his younger brother. Disappointed Democratic aspirants for the judgeship demanded that Dickerson decline to serve, but the former secretary of the navy, although perplexed that the president had not consulted him about the appointment, faithfully cooperated.[32] He denied allegations that he was merely holding the judgeship for his brother until after the 1840 elections, but New Jersey Whigs denounced the appointment as a "mere contrivance."[33] With the nomination coming only two days before adjournment, Whigs in the upper house apparently did not have time to understand the full meaning of the nomination, and the Senate quickly confirmed Dickerson. If Van Buren's former secretary of the navy was not aware of the president's intentions when nominated, he surely was not innocent of subsequent events. After Philemon Dickerson lost his bid for reelection, Mahlon, in February, 1841, resigned the judgeship. Van Buren immediately nominated the younger Dickerson, whom the Senate confirmed without opposition.[34]

Van Buren distributed district court judgeships in a party-directed fashion, but he did not fully implement his policy of party harmony. In making these nominations, he endeavored to consolidate existing administration support by selecting nominees from factions of the various southern state Democratic parties already favorable to the administration. He gave higher priority to placing Democrats of known loyalty on the federal bench than to using this patronage to convert potential supporters. Throughout, he proceeded with caution, avoiding the bickering between the executive and Senate that had consumed much of the energy of the Jackson administration, while successfully Jackson administration, while successfully thwarting attempts by Democratic senators to control the judicial patronage.

Significant nonpartisan influences shaped Van Buren's district court patronage strategy. The president discriminated among Democrats; he sought to place on the federal courts of the South candidates with a firm attachment to the Union. The popular image of Van Buren as partisan expedient concealed his principled commitment to maintenance of the Union through the appointment of district judges favorably disposed to the ascendancy of the national government. Furthermore, within an essentially modern, party-directed mode of selection, the vestiges of a traditional process persisted.

III

In selecting territorial judges, Van Buren also departed from his commitment to establishing harmony among the divergent factions of the Democratic party. The president nominated a total of nine judges to Iowa, Wisconsin, and Florida territories. Rudimentary two-party systems had evolved in each territory, but factionalism and dominant personalities, rather than coherent party organization, typified political culture on the frontier. In concert with his plan to reduce the level of political acrimony, Van Buren balanced the wishes of nascent territorial Democrats against the demands of state party leaders. Viewing the political and constitutional wisdom of removing territorial judges with a circumspection equal to that of his predecessor, he refused to replace judges before their terms expired.

Congress, in June, 1838, organized Iowa from the southern portion of Wisconsin territory, establishing a court whose three judges were to serve four-year terms. Until 1840 political activity in Iowa was an extension of factional divisions in Wisconsin that pitted former Michigan territorial judge and nascent Whig, James D. Doty, against the Democratic territorial delegate, George W. Jones.[35]

The president ordered that Iowa residents should hold two of the judgeships. In response to Van Buren's invitation that he recommend the nominees, Wisconsin Territorial Delegate Jones endorsed two former constituents: Charles Mason, the prosecutor of Des Moines County, and Thomas S. Wilson of Dubuque. Both candidates had assisted Jones in forging the rudiments of Democratic party organization in that section of Wisconsin territory incorporated into Iowa. Mason was a former New Yorker who before coming to Wisconsin had briefly edited William Cullen Bryant's pro-Jackson *New York Evening Post.* Wilson, at twenty-five, was eleven years younger than Mason and had been elected the first territorial delegate from Iowa. He resigned the post, without ever going to Washington, to accept the judgeship. In mediating the selection process, Jones rewarded two instrumental political friends whose presence on the Iowa bench promised to enhance the development of the territorial Democratic party.[36]

In response to intense political and personal pressures, Van Buren decided that the third judge should be appointed from Pennsylvania. The old division between Family and Amalgamator factions in the Democratic party of that state had dissolved by 1835 into two new factions led respectively by George Wolf and Henry A. Muhlenberg. Tension between the "Wolves" and the "Muhles" in the party lasted until the mid-1840s. The disastrous state elections of 1835, in which Anti-Masons had won impressive victories, had prodded the two Democratic factions into an uneasy alliance that gave Van Buren a narrow victory in the presidential contest of the following year. Once in power, the president cautiously avoided offending either faction; he refused until 1840 to select a Pennsylvania Democrat for his cabinet. He appointed the two Democratic leaders to major posts: Wolf became the collector of the port of Philadelphia, and Muhlenberg, the first American minister to Austria.[37]

The two Democratic factions expected the administration to bestow federal patronage upon them in return for their loyalty. Their divergent recommendations for the third Iowa judgeship constituted only one of many instances in which they offered the administration competing candidates. On this occasion, however, Muhlenberg Democrats pressed more vigorously than did the Wolf adherents for their candidate, although both agreed that the influx of former Pennsylvania residents into the new territory gave them a special interest in the outcome of the selection process. Muhlenberg threw his full support behind Joseph Williams, the assistant clerk of the Pennsylvania House of Representatives and the editor of a proadministration newspaper in Delaware County. Muhlenberg Democrats in the federal House of Representatives and Supreme Court Justice Henry Baldwin added their endorsements. So, too, did Muhlenberg's Senate protégé, James Buchanan, who acted not only at the behest of the party leader, but also in response to the incessant demands of Jeremiah Sullivan Black, a friend, fellow law student, and former law partner with Williams.[38] The Wolf faction recommended James Thompson, the Speaker of the Pennsylvania House, but he did not receive the personal endorsement of Wolf or benefit from friendship connections similar to those that served Williams.[39] In view of the overwhelming endorsements by Muhlenberg Democrats and his sympathy with the general proposition that former Pennsylvania residents ought to have judges familiar to them, the chief executive appointed Williams.[40]

The president dispensed the Iowa judgeships in a party-directed fashion, relied on Democratic leaders in Congress to identify nominees, facilitated the growth of an indigenous Democratic party in the territory, and rewarded Muhlenberg Democrats. Nevertheless, personal and instrumental friendship connections within the party contributed to the composition of the Iowa judiciary.

Van Buren between 1838 and 1840 also filled five judgeships in Florida. During these years the evolution of territorial politics affected the mediation of the judicial selection process. After 1835 the Tallahassee Nucleus splintered; some former Jacksonians organized in the Democratic party, while others formed an effective, if loosely knit, opposition that subsequently developed into the Whig party. Judge Robert R. Reid and territorial legislator David Levy organized the Florida Democracy. Simultaneously, Richard Keith Call, whom Jackson had appointed governor in 1836, and Charles Downing, who was elected territorial delegate in the same year, led the opposition.[41]

Call and Downing broke with the national administration and the emergent Democratic party of Florida over three issues. First, they blamed the collapse of territorial financial institutions, especially the Union Bank of Tallahassee, on the inability of the national administration to stem the depression following the Panic of 1837. Second, they insisted on statehood and government assistance to territorial banks as appropriate measures to revive the faltering economy of Florida (Reid and Levy in the 1838 constitutional convention successfully opposed these schemes as inequitable intervention by the government in business affairs). Third, the brutal Second Seminole War poisoned relations between Governor Call and the national administration. Call blamed the federal army for military blundering that perpetuated the Indian uprising, while Secretary of War Poinsett made a similar accusation against the territorial militia.[42]

Van Buren in mid-1838 pursued his policy of party harmony in Florida territory. Congress in that year created a new judgeship for the Apalachicola District. Territorial delegate Downing sponsored the original legislation as a reform that would expedite settlement of land

and admiralty litigation. Previously, the judge of the Middle District, who resided in Tallahassee, had often been unable to complete federal court business in Apalachicola because he had to devote most of his energies to the crowded docket in Tallahassee. Van Buren solicited from Call and Downing their recommendation for the judgeship. Over the protests of Reid, the president appointed their candidate, Richard C. Allen, a cashier of the Union Bank, federal law agent in middle Florida, prominent land speculator, and a friend and business partner of Call.[43]

The second vacancy in 1838 occurred in the Western District of the territory upon the death of John A. Cameron, a native of North Carolina. The Democratic senators from that state immediately asserted a proprietary right to designate Cameron's successor. Van Buren concurred; he nominated their candidate, Dillon Jordan, Jr., a Fayetteville lawyer experienced in deciding claims against the government involving Indian depredations.[44]

Florida politics in 1839 underwent a profound change. Tension between the president and Governor Call escalated as the territorial official publicly flayed the national administration for the military successes of the Seminoles. Van Buren resented these charges of ineptitude; he fixed responsibility for the protracted conflict on his chief accuser's incompetent leadership of the territorial militia. At the same time, Levy and Reid broke from Call and Downing and sought the patronage of the national government to sustain their new party organization. These events bankrupted Van Buren's policy of playing honest broker in making Florida judicial appointments; further cooperation with Call and Downing would frustrate the organizational efforts of the new Democratic party.[45]

Florida Democrats had no qualms about exploiting the political potential of the judicial patronage, but they offered Van Buren contradictory advice about how best to proceed. Reid recommended the president stimulate party growth by replacing the judges as their terms expired with lawyers already in Florida, rather than "disappointing the . . . Democratic party" through the selection of nonresidents, "unknown and without influence."[46] Levy advocated a bolder approach. The president could facilitate party development by promptly removing unacceptable judges aligned with Call and Downing and replacing them with nonresident Democrats. "To form a nucleus to the Democratic party, afford leaders and infuse vigor into its organization," Levy explained to the president, *"all the offices in Florida, from highest to lowest,* should be immediately filled with active thorough-going Democrats mostly from the states." Van Buren could diminish the influence of Call and Downing, Levy concluded, by selecting Democrats "*all* from the . . . different states as have furnished most of the immigrants."[47]

Van Buren developed a judicial patronage policy that incorporated parts of both of these views. His patience worn thin, the president removed Governor Call and appointed Reid in his place.[48] The chief executive, however, refused to extend the removal power to the judiciary; instead, he selected new judges, two of whom were nonresidents, when three vacancies occurred through resignations and an expired term.

Judge James Webb of the Southern District at Key West in early 1839 created the first of these openings when he resigned in order to move to Texas. The selection of his successor precipitated the only controversy over a judicial nominee during the Van Buren administration. The conflict stemmed from tensions created by the rise of the Democratic party and exacerbated by the competing expectations of coastal shippers and salvage operators who were affected by decisions of the southern district court. The treacherous shoals and keys off the Florida peninsula regularly snared a heavy toll of vessels entering and leaving the Gulf of Mexico. The decrees of the court in salvage cases amounted yearly to hundreds of thousands of dollars, most of which represented, even with insurance, losses to the shipping community of New York City.[49]

Charles Walker and District Attorney William Marvin, both of Key West, were the leading applicants. Downing and the shipping interests of New York recommended Walker, who, before moving to Florida in 1838, had been counsel for the New York Dry Dock Company, a firm engaged in coastal shipping and salvage operations around the Florida Keys. Spokesmen for the New York shippers pleaded that Walker's "appointment would give great satisfaction to that class of men who suffer most by the Florida salvage decrees."[50] Downing argued that the appointment of a judge sympathetic to the interests of New York shippers was essential if American commerce were to continue to flow regularly around the tip of Florida.[51]

Robert R. Reid recommended Marvin as the candidate most familiar with the operations of the court and sensitive to the interests of the Florida salvage operators. Marvin in 1835 had accepted appointment as federal attorney in order to be near his extensive Florida landholdings. In this post he incurred the ire of the shipping interests, who charged that he was too lenient in prosecuting the often aggressive tactics of salvage operators. The bar of Key West, however, endorsed Marvin; his experience would insure continuity and competence in the disposition of the extensive admiralty and maritime business before the court.[52]

The president deliberately postponed making the nomination until he learned the sentiments of Florida Democrats. The delay meant that an office which should have been filled while the Congress was in session was not filled until after it adjourned. Webb's resignation reached Van Buren by mid-February, well before the end of the Twenty-fifth Congress on March 3, 1839. Eight days after adjournment and three days after receiving Reid's recommendation, the president granted the district attorney a recess judicial commission.[53]

Downing and the New York shipping interests attempted, at the beginning of the Twenty-sixth Congress, to block the submission of Marvin's name for a regular appointment. They alleged that Marvin had exploited his new office for personal gain. The otherwise faulty accusations had enough substance to prove a potential embarrassment to the president. Prior to his recess appointment, Marvin, in the capacity of a private citizen, had appeared before Judge Webb seeking to foreclose a mortgage. Webb issued the foreclosure order, but the marshal sealed the proceedings after Marvin had taken the oath of office; thus, the new judge seemingly had employed his office to expedite personal business. Van Buren proceeded with cautious determination; he immediately directed Secretary of State Forsyth to secure from Marvin a full explanation.[54] The judge admitted some "judicial indelicacy," but stressed in self-defense that Webb, not he, had issued the foreclosure order.[55] Persuaded of Marvin's innocence, if not his common sense, and unwilling to capitulate to Downing, Van Buren on March 16, 1840, nominated the judge. After a delay of more than one month, during which the Senate Committee on the Judiciary heard and rejected the same charges, the full Senate added its confirmation.[56]

Van Buren selected the two other Florida nominees from outside the territory. The conduct of Judge Thomas Randall, of the Middle District of Florida, raised once again the issue of whether a president could remove a territorial judge. In addition to his judicial duties, Randall was adjutant general of the territorial militia and, with Call, an outspoken critic of Van Buren's war policy. Furthermore, Democratic lawyers in Tallahassee complained that Randall was highhanded and short-tempered on the bench, and they demanded his removal. Van Buren pondered the available constitutional remedies; he requested Attorney General Felix Grundy to clarify the scope of the president's power to remove judges. Grundy responded with a ringing opinion that established the absolute power of the chief executive to remove territorial judges. Much as had Jackson, Van Buren eschewed such sweeping power; instead, fearful, perhaps, of Senate repercussions, he bided his time until the judge's term expired. In 1840 he replaced Randall with Alfred Balch, a Nashville, Tennessee, lawyer recommended by Andrew Jackson and James K. Polk. The appointment signaled to Tennessee Democrats the continued good will of the administration and rewarded Balch for his early and sustained support of Van Buren.[57]

The last Florida judgeship went to an instrumental political friend of the president. Jackson had frequently resorted to political cronyism in appointing territorial judges, but only in this single instance did Van Buren even appear to accept the practice. The vacancy occurred when Van Buren elevated Reid from judge of the district court for east Florida to governor of the territory. Reid recommended the president select a resident Democrat; instead, Van Buren nominated a former Democratic congressman, Isaac H. Bronson, of Watertown, New York. Not only was Bronson personally known to the president, but the New York Democrat while in the House of Representatives had been derided by Whig colleagues as one of the "Kinderhook Oligarchy." After losing a bid for reelection in 1838, Bronson had accepted a judgeship in the Fifth District Court of New York State. Plagued by poor health, he wanted to move to the warmer climate of Florida, but only if he could secure a federal post that would insure him a steady income. His brother-in-law and law partner, former congressman Micah Sterling, relayed these wishes to the administration, sparing Bronson what he called the "humiliation of seeking after public office."[58]

The growth of the Florida Democratic party altered the conduct of the selection process. With an indigenous Democratic party in the territory, Levy and Reid supplanted Call and Downing as the principal mediators of the selection process. The president accepted Levy's argument that the Democratic party of Florida would develop most rapidly through the infusion of nonresident judges, but he refused to impede the traditional independence of the judiciary through the removal power.

Van Buren pursued a party-directed selection process that contrasted sharply with the practices of his predecessor in filling vacancies in the territorial courts. The traditional forces of personal interest that bulked large in Jackson's administration were less significant during Van Buren's. The New Yorker respected the wishes of territorial Democrats, but he also understood that the calculus of territorial and national politics required appointment of party supporters from outside the territories.

IV

"Martin Van Buren," John Randolph of Roanoke observed, had a habit of "rowing to his object with muffled oars."[59] Too frequently historians have interpreted this shrewdness as mere expedience without appreciating the handicaps under which Van Buren labored or the achievements he wrought. More than his predecessor, Van Buren intended, through a restrained and cautious judicial patronage policy, to enhance the development of the Democratic party. To this end he defused, through cooperation and attention to the qualifications of his nominees, the institutional conflict that had, during Jackson's administration, pitted the chief executive and the Senate against one another. He not only won Senate cooperation, but also retained the presidential initiative in the selection and appointment processes. The gathering momentum of two-party competition was accompanied by an intensification of the role of party in the selection of federal judges and a diminution of traditional personal interests. From within the Democratic party, however, Van Buren rewarded only those partisans loyal to the administration and, in the South, committed to the Union. Van Buren's belief in a decentralized and state-oriented Democracy allowed him to bend to local party demands without sacrificing his broader political purposes. Ultimately, that broader strategy failed and Van Buren bequeathed the Jacksonian tradition of a forceful role for the president in the selection process to a Whig successor.

3

A DOOMED MAN

Mr. Tyler is weak. . . . The members and senators of both
parties tell me on all sides that they hardly ever know anything of appointments in their Districts till the name goes
in.—James D. Westcott, 1842[1]

The presidential election of 1840 crystallized the nation's first
mass two-party system. In the boisterous "Log Cabin" campaign of
that year, almost 80 percent of the eligible electorate voted for either
Martin Van Buren or William Henry Harrison. The Democratic and
Whig parties emerged as modern "electoral machines" capable of
mustering impressive numbers of voters. A subtle revolution under-
girded this transformation of politics: local and state central committees fostered organizational coherence in party operation, and the
stigma attached to partisan opposition diminished. The "Shrine of
Party" superseded traditional notions of deference and antipartyism.

The transformation was far from complete. A competitive two-
party system distinguished the antebellum political culture, but the
Whig and Democratic parties, for all of their abilities to mobilize
voters, remained loose-knit, parochial coalitions. The Democrats did
not form a national party committee until 1848; the Whigs never
forged a formal continuing national organization.[2] These decentralized party structures perpetuated the presidential isolation
prevalent during the 1830s. The sheer bulk of territorial acquisitions
canceled the centralizing effects of technological advances in communications and transportation during the next two decades. Nativist
fears fueled by massive foreign immigration and sectional pressures
associated with the expansion of slavery, especially after the Mexican
War, increasingly strained the new mass two-party system. While the
full consequences of these centrifugal pressures lay in the future, the
Whigs' 1840 national ticket revealed the dynamics of coalitional two-
party politics: the state rights advocate John Tyler of Virginia was
paired with the more national-minded William Henry Harrison of
Indiana.

The selection of Tyler as the aged Harrison's running mate was,
like most vice-presidential nominations, a tactical maneuver whose

44

strategic consequences were perceived only dimly. The Whigs nominated the state rights Democrat-turned-Whig with the intention of enlisting conservative Democrats in the South to complement Harrison's strength in the North and West. As a Tyler critic observed: "At the time of his nomination for Vice President no one ever thought of him as fit for the Presidency . . . it was offered merely as proprietary to the South, not personally."[3] Harrison's sudden death vaulted Tyler into the White House and created for Whigs "a crisis as a party."[4] The powerful Kentucky senator Henry Clay expected Tyler to concur with the Whigs' new-won majority in the Congress in the enactment of a national economic program. After a brief period of cooperation, the new president and the Kentucky senator clashed over fiscal, economic, and patronage policies. Any hope of reconciliation vanished in September, 1841, when the chief executive vetoed for a second time Clay's cherished national bank. In response, the cabinet, with the exception of Secretary of State Daniel Webster, resigned, and most congressional Whigs formally renounced the president.

Whigs in the upper house denounced the president's patronage policy. Tyler's conception of the presidential power to appoint and remove officeholders evolved in response to changing political circumstances. As a senator during Jackson's administration, Tyler protested the advent of the spoils system and Old Hickory's alleged disdain for the Senate.[5] Once in the presidential office, Tyler temporarily persisted in this Whiggish theme of limited executive authority: he promised to appoint and remove federal officeholders strictly on the basis of ability and honesty. "Executive control of the patronage," Tyler proclaimed in 1841, had "become so powerful as to create great alarm." He demanded that Congress reform the patronage system, but the new Whig majority balked at the prospect of losing the bounty of its recently acquired power.[6] "I am much ashamed," Whig Congressman William B. Campbell of Virginia observed, "that I ever abused the Van Buren party so much for their spoils principles, as I see the same principles overflowing in the bosoms of the Whigs generally." Tyler avoided wholesale removals, but his lofty disinterestedness dissolved into pragmatic political concern, and he vigorously defended the executive prerogative.[7]

Tyler by mid-1842 was using the distribution of federal offices to build a third party committed to his reelection. "The appointments will be made," concluded William Campbell, "with a view of Tyler's popularity—to secure him strength."[8] As the new minority in the upper house, Senate Democrats challenged the removal of Van Buren appointees by demanding, much as had the Whigs in the

1830s, a written explanation from the president. After the second bank veto, Clay Whigs joined the attack. With the exception of conservative state rights members, senators from both parties flayed Tyler for appointing neither sound Democrats nor thoroughgoing Whigs; instead, "his favors," they claimed, were "reserved principally for those men who have been vacillating between parties."[9] "Tyler," observed the editor of a hostile Whig paper in Pennsylvania, was "the first President who had ever set himself up as a political cannibal to . . . devour the men and the party who elevated him to power."[10]

Tyler's mercurial partisanship and the Senate's hostility toward him affected the judicial selection and appointment processes in three ways. First, Tyler became the only antebellum president to appoint consistently both Whigs and Democrats to the lower federal bench; of twenty-two nominees, ten were Whigs and twelve Democrats. Until June, 1842, he most frequently selected Whigs, but thereafter he nominated only Democrats. Second, Tyler encountered stiff Senate opposition; the upper house rejected three nominees and forced the withdrawal of a fourth. Tyler's changing partisan allegiance precluded senatorial courtesy; neither Senate Whigs nor Democrats could expect to exercise a decisive role in the selection of judges for their states. Third, the president's reputation for "political cannibalism" prompted judicial nominees, for the first time during the era of the second party system, to refuse commissions. These refusals also reflected a growing disparity between the prestige and financial rewards of federal service and the attractions of private law practice, state judicial service, and political careers.

Tyler's willingness to cross party lines in making his nominations did not mean that, in the midst of a new mass party system, the selection of federal judges reverted to a traditional patron-client method. Carl Russell Fish concluded that the president, instead of following partisan affiliation, made nominations "from the ranks of his personal and political friends, with the personal element fully as prominent as the other."[11] This conclusion only partially accounts for Tyler's choices. Twenty-three percent of his nominees had kinship connections to principal mediators—including the president—of the selection process, although one of these was the president's brother-in-law. While Tyler switched parties, he did not forsake partisanship.

Tyler made two decisions which contributed to a formal, party-directed selection process. First, he adopted the administrative routine followed by previous administrations; his three secretaries of state—Daniel Webster, Abel P. Upshur, and John C. Calhoun—supervised the stream of applications and recommendations for judicial office. Second, he allowed Webster to become, according to John C. Calhoun, the administration's "controlling spirit."[12] Webster believed that his own future prospects and the success of Tyler's administration depended upon the degree to which Clay's Senate opposition could be neutralized.[13] Equally significant was Webster's insistence that the selection process reflect his concern with the competency and political correctness of the federal judiciary. During his service in the House and the Senate, Webster had sustained the federal judicial power, had called for extension and reform of the circuit court system, and had protested against federal judges who lacked technical legal ability and propounded radical views of property rights and the sanctity of the Union.[14] More than any previous secretary of state, Webster, so long as Tyler wished a connection with the Whig party, dominated the selection process.

II

An intransigent Senate and uncooperative nominees plagued Tyler's recruitment of federal judges. The upper house rejected three district court nominees: one to the Eastern District of Pennsylvania and two to the Eastern District of Virginia, the president's home state. The chief executive also had difficulty in persuading appointees to serve; of twenty-two nominees, four declined commissions. Together, these rejections and refusals produced prolonged delays in filling district court vacancies, particularly in Louisiana, Pennsylvania, Indiana, and Virginia. Only in Massachusetts and Vermont did the selection process proceed without incident.

Especially after 1842, fundamental changes occurred in the selection process. Abel P. Upshur and John C. Calhoun independently observed that the president kept his own counsel in patronage matters; he "rejected as much advice as he accepted."[15] They, however, viewed Tyler's actions from the perspective of the period after mid-1842, when the president had begun his trek back into the Democratic party. During the first eighteen months of his administration, Tyler accepted advice about nominations, particularly recommendations offered by Webster. The decline of the secretary of state's influence and the increasing isolation of the president began in June, 1842, when he abruptly assumed direct supervision of the selection of judges for Iowa territory.

During the first session of the Twenty-seventh Congress, Webster influenced the selection of judges for the district courts of Louisiana and Massachusetts. In Louisiana Judge Philip K. Lawrence, who was facing possible impeachment, died unexpectedly in May, 1841. Tyler in July nominated Abner Nash Ogden, a judge of the Louisiana Supreme Court and an organizer of the Whig party in that state. Ogden declined, however; he considered service on the state supreme court of greater significance than duty on the federal district bench.[16]

Ogden's declination produced a four-month delay. The president, shortly before Congress recessed in September, settled on a more willing nominee, youthful Theodore Howard McCaleb. The thirty-one-year-old federal attorney for the Eastern District of Louisiana benefited from influential family, personal, and political connections. McCaleb's father, David McCaleb, had an extensive circle of political acquaintances in Mississippi, including Sen. John Henderson and prominent Whig leader S. S. Prentiss, who endorsed the nomination. More important, Theodore McCaleb was known to Secretary of State Webster; he had studied in the law office of Webster's friend, Sen. Rufus Choate of Salem, Massachusetts. With support from the major factions in the Whig party, McCaleb's nomination sailed through the upper house.[17]

Webster also influenced the selection of a successor for Judge John Davis of Massachusetts, his home state. Davis announced his resignation in May, 1841; during the next four months John Pickering, the son of former Federalist Timothy Pickering, Massachusetts Supreme Court Justice Theophilus Parsons, and Peleg Sprague solicited the blessings of Webster and the Whig senators from Massachusetts. Sprague was ultimately successful. He had, as a representative and senator from Maine, consistently aligned himself with Webster; in 1839 he had been a Massachusetts delegate to the Whig convention, and the following year he had served as a presidential elector for Harrison. The former Maine senator, however, had a history of poor health, including failing eyesight. Sprague's physician assured Webster that the former senator was physically sound. The Massachusetts senators added their endorsements to Webster's recommendation, and four days after Davis resigned, the Senate confirmed Sprague.[18]

Tyler acted with greater independence in making territorial appointments. His last nominations during the first session of the Twenty-seventh Congress were to Florida. The Whigs of that territory were poorly organized and divided over the patronage policy of the national administration. Tallahassee lawyer William Wyatt insisted that the infusion of nonresident Whigs of proven principles would hasten the development of an indigenous Whig party. Gov. Richard K. Call, whom Harrison had restored to office, expected

Tyler to stimulate party loyalty by rewarding Florida residents, especially since Democrats controlled the territorial government.[19]

Contrary to Webster's wishes, Tyler attempted through personal politics to cultivate Democratic support. The president was unsympathetic to the plight of Florida Whigs; he nominated two Democrats, both with Virginia backgrounds, and one Whig to fill vacancies in the Apalachicola and middle districts. Only the selection of Samuel Carmack for the latter post was party-directed; the Lincoln County, Tennessee, lawyer, who was recommended by the leading Whigs of that state, had supported Harrison and Tyler during the 1840 campaign.[20]

The other judgeship, however, was filled for altogether different reasons. Relying on his personal knowledge of the nominee, Tyler selected William H. Brockenbrough, whom Van Buren had earlier appointed federal district attorney for the Apalachicola district. He was a native of Virginia, an acquaintance of Tyler's, and a nephew of prominent Virginia Democrat Thomas Ritchie. Florida Whigs bitterly opposed the nomination. Wyatt denounced Brockenbrough as "a whole Hog Jackson and Van Buren man and consequently unacceptable to the Whig party." The nominee, however, declined to accept; he wanted no part of Tyler's third-party strategy and protested as well the "utter inadequacy of the compensation." This nomination of a Democratic friend was no aberration, however; Tyler on October 13 issued a recess commission to another Virginia Democrat, Samuel J. Douglas, a neighbor and political supporter from Southampton County.[21]

During the first ten months of his administration, Tyler pursued an inconsistent but uncontroversial judicial patronage policy. While still aligned with the Whig party and attentive, at least in making district court selections, to the wishes of Secretary of State Webster, the president also bestowed territorial judgeships on Democratic friends. Beginning in January, 1842, however, Senate Whigs challenged Tyler's distribution of not only judgeships but all federal offices. The president responded by accelerating his plan to fashion a new party composed of dissident Democrats and Whigs. The result was increased acrimony between Senate Whigs and the chief executive.

The death on January 15, 1842, of Joseph Hopkinson of the Eastern District of Pennsylvania created the administration's first major judicial appointment crisis. Factional divisions among the Whigs of that state limited Tyler's freedom in selecting a successor to Hopkinson. The cohesion produced by the Whig victory in 1840 had quickly

dissipated with Harrison's death. Former National Republicans in
Philadelphia particularly distrusted Tyler.[22] "President Tyler," observed George Sidney Fisher, was "a poor, weak, vacillating fellow
heartily despised by everyone." Prominent party leaders Nicholas
Biddle and Jonathan Roberts charged that Tyler had "surrendered
every genuine impulse in seeking reelection."[23] These Whigs expected Daniel Webster to lead the administration.

Tyler also had supporters in Philadelphia. The most important
was J. Washington Tyson, the surveyor of the port and rival of
Roberts for control of the customhouse's patronage. To the dismay of
Roberts, Tyson wished to enlist the Catholic and Irish immigrants of
the city and to forge a reciprocal alliance with the national administration.[24]

Passage by Congress during the previous August of legislation
granting bankruptcy jurisdiction to the district courts lent special
urgency to the selection. The law provided that individuals could file
voluntary and involuntary bankruptcy petitions. The first of these
petitions from Philadelphia, which had been hard hit by the depression following the Panic of 1837, reached the district court at about
the time of Hopkinson's death. All of the petitions would languish
until the president filled the judgeship.[25]

Webster wanted to defuse the potentially volatile situation
through a politically safe appointment. On his recommendation Tyler
nominated Horace Binney. Webster hoped to recruit the most able
Whig lawyers for the federal bench; Binney commanded enormous
prestige as one of the most esteemed lawyers in the nation. Webster
also believed that the appointment of such an eminent figure would
forestall complaints by other office-seekers, preclude rancor among
the rival Whig factions, and insure immediate Senate approval.[26]
Binney refused; it was "an inferior judicial station," the conduct of
which "his heart would not be in." He also resisted on personal
grounds; he admired Webster, but considered Tyler a "vain and weak
man" who sought to exploit him for political purposes.[27]

Binney's refusal opened the selection process to the divisive pressures of Whig factionalism. William Rawle and Thomas Bradford,
both of Philadelphia, emerged as the most prominent candidates.
Rawle was a former Jacksonian Democrat and state supreme court
reporter who had bolted the party after Old Hickory's Bank veto.
Tyson and dissident Democrats in eastern Pennsylvania anxious for
an alliance with the national administration supported him. Biddle,
Binney, and other conservative Whigs determined to nullify Tyson's
influence supported Bradford, a one-time common pleas judge who

had an extensive practice before the federal courts.[28] His allegiance to the administration was unquestionable; he had, in late January, presided over a massive pro-Tyler rally in Philadelphia. Biddle appealed to his old friend Webster to press for Bradford's nomination. Once again the secretary of state prevailed; Tyler nominated Bradford.[29]

The selection precipitated a clash between Senate Whigs and the president that Webster had hoped to prevent. Both Democratic senators from Pennsylvania endorsed the nominee, but Henry Clay rallied Senate Whigs against confirmation. The Kentucky senator accused Tyler of subverting the federal judiciary by rewarding active politicians with appointments. He denounced Bradford's participation in the Philadelphia pro-Tyler rally. The Senate on February 24, 1842, voted seventeen to twenty-two to reject Bradford. The nominee fell victim to his own partisans; only five of twenty-eight Whig votes were cast for Bradford.[30]

Bradford's rejection heightened the administrative and political pressures on the administration. It further delayed reopening the court, much to the dismay of lawyers and litigants seeking to file under the bankruptcy act. It also pushed Tyler to consider more fully an alliance with Democrats. Biddle urged such a solution; he recommended that the president nominate a Democrat from "the interior . . . but still within the district so as to get out of the City intriguers and select a popular man." He cautioned that after Bradford's rejection the selection of Rawle "would be an acknowledgement of defeat."[31] Webster, however, refused to abide the selection of any Democrat, and the Tyson faction demanded the nomination of a city resident.[32]

Biddle broke the deadlock by persuading Webster to intervene with the president on behalf of a compromise candidate. Archibald Randall, a Democrat-turned-Whig, had been during the previous eight years a judge of the Court of Common Pleas of Philadelphia County. In that position he had impressed Biddle and other former National Republicans with his sensitivity to creditor interests while presiding over suits involving the defunct Second Bank of the United States and insolvent debtors. The Tyson faction was also enthusiastic; Randall's Catholicism and his good relations with the Irish community promised to broaden Whig support. Moreover, Randall, who had "not mixed in party politics," was acceptable to the Whig majority in the Senate.[33]

Webster and Senate Whigs also influenced Tyler's decisions about his last two district court nominations during the second session of the Twenty-seventh Congress. At the urging of the secretary of state, Tyler avoided further controversy by nominating Sen. Samuel Prentiss of Vermont to be district judge for that state. Senate Whigs quickly confirmed one of their own.[34] A vacancy on the Indiana bench, however, stirred controversy and revealed once again the difficulty of the Tyler administration in attracting able judges.

Whig domination of Indiana politics in the early 1840s concealed serious internal party divisions. Most of Harrison's supporters were skeptical of the new Virginia president; indeed, as a former Democrat, Tyler became a divisive issue. Former governor William Hendricks and Congressmen James H. Cravens and Joseph L. White led an opposition faction critical of Tyler's Bank veto. The proadministration faction included former congressman Johnathan McCarty and Commissioner of the General Land Office Elisha Mills Huntington, a Harrison appointee. The Whig senators from Indiana—Albert S. White and Oliver H. Smith—adopted a neutral position, although they occasionally joined Clay in voting against the president.[35]

When Judge Jesse Lynch Holman died on March 18, 1842, Webster immediately identified a replacement. The secretary of state adopted a strategy similar to that followed in filling the Pennsylvania judgeship; he sought to preclude Whig dissension by nominating a candidate of unimpeachable qualifications. Supreme Court Justice John McLean, whose circuit included Indiana, encouraged Webster's pursuit of excellence. On learning of Holman's death, he immediately wrote the secretary of state, expressing his "natural . . . solicitude" about a successor and protesting "most solemnly against the appointment of a mere stump partisan, who had no other merit." While he had "no wish for any particular individual," the justice recommended the nomination of one of the three judges of the Indiana Supreme Court.[36]

Webster persuaded Tyler, six days after Holman's death, to nominate Charles Dewey, a six-year veteran of the Indiana Supreme Court. A native of Sheffield, Massachusetts, Dewey was one of the secretary of state's most enthusiastic Indiana adherents. Webster decided upon Dewey, as he had Binney, without the nominee's knowledge. The strategy appeared to work; the Indiana senators joined their colleagues in confirming Dewey the same day he was nominated.[37]

Once again, the exigencies of federal district court service undermined administration political strategy. Dewey declined the commission; the federal post offered tenure during good behavior, but he preferred the prestige and the additional $1,500 in salary that the state judgeship commanded.[38]

Dewey's refusal fomented factional discord. The two leading

candidates—Judge Miles C. Eggleston and former governor William Hendricks—were endorsed by Whigs sympathetic to Clay. As a circuit court judge, Eggleston escaped charges of conflict of interest levied against Hendricks and other candidates who had bankruptcy litigation pending before the federal court. In Washington, Whig Congressman Joseph L. White sought to mediate the selection of Eggleston, channeling recommendations and advice to the administration.[39] Johnathan McCarty worked vigorously against both candidates, denouncing what he termed a "systematic arrangement" by Hendricks and Clay Whigs in Indiana to have the "administration . . . sustain enemies against its friends."[40]

The president and the secretary of state attempted to defuse McCarty's political protest and the problem of conflict of interest by reaching inside the administration. They ignored recommendations for other Indiana Whigs and selected Commissioner of the General Land Office Elisha Mills Huntington. A native of New York, Huntington had served as a state legislator, a delegate to the 1839 Whig National Convention, a prosecuting attorney, and judge of Indiana's seventh circuit before accompanying Harrison to Washington.[41]

The nomination stunned Indiana Whigs. Congressmen James H. Cravens and Joseph L. White condemned the selection as "hasty and secret" and charged that the president had ignored the better-qualified candidates they had recommended. Huntington had not received a single endorsement from the Indiana delegation; therefore, they demanded the Senate Committee on the Judiciary conduct a thorough investigation.[42] Senators Albert S. White and Oliver H. Smith straddled the conflict; they notified the judiciary committee of the congressmen's complaints, while simultaneously soliciting letters testifying to Huntington's previous satisfactory judicial service, an indication, perhaps, that they had known of and agreed to the nomination before Tyler made it. The committee's investigation disclosed that the president had, indeed, nominated Huntington without a single endorsement, but that the nominee was nonetheless qualified. The full Senate confirmed Huntington without objection.[43] The business of the court, however, had languished during the two months since Holman's death.

Webster wanted the administration to remain within the Whig party. In selecting an Indiana judge he expected to fulfill this goal by quickly nominating a candidate whose impeccable legal credentials would disarm critics in the state and the Senate and diminish the disruptive consequences of Whig factionalism. The meager salary paid the federal judge for Indiana exploded the strategy. As the connection between the national administration and the state Whig parties became increasingly brittle, Tyler jettisoned Webster and Whiggery.

III

Beginning in June, 1842, Tyler shifted the partisan basis of his lower court nominations. This coincided with the president's decision to nurture his third party movement and election by appealing to Democrats. During the next two years all of his ten judicial nominees were Democrats; seven were selected for Florida and Iowa territories and three for the Eastern District of Virginia. As a result of the president's new partisan alignment, Webster's once dominant role in the selection process ended, but conflict with Senate Whigs intensified.

Tyler distributed the judicial patronage in Florida and Iowa territories with the expectation of winning Democratic support.[44] He wanted to insure that when statehood conventions met, which promised to occur in both territories by 1844, Democrats sympathetic to the national administration would control the major appointive offices. The zeal with which the president pursued this policy in Iowa stirred the ire of local Whigs and alienated the secretary of state.

Two-party development in Iowa proceeded with unusual rapidity; by 1840 Whigs and Democrats had installed party organizations that included central committees and subordinate county organizations. Unable to participate in the presidential election, the parties in 1840 concentrated on territorial issues, the most important of which was the statehood question. Democrats endorsed early statehood, but Whigs opposed it, fearing that creation of a state government would make the Democratic majority permanent. In the 1840 election Whigs achieved substantial gains, but Democrats sent Augustus C. Dodge to Washington as territorial delegate.[45]

Isaac S. Leffler of Muscatine and Francis Springer of Iowa City led the Iowa Whig party. Leffler had once served with Tyler in the Virginia House of Delegates. Springer was an Indiana immigrant who, like Leffler, served in the territorial legislature. From the time of Harrison's death, they distrusted Tyler, principally because of his refusal to cooperate with Henry Clay.[46] The struggle in mid-1842 over the fate of the three Democratic judges appointed to the territory further strained relations between the president and Iowa Whigs.

As Martin Van Buren anticipated when he appointed them, Chief Justice Charles Mason and Associate Justice Joseph Williams combined judicial service with Democratic party politics. Francis Springer denounced both judges as "political demagogues" who "poured forth tirades of abuse against . . . the administration." He held a more generous view of Associate Justice Thomas S. Wilson; he "did not meddle in politics" and had become "a very popular man and a very popular judge with all parties."[47] Wilson's uncle, Whig Congressman Samuel Stokely of Ohio, and Supreme Court Justice John McLean added their recommendations. Under Springer's direction Iowa Whigs in the judicial districts served by Mason and Williams gathered petitions demanding new judges and charging the incumbents with violating judicial propriety by interfering in politics. They also claimed that Williams had defrauded litigants in his district through improper handling of court fees.[48]

To replace Mason and Williams, Iowa Whigs recommended Leffler and Stephen Whicher. A sense of propriety prevented Leffler from appealing directly to his "personal friend," the chief executive, but he did solicit the assistance of Abel P. Upshur, a trusted Tyler advisor. Whicher, who had run unsuccessfully in 1840 for territorial delegate, went in the spring of 1842 to Washington in the hope of persuading the president to nominate him to Williams's seat.[49]

Webster urged the president to give Whigs control of the Iowa judiciary. He recommended Wilson as chief justice and Leffler and Whicher as associate justices. "Williams," he observed, was "not strongly supported . . . and Mason still less." Whicher, on the other hand, was "exceedingly well recommended"; furthermore, while in Washington, he had conducted himself with "sense and character." Webster preferred Leffler on less objective grounds: he was a Virginian and his father had been "a valued former acquaintance."[50]

The president rejected Webster's advice. Tyler on July 15 nominated Wilson chief justice, but he designated Charles Mason and a Kentucky Democrat, William Brown, associate justices. Brown was to replace Williams; apparently, Tyler accepted as true the accusations of misconduct leveled against the judge. Democratic territorial delegate Augustus C. Dodge opposed Brown, partly because the nominee was a nonresident and partly because he believed Williams had been falsely accused. The Iowa delegate persuaded the Senate to delay consideration of the nominations until Williams, who had already left for Washington, had conferred with the president. Following a personal interview with the judge on July 24, Tyler reversed himself: he withdrew Brown's nomination, renominated Williams, and, on Williams's recommendation, switched the chief justiceship back to Mason.[51]

Iowa Whigs and Democrats reacted differently to Tyler's reap-pointment of the incumbent judges. The former condemned the president for squandering the valuable patronage. The latter faintly praised him for maintaining continuity on the territorial bench, for appointing residents, and for acting "with . . . creditable independence." These same Democrats, however, subsequently refused to endorse the president's bid for a second term.[52]

Tyler's realignment with the Democratic party prompted a reshuffling of the cabinet. Webster protested the distribution of federal offices to Democrats and the president's enthusiasm for the annexation of Texas. Increasingly isolated and without influence, Webster resigned in March, 1843. He was replaced successively by two Democrats: Abel P. Upshur and, in February, 1844, John C. Calhoun. At the same time Tyler brought Calhoun into the cabinet, he created a vacancy in the Eastern District of Virginia by appointing the judge of that court, John Y. Mason, secretary of the navy.[53]

The vacancy in the Virginia judgeship occurred at the end of a metamorphosis in the two-party system of that state. Led by Senator William C. Rives, in the late 1830s conservative Democrats in the Old Dominion revolted against the Van Buren administration. In 1839 Rives, John Y. Mason, and Tyler battled for a seat in the United States Senate. Regular Democrats supported Mason while conservative Democrats and most Whigs backed Rives. With no hope of success, Tyler accepted the Whig vice-presidential nomination. Rives prevailed over Mason, the latter receiving from Van Buren in 1840 the judgeship in eastern Virginia. During the subsequent four years, while Tyler moved back to the Democratic party, Rives gravitated toward Henry Clay. In the upper house Rives and his Whig colleague, William S. Archer, routinely attacked Tyler's Virginia nominations and sided with Clay on legislative matters.[54]

Tyler wanted to appeal to both factions of the divided Virginia Democratic party. A minority Calhounite faction, led by James A. Seddon and Robert M. T. Hunter, clashed over annexation of Texas with the older Jacksonian faction identified with Thomas Ritchie. Calhoun Democrats shared Tyler's enthusiasm for annexation, but to remain in the White House the president also had to enlist regular Democrats. Thus, Tyler brought both Mason and Calhoun into the cabinet at the same time. In order to extend this strategy to the entire state, the president removed Whigs; indeed, the editor of the Richmond Whig wryly observed in early 1844 that the "Tyler Grip" was sweeping the federal officeholders.[55]

Tyler lacked the personal discipline necessary to implement his political strategy. In selecting a judge for the Eastern District of Virginia, he capitulated to personal interests. From the time the judgeship became vacant, one candidate pressed the chief executive for nomination: state district court judge John B. Christian—Tyler's brother-in-law.[56] Among those persons from whom he solicited recommendations was Supreme Court Justice Peter V. Daniel, an old friend. The justice dismissed any misgivings the president harbored about appointing a kinsman; he assured Tyler that Christian was so well qualified that the Virginia Whig senators would not dare oppose his nomination.[57]

Even if he had not been the president's kinsman, Christian would have been a controversial nominee. Since the beginning of the administration, he had served Tyler as a confidential personal and political advisor. In 1843 and 1844, while ostensibly conducting judicial business, Christian had organized Tyler rallies in his judicial district, frequently taking to the stump to cajole wavering Democrats to support the president. Whether gripped by doubt or discretion, Tyler delayed nominating Christian until April 2, three weeks after Mason left his post.[58]

The nomination ignited a storm of protest. Democratic aspirants for the judgeship, "who had no interest at court," derided as insincere the president's professed desire to accommodate them.[59] The *Richmond Whig,* on the other hand, ridiculed Christian for clamoring after the federal post on the basis of his family ties and for meddling in politics while holding a judgeship.[60] Christian pleaded with Rives and Archer to ignore "these most unjust insinuations," but the Virginia senators, contrary to Daniel's prediction, objected to the nomination.[61]

Christian's nomination produced a political and administrative debacle. The Whig-dominated judiciary committee on June 15 reported the nomination without recommendation. The full Senate then rejected the nominee on a straight party vote: twenty Democrats for and twenty-four Whigs against. Not only did Tyler lose in the Senate, but during the three months the upper house considered the nominee, more than three-hundred petitioners seeking relief under the bankruptcy law waited impatiently for a new district court judge.[62]

Tyler replied to Christian's rejection with another controversial nominee. The president immediately nominated Robert R. Collier of Petersburg, a former delegate to the Virginia legislature, a prosperous lawyer, and a member of the Calhoun faction of the Virginia Democracy. Collier's essays on the constitutional ascendancy of state rights over the national government had a small but influential following in Virginia that included the president. The nominee was also outspoken in his advocacy of the immediate annexation of Texas. Archer objected to the appointment of any federal judge with such views; he successfully moved by a vote of twenty-four to fifteen to table the nomination. Once again, party lines held firm; only two Democrats voted in favor of Archer's motion.[63]

Unable to force his will upon the Whig majority, Tyler retreated to a third, less politically controversial candidate. On June 15 he nominated, on the recommendation of Christian, James D. Hallyburton of New Kent Courthouse. As commonwealth's attorney in Christian's state judicial district, Hallyburton was considered a technically competent lawyer untouched by political activism. Christian believed him to be an excellent compromise candidate; he was a state rights Democrat acceptable to Senate Whigs because he had "never courted public life or public favor." He was confirmed without a vote.[64]

Tyler was politically obtuse in filling the Virginia judgeship. Beginning in mid-1842 the president pursued a party-directed mode of selection intended to assist his reelection by distributing federal judgeships to Democrats. He lacked, however, the personal toughness and sufficient existing political strength necessary to implement such a policy. By succumbing to the personal demands of his controversial brother-in-law, Tyler precipitated an interparty conflict in the upper house that he could not win. Nepotism furnished Senate Whigs with precisely the issue they required to challenge successfully the independence of the reconverted Democratic president. Senate Democrats, on the other hand, by supporting his nominees, willingly assisted the president in administering his self-inflicted wounds. Ultimately, Virginia Democrats, imbued with a sense of partisan self-interest, reconciled their differences; in 1844 they deserted their native son in favor of James K. Polk.[65]

IV

"Captain Tyler, poor soul," mocked Democrat William L. Marcy of New York, "thinks the people have discharged all their party leaders and are coming en masse to his relief. . . . He is a doomed man."[66] Marcy full well understood that by shifting partisan affiliation in an era of hardening partisan commitment, the president sealed his political fate. Tyler certainly imbibed some of the new partisan ethic; he adopted a party-directed patronage policy designed to win a second term in the White House. Like many of Jackson's Whig critics, Tyler conveniently forgot much of his earlier criticism of the evil consequences of partisan distribution of the patronage. Three conditions impaired Tyler's success. First, as a Democrat-turned-Whig, Tyler could not command the most influential leaders of either party; the expedient nature of his selection as vice-president only exacerbated his problems as president in trying to lead a party that never intended for him to lead it. Second, when, in mid-1842, he asserted his independence, Tyler had already alienated much of the Whig majority in the upper house. The Senate Whigs imposed a strict standard of political conduct on his nominees, often forcing him to select second and third candidates. An absence of broad popular support, the personal disdain for the president expressed by some nominees, and the increasing unattractiveness of federal judicial service combined to further erode the president's independence. Third, these difficulties notwithstanding, Tyler too often lacked the personal toughness and political sagacity essential to the success of his patronage policy.

John Tyler became a disposable anomaly in a political culture swept by the forces of political modernization. While unprecedented numbers of voters displayed a new and tenacious commitment to party, the chief executive was unable to make a comparable commitment. Frustrated by his unique ascent to the White House and committed to the ideal of party government but too weak to make it work, Tyler was unable to harness his political fortunes to the new engine of party. Under his successor, however, the ethic of partisanship combined with Democratic control of the Senate and the executive mansion to infuse order and discipline into the selection of lower court judges.

4

GALVANIC ANIMATION

I made an appointment upon the letter of recommendation
of a senator . . . and it was rejected . . . at the instance of the
same Senator. I said to him, well, you rejected that man I
nominated; O yes, he replied, . . . we are obliged to recommend our constituents when they apply to us.—James K.
Polk, 1845[1]

Coalitional politics in the American party system has muted most
disruptive elements in the political culture. To bring this about has
required consummate political leadership. As James MacGregor
Burns has observed, even under the best conditions a majority party
maintains internal cohesion only by balancing the expectations of its
executive and legislative wings.[2] Such in 1845 was the task confronting James K. Polk and the resurgent Democratic party. The president
had to preserve Democratic unity from the sectional pressures of
slavery and territorial expansion and to protect the executive prerogative from infringement by the Senate Democratic majority.

Throughout the Polk administration factionalism threatened
cooperation between the executive and legislative wings of the Democratic party. Several Senate Democrats, notably John C. Calhoun,
Simon Cameron, James D. Westcott, and Ambrose H. Sevier, were
informally allied to Whigs in their home states, in Congress, or both.
Beyond Capitol Hill, free-state Democrats disagreed over the tariff,
fiscal policy, internal improvements, and, most notably, the extent
and pace of expansion of the American empire and slavery into the
West. Slave-state Democrats differed over many of the same issues,
but they insisted on the legitimate constitutional right of slaveholders
to take their peculiar property into the new territories. At least in
Congress the modernizing thrust of the new party system diminished
the destructiveness of this factionalism; typically, Democrats and
Whigs voted as partisans, not as sectionalists.[3]

Factional differences within the Democratic party also threatened
to disrupt distribution of the federal offices. Polk appreciated the
inherent dilemma in patronage decisions: federal appointments enabled the chief executive to discipline party members, but they also

endangered party unity when the candidates of congressional Democrats were not appointed. Polk complained that the limited number of offices and the multiplicity of applicants made "the dispensation of the public patronage . . . a weakening operation."[4]

Both Polk's contemporaries and historians have disagreed over the success of the Tennessean's patronage decisions. Influential Missouri Democrat Francis Preston Blair blamed the collapse of the party in 1848 on Polk's "perfidy" in ignoring the recommendations of his staunchest friends in Congress and the States.[5] Others were less critical. They viewed the deficiencies in the president's policies within the often troubled context of the administration. Polk had to diminish Democratic factionalism while he was also engaged in prosecuting the Mexican War, facilitating territorial expansion, and enlarging the federal bureaucracy.[6]

Polk abetted such contradictory assessments. The twelfth president intended to be both an efficient administrator and an adroit party leader. He devoted long hours and often feverish attention to major appointments. Polk adopted Jackson's conception of the president as the tribune of the people, accountable for the quality of governmental officeholders. He retained some Whigs "who were faithful and good officers"; he demanded "honesty and competency" of Democratic appointees. As an administrator he sought independence from the Senate and resisted partisan expediency. He was, as a result, suspicious of congressional advice. "Men of high station," Polk observed, often signed "papers of recommendation . . . without meaning what they say" and thus induced the president "to make bad appointments." He refused to nominate members of Congress, although he recognized "the almost certain hazards of incurring . . . [congressional] displeasure" that would reduce his "administration to a minority in both Houses."[7]

The president was sensitive to the exigencies of Democratic politics. He realized that failure to cooperate with the congressional wing of the party would diminish his appointment prerogative and undermine administration-supported legislative measures. The taciturn and disciplined Polk often endured hours of frustration listening to the pleas of congressionally endorsed office seekers who thoroughly disgusted him. He retained some "faithful" Whigs, but he removed at least 340 others, the most extensive purge to that time of federal officials. His grudging attention to the prerogatives of the congressional wing of the party produced results; the Senate rejected only forty-two nominees, none of these to the lower federal courts.[8]

Polk maintained a coherent view of the federal judiciary and the judicial function. He applied to lower court nominations the same criteria he followed in making other major appointments, including justices of the Supreme Court. He deemed appointment of judges with prior judicial or public legal service essential to maintenance of the federal judiciary as an "independent coordinate branch of government." All of Polk's nominees had such experience. The chief executive also expected his nominees to believe in state rights, unionism, and a traditional Jeffersonian scheme of limited government. Polk knew that the selection process offered an opportunity to implant such beliefs on the federal bench, but he also realized that competing pressures often eliminated candidates with the most acceptable constitutional and political views. Thus, at the inception of his administration Polk established a general rule with regard to the political and constitutional views of judicial appointees. "I resolved," he concluded, "to appoint no man who was not an original Democrat and a strict constructionist."[9]

Polk orchestrated the selection process with only minimal assistance from his secretary of state. The president considered James Buchanan of doubtful political loyalty, and, in any event, a forceful administrative presence for the secretary did not comport with Polk's style of governing. The chief executive immersed himself in the details of administration and scrutinized judicial candidates, usually informing the secretary of state of his decision through a brief note written on a letter recommending a successful applicant.[10] The small number of judicial vacancies facilitated direct control. While the need to replace Whigs with Democrats and the growth in the number of federal offices increased the total positions susceptible to presidential discretion, the number of judicial vacancies remained small: Polk nominated only sixteen lower court judges.

During the Polk administration traditional patron-client relations and a modern party-directed selection process reinforced one another. One-quarter of his nominees had family ties to principal mediators. These informal and nonpartisan connections, along with the president's acquaintance with at least four of the nominees, were important in determining which Democrats received appointments. These personal connections, however, were usually subordinated to partisan exigencies. More than any previous president, Polk allowed the congressional wing of the Democratic party to mediate the selection process. He retained, however, a keen sense of the presidential prerogative and employed the power of his office to cooperate with rather than capitulate to congressional Democrats.

II

While war in Mexico and diplomacy in Oregon initiated a new wave of territorial growth, Polk realized the final fruits of a previous era of expansion. Before the president left office, the territories of Florida, Wisconsin, Iowa, and Texas entered the Union. These new states provided the president five of his eight district court nominations. The remaining three were to the Circuit Court for the District of Columbia, the Western District of Virginia, and the Eastern District of Pennsylvania. No district court nominee refused Polk's call to service.

In filling these vacancies, Polk attempted to accommodate congressional Democrats, but he insisted on loyalty to the administration as the price of cooperation. Through the aegis of party, the president recruited experienced judges, balanced the demands of congressional Democrats and rival state party factions, and enhanced the executive's independence.

The first vacancy occurred during the recess between the special and first sessions of the Twenty-ninth Congress. On August 30, 1845, Buckner Thruston, one of the three judges of the Circuit Court of the District of Columbia, died. The court was unique; it heard suits involving the various bureaus of the federal government, inhabitants of the nation's capital, and residents of the contiguous states. These multiple constituencies maneuvered to shape the selection process to their interests. In the absence of congressional representation, Democratic lawyers from the District expected to mediate the selection of Thruston's successor. On the other hand, Maryland and Virginia Democrats attempted to exploit the political dependency of the District.[11] Democrats in northeastern Virginia argued that the District was "the market for the beef and produce of this whole section of the state." They expected the federal judiciary in the District to insure the security of the slave property that transported their produce to the marketplace. "Northern Emmissaries," warned a local Democratic leader from Warrenton, Virginia, might "attempt to kidnap or assist away . . . slaves" who crossed into the District. "No appointment," he cautioned, would generate "a deeper sensation in Virginia, nay in the South, than those of the Judiciary . . . in the District of Columbia." "Southerners generally," he warned Polk, would view with "deep sensibility the appointment of any citizen . . . to a court exercising jurisdiction over [their] peculiar institutions."[12]

The vexing administrative and political problem of whether to select a District lawyer subsumed the slavery issue. As a slaveholder and critic of abolitionism, Polk accepted the judicial power as a proper means to sustain slaveholders' property rights.[13] The legal community of Maryland and Virginia claimed that the population of the District was too small to produce a lawyer with sufficient experience to oversee the complex and lucrative litigation that involved the federal government.[14] The bar of the District maintained that the circuit court "was a local office" to which the president should nominate only resident lawyers with "intimate knowledge of its peculiar jurisprudence." To achieve the strongest possible position before the president, Whig and Democratic members of the Bar Association of the District of Columbia set aside party differences and united in recommending James Dunlop, a wealthy Georgetown lawyer, slaveholder, Democrat, and judge of the Criminal Court of the District.[15]

The president heeded this unified voice. Dissident Democrats in Alexandria, who resented their forced inclusion in the District and believed that a Virginia resident would better represent them on the court, presented the only opposition to the recess appointment and eventual confirmation of Dunlop. District lawyers, however, applauded Polk's willingness to "concede to the . . . inhabitants of this District, in the matter of local judicial appointments, the same . . . respect for the people and the bar . . . which has been heretofore extended to . . . the States."[16]

The first test of the president's ability to cooperate with congressional Democrats occurred at the same time the Senate confirmed Dunlop. On December 6, 1845, Judge Isaac S. Pennybacker of the Western District of Virginia resigned to enter the Senate. To replace him, Polk had to contend with the demands of competing state party factions and a divided Democratic congressional delegation.

Differences within the Virginia Democracy stemmed from traditional economic tensions between the tidewater east and the mountainous west and from disagreement over annexation of Texas. As the Richmond Junto dissolved during the 1830s, Thomas Ritchie had sought fuller cooperation with western Democrats. The strategy bore fruit in 1842 with the election of westerner James McDowell as governor. Ritchie and McDowell then rallied Van Buren supporters in the state against the Whigs and the proannexation Calhounite faction led by James A. Seddon and Robert M. T. Hunter.[17]

Cooperation in 1844 returned handsome dividends: Polk carried the state, while Democrats won fifteen of sixteen congressional seats and expanded their majority in the state legislature. In August, 1845, divisions reappeared when the legislature selected a successor for

Whig Senator William C. Rives. The Calhounite faction, distressed over the anti-Texas position of the governor's brother-in-law, Sen. Thomas Hart Benton of Missouri, denied McDowell the Senate seat. Instead, the post went to another westerner, Judge Pennybacker.[18]

The expectations of the Virginia congressional delegation and the president quickly diverged.[19] The former recommended the selection of one of two colleagues: George W. Hopkins of Abington, a leader in the late 1830s of the conservative Democratic revolt, and William Taylor of Lexington, a Van Buren Democrat who believed that judicial service would provide the opportunity to regain his failing health. The president was intransigent, however: he refused to select a former Whig; he rejected the idea of nominating a sick man to the federal bench; and he reiterated his vow not to bestow federal offices on members of Congress.[20]

Polk wanted the Virginia delegation to forge a compromise without his direct intervention. The House delegation responded by shifting attention to two other candidates: John W. Brockenbrough of Lexington and Benjamin R. Floyd of Winchester. Of the two, Brockenbrough had superior legal credentials and fuller political support. He had served four years as prosecuting attorney for Hanover County and had published a respected two-volume edition of John Marshall's circuit court opinions. As the editor of a Lexington newspaper, Brockenbrough appealed to both major factions of the Virginia Democracy by endorsing Polk's candidacy and the annexation of Texas. He also benefited from the intervention of Thomas Ritchie and John Brockenbrough, his uncles and former leaders of the defunct Richmond Junto. The youthful Floyd, son of a former governor, belonged to the conservative wing of the party. Congressman George W. Hopkins insisted that Brockenbrough was too closely allied to the Calhoun faction; that his selection would dismay conservative Democrats in the state who had only reluctantly endorsed Polk's candidacy; and that the nomination of Floyd would renew conservative confidence.[21]

The president allowed Virginia Democrats to settle the dispute. He refused to submit a nomination until the Democratic congressmen from western Virginia had reached agreement. On December 22, with the exception of Hopkins, they unanimously recommended Brockenbrough. Following immediate nomination by the president, the Senate quickly added its confirmation.[22]

Cooperation between the executive and legislative wings of the Democratic party structured the selection process. Unlike Jackson, Polk rejected confrontation; instead, he expected to maintain his avowed principles of judicial selection by tapping the strength of party. He acted only after Virginia Democrats in Congress had reached accord. Family connections undoubtedly assisted Brockenbrough's candidacy, but in Polk's scheme of party government they were secondary to the endorsement and cooperation of congressional Democrats from western Virginia. Through independence and cooperation Polk nominated a judge with an excellent legal reputation and political views similar to his own.

Polk's patience with congressional Democrats was finite. The president, in filling vacancies in Florida, ruthlessly proscribed Democrats who refused to cooperate with the administration.

The Florida Democracy in 1844 boasted a state-wide organization that emphasized popular participation in party affairs through local and state conventions. In the transition from territory to state, Democrats captured the governor's mansion and a majority in the state house. They also controlled the congressional delegation, sending David Levy Yulee and James D. Westcott, the two most influential Democrats in the state, to the Senate and William H. Brockenbrough to the House of Representatives. The party, nevertheless, suffered serious divisions. Yulee was identified with the landed interests of east Florida, while Westcott and, to a lesser extent, Brockenbrough represented the commercial and plantation economies of middle and west Florida. Yulee usually sustained administration policies, although he occasionally joined a knot of dissident southern Democratic senators. Westcott, however, consistently opposed Polk; indeed, the president confided to his diary that he "considered Mr. Westcott a Whig."[23]

Polk had to contend not only with party factionalism but with a poorly conceived law that designated the entire state of Florida a single judicial district. It assigned one judge to assume the legal responsibilities for an area previously served by five territorial judges. The Florida Democratic congressional delegation in the spring of 1845 denounced the law, asserting that a single judge could not negotiate the hostile terrain of Florida and complete the yearly docket of the federal court. They denounced a provision in the law that directed the judge to spend only one month at Key West hearing admiralty and maritime suits.[24]

The Florida delegation successfully urged Polk to postpone making a nomination until the opening of the first session of the Twenty-ninth Congress. During the interim the territorial judges dispensed federal justice. When Congress convened in December, 1845, Yulee submitted a list of potential federal appointees, but he withheld the name of a judicial candidate. Instead, the Florida delegation introduced a bill that would carve the state into three districts with a judge assigned to each.[25]

Further delay posed a difficult constitutional problem for the administration. Could territorial judge assume the jurisdiction of a district court without violating the intent of Article III of the Constitution? Attorney General John Y. Mason concluded negatively; Congress had already authorized the president to appoint a district court judge. With no prospect of quick congressional action on the Florida bill, Polk in April, 1846, bowed to constitutional scruples and informed a still reluctant Yulee that the "public interest" required action.[26]

Choosing a judicial nominee divided Florida Democrats. By March, 1846, an original list of ten applicants, which had included all of the territorial judges, was reduced to three: Isaac H. Bronson of St. Augustine, William Marvin of Key West, and George S. Hawkins of Tallahassee. The first two were territorial judges who declined appointment to the state supreme court in the hope of receiving a seat on the federal bench. Yulee and Brockenbrough endorsed both judges, who had been aligned with them in territorial politics, although they advised Polk that, if he could select only one, Bronson was preferable; he had not taken as active a part in politics as had Marvin, and east Florida litigation had stirred less legal controversy than had the clash among commercial, salvage, and insurance interests in Marvin's court at Key West. Should Congress approve the pending Florida court bill, Marvin was their choice to serve in south Florida—a contingency warmly approved by the bar of Key West.[27] Westcott denounced both candidates as "political opponents"; instead, he recommended Hawkins, the federal attorney for the Middle District of Florida territory.[28]

By nominating Bronson on May 5, 1846, Polk rebuked the inconsistent Westcott. The outraged senator threatened "to join the Whigs," but the president concluded that "it was a matter of indifference to me whether he was dissatisfied." Bronson's confirmation was delayed, however, until the last day of the session, when Congress tabled the Florida court bill. Six months later it did pass revised legislation that established a southern district; Polk, once again on the recommendation of Yulee and Brockenbrough, nominated Marvin.[29]

Polk forcefully displayed in making the Florida nominations the bases of his cooperation with the congressional wing of the party. Democratic affiliation bound the president and the Florida congressional delegation in an institutionalized relationship that placed partisan over personal interests. The chief executive heeded the advice of

Democrats in Congress, but he retained his prerogative to act independently; the recalcitrant Westcott learned the hazards of feigning
Democratic allegiance while opposing administration policies.
Throughout, the president balanced partisan interests with public
necessity; he acted despite Yulee's request for further delay and
selected candidates well qualified by previous experience and acceptable to the bar of Florida.

During the spring of 1846 these same concerns—for cooperation
between the executive and legislative wings of the party and for the
quality of the judiciary—surfaced in Polk's selection of the first district
judge for Texas. The president also weighed the political and constitutional beliefs of the Texas judicial candidates.

Democrats dominated early Texas politics. A personal and informal style of politics divided Democrats between their two most powerful leaders: Sam Houston and Mirabeau B. Lamar. The former enjoyed a following among immigrants from the upper South generally,
while the latter claimed support among one-time residents of the
lower South. The Texas Senate delegation in the spring of 1846 reflected these differences: Houston favored the administration, but
Thomas J. Rusk, a protégé of Lamar, adhered to John C. Calhoun.[30]

These Democratic senators clashed over the district court appointment. Between October, 1845, two months before statehood,
and May, 1846, when Polk nominated a judge, only three of ten
candidates received serious consideration: James Webb of Austin,
Anthony B. Shelby of Houston, and John C. Watrous of Galveston.
Webb was a former Florida territorial judge who in 1837 migrated to
Texas. He became a friend and political ally of Lamar, who appointed
him secretary of state and attorney general. Lamar instructed Rusk to
secure Webb's nomination. Houston, however, objected to the close
association between Lamar and Webb and to the candidate's previous
association with National Republicans while a judge in Florida. The
senator endorsed Shelby, a former justice of the Texas Supreme
Court whose volatile personality and fascination with hard liquor had
disgusted his former colleague on the bench, Thomas J. Rusk. Not
surprisingly, the Texas senator denounced Houston's candidate as
unfit. Neither Webb nor Shelby relied wholly on their respective
senatorial advocates; they won interviews with the president and lob-
bied for additional support in Congress.[31]

The vacant judgeship posed for Polk a political and administrative
dilemma. He wished to retain Houston's support and to avoid further
convulsion of the Texas Democracy. He was equally anxious to select
a skilled lawyer with constitutional beliefs parallel to his own. He

explained to Houston in January, 1846, that he intended to "appoint some able lawyer, who is sound upon the constitutional questions, according to the Jeffersonian faith." "I will not, if I know it," observed the president, "appoint any latitudinarian Federalist to the Federal Judiciary."[32] He applauded Shelby's political beliefs, but objected to the candidate's character and judicial temperament. He was not only apprehensive about Webb's former National Republicanism, but insisted on seeking the fullest possible cooperation with Houston. This effectively slammed the door shut on Webb; Houston refused to endorse him. With the selection process knotted, the president adopted a strategy of delay, waiting for the senators to reach agreement.[33]

When the president eliminated Shelby, Lamar observed that "Watrous and Webb" were "the final two candidates for the position." Lamar reiterated his commitment to Webb: the former territorial judge was the best choice because he had "filled judicial office before."[34]

Watrous occupied a middle position between the two Democratic factions. The Connecticut native had migrated to Texas in 1837 after spending nine years studying and practicing law in Tennessee and Alabama, making Polk's acquaintance in the process. After Watrous moved to Texas, President Lamar appointed him attorney general, but he quickly resigned because of a conflict of interest arising from his extensive land holdings. Houston immediately offered to make him a law partner, but Watrous declined. Between 1838 and 1845 his law practice prospered as he won prominence for his skill in litigating conflicts involving disputed Mexican, Spanish, and American land claims. Alabama Senator Dixon H. Lewis, a friend of Watrous, assured Polk that the candidate was not only professionally qualified to preside over the federal court but that he was an "orthodox Democrat of the state rights constitutional school."[35]

In late May of 1846 the president's strategy of delay finally forced action. During the preceding month, Watrous and Webb had conferred about the possibility of one of them withdrawing, but neither budged. With the candidates unwilling to agree and with Houston adamantly opposed to Webb, Rusk relented; he restated his recommendation in favor of Webb, but informed Houston that Watrous was "a first rate lawyer of excellent character" whose nomination he would accept. The president promptly nominated Watrous; the Senate quickly confirmed him.[36]

Polk once again pursued a party-directed mode of selection. Texas's Democratic senators fulfilled the important administrative function of identifying potential nominees for the distant national

administration. Polk's familiarity with him and the soundness of his
constitutional views enhanced Watrous's candidacy, but it was his
neutral position in the Texas Democratic party that ultimately made
him acceptable. Unlike Jackson, Polk used Democratic affiliation to
instill genuine coherence in the selection process. Polk skillfully retained his independence by avoiding confrontation; he allowed Rusk
and Houston to reach accord before he acted. Polk maneuvered,
much as had Van Buren, to diminish opposition before it formed. He
was not subservient to senatorial wishes; he eliminated Shelby and
Webb from consideration while impressing upon the district
judgeship a candidate acceptable to Texas Democrats and congenial
to his own constitutional views.

Cooperation between the executive and legislative wings of the
Democratic party remained vulnerable to party factionalism. The
most serious breakdown occurred following the death on June 6,
1846, of Judge Archibald Randall of the Eastern District of Pennsylvania. The selection of his successor disrupted the Polk administration, Senate Democrats, and the already contentious Pennsylvania
Democratic party.

Factionalism plagued the Pennsylvania Democracy. No single faction had unequivocally accepted Polk, and the president had included
leaders of both major factions in the administration. Gov. Francis P.
Shunk and James Buchanan, whom Polk made secretary of state, led
one faction. Philadelphia Van Burenites Henry Horn (perhaps Polk's
most loyal follower), John K. Kane, and Vice-President George M.
Dallas composed the other. While the Van Burenites wanted to curtail
Buchanan's influence, the secretary of state was equally anxious to
curb Dallas's role in the new administration.[37]

There were also two important minor divisions within the party.
Former supporters of John Tyler constituted the first. The other
consisted of the once powerful anti-Jackson Muhlenberg Democrats,
led by Simon Cameron. They excoriated Polk's free-trade policies and
joined Whigs to vault Cameron into the Senate seat left vacant by
Buchanan's resignation. Cameron reciprocated by supporting Whig
policies, including a protective tariff.[38]

Before the district court vacancy, discord among Pennsylvania
Democrats had already disrupted Polk's patronage policies. Cameron
in December, 1845, blocked confirmation of Henry Horn as collector
of the port of Philadelphia and George B. Woodward of that city as
associate justice of the Supreme Court. A handful of disgruntled
southern Democrats, led by James D. Westcott of Florida, and Whigs
anxious to embarrass Polk united with Cameron. The Pennsylvania

senator also recieved the tacit support of Buchanan, who opposed
Woodward's elevation to the Supreme Court. Buchanan threatened
resignation; Polk's refusal to consult him on patronage matters in his
home state was "unprecedented in the history of the relations between
the Presidents and their cabinets."[39]

The vacant district judgeship subjected the president to difficult
political and administrative pressures. On the one hand, he had to
contend with the divided Pennsylvania Democracy, especially Cameron, whose dissent threatened to spread party conflict beyond the
state. An angry Polk concluded that the Pennsylvania senator, much
like Westcott, was "a managing tricky man, in whom no reliance is to
be placed."[40] There was, as well, the frustrated secretary of state,
apparently interested in a seat on the Supreme Court and determined
to curtail the control of Vice-President Dallas and the Philadelphia
Van Burenites over the federal patronage. On the other hand, he had
to fill a vacancy on the Supreme Court for the circuit that included
Pennsylvania; as a result, there was no circuit court judge to assume
temporarily the federal district court business that Randall's death left
unfinished. The president had to act promptly to restore federal justice.

Philadelphia Van Burenites divided their recommendations
among three candidates: Edward King, Thomas Pettit, and John K.
Kane. Vice-President Dallas and Henry Horn, who frequently disagreed on patronage matters, independently recommended King, a
common pleas judge who had been nominated to the Supreme Court
by Tyler but rejected by the Senate. Horn, along with John W. Forney, editor of the *Pennsylvanian* and political ally of Buchanan, endorsed Pettit, Polk's appointee as federal attorney for the Eastern
District. The commercial and insurance community joined in recommending Pettit; his experience would facilitate continuity in the operation of the court.[41]

Governor Shunk, Vice-President Dallas, and Sen. Daniel Sturgeon, a neutral in Democratic party factionalism, endorsed Kane. In
addition, William J. Leiper, Kane's influential brother-in-law, intervened with Polk and Buchanan; he traveled to Washington to urge
the selection as a "personal favor."[42] The socially prominent Kane had
held a variety of state and local posts, most recently that of attorney
general of Pennsylvania.

Kane was anathema to Muhlenberg Democrats. In August, 1844,
he had become involved in a scheme to alleviate Polk's stigma as a
free-trader in tariff-conscious Pennsylvania. The presidential candidate wrote a public letter to Kane in which he expressed a willingness

to accept a high tariff to protect the manufacturing, iron, and coal industries of Pennsylvania. After carrying the state by a narrow margin, Polk dismayed Muhlenberg Democrats by introducing the Tariff of 1846, which promised less, not more, protection on many Pennsylvania goods.[43]

Polk had to resolve two crucial political unknowns before he nominated any of these candidates. The first was the attitude of Cameron. The bar of Philadelphia expected quick action. "The business of the court," noted a disgruntled lawyer, was "suffering . . . and daily accumulating" because of the long delay in making the Supreme Court appointment and Randall's untimely death. Too hasty a nomination, however, might precipitate a clash with Cameron similar to that over Horn's nomination. Polk excluded the senator from participation in the selection process; Cameron seems not to have endorsed any candidate. Instead, William J. Leiper kept Polk posted on Cameron's position. He assured the president that the senator believed that there was "no man whose nomination he would prefer to Mr. Kane's."[44]

Buchanan was the other unknown. On June 10, the same day Leiper informed the president of Cameron's position, Polk apprised his secretary of state that he intended to nominate Kane immediately unless Buchanan had "insuperable objections." The secretary admitted that the Philadelphia lawyer was not his "first choice," but said that he "would not object." Buchanan demanded and won an important concession for this grudging acquiescence. The president had humiliated Buchanan by refusing to nominate Philadelphia attorney John. M. Read, a Muhlenberg Democrat and former Federalist, to the Supreme Court. Buchanan demanded that Polk request Governor Shunk to appoint Read in place of Kane as attorney general. Polk's endorsement of Read, Buchanan observed, "would harmonize and reunite the party in the State."[45] Incidentally, it would save face for the secretary and reaffirm his influence with the president. Polk agreed to the proposal, and, the next day, apparently certain of Cameron's support, he dispatched Kane's nomination to the Senate and sent a letter to Shunk urging Read's appointment.[46]

Leiper's assurance of Cameron's support proved faulty. When Kane's nomination reached the Senate, Cameron immediately objected. His dissent transformed the intraparty selection process into an interparty struggle. Whigs welcomed the opportunity to attack indirectly the administration's tariff program; every Whig senator present voted against consideration of the nomination. They were not, however, joined by other dissident Democrats; only James D.

Westcott voted with Cameron. Party discipline prevailed; the Senate agreed twenty-eight to twenty-three to consider the nomination. Having lost this crucial test vote, Cameron withdrew his objections; the Senate on June 17 confirmed Kane by a vote of thirty-three to two.[47]

Administrative pressures forced Polk to abandon his usual strategy of defusing factional discord through delay. The death of the judge for the Eastern District of Pennsylvania, in view of the longstanding vacancy on the circuit court, created a vacuum in federal judicial authority. As he had done in filling the Florida judgeships, Polk made loyalty to the administration a condition for mediating the selection process. He relied upon party discipline to foil Cameron. Senate Democrats obliged the president rather than their colleague; they lacked the independence to respond institutionally to Cameron's invocation of senatorial courtesy.

More than any of his predecessors during the era of the second party system, Polk relied on the legislature wing of his party to organize the selection of district court judges. A disciplined Democratic majority in the Senate prompted Polk to seek cooperation rather than confrontation. Through a skillful reading of the political sensibilities of his fellow partisans on Capitol Hill, Polk retained the independence and the prerogative of the executive in the selection and appointment processes; he ignored recommendations by Senate Democrats hostile to the administration; and he applied to candidates standards of ability and political belief. While kinship and instrumental friendship connections between nominees and principal mediators persisted, they were subordinated in this modernizing selection process to party interests.

III

Polk appointed territorial judges only to Iowa and Oregon. In the former, he pursued a policy similar to that adopted in making district court selections; he cooperated with the congressional wing of the party and heeded local Democratic demands. On the recommendation of Iowa Democratic territorial delegate Augustus C. Dodge, Polk in June, 1846, renominated the three-man territorial bench.[48] The Oregon judicial selections were a knottier patronage problem.

When Congress in August, 1848, organized Oregon territory, only the rudiments of a two-party system existed. Neither Whigs nor Democrats had established party organizations; instead, factions predicated on "local jealousies" that only roughly coincided with the national party system competed for political control of "isolated Oregon." The Whiggish Missionary faction, which included the Protestant Methodist missionaries and settlers, coveted eventual statehood. The American faction, which included many of the future Democratic leaders of the territory, was composed of mountain men, independent settlers, and non-Protestants who favored independence. The provisional government had reflected these divisions: the Missionary faction, under the leadership of Gov. George Abernathey, had controlled the executive office and the supreme court, while the American faction had dominated the legislature.[49]

Both factions were determined to influence Polk's patronage decisions. In October, 1847, Abernathey quietly dispatched provisional Supreme Court Justice J. Quinn Thornton to Washington with instructions to win nomination of candidates favorable to the Missionary faction. When the American-controlled legislature learned of the governor's action, it promptly sent its own emissary, provisional Sheriff Joseph L. Meek. The American faction expected the envoy to have special access to the chief executive; Meek was a kinsman of both the private secretary and the wife of the president.[50]

Midwestern and southern Democrats also demanded the president's attention. Thomas Hart Benton of Missouri, Stephen A. Douglas of Illinois, and Edward A. Hannegan of Indiana had contributed to Polk's expansionist policies in the Pacific Northwest; they expected a portion of the patronage in the new Oregon territory in return for their efforts. They were also motivated by a host of economic and political considerations and a concern about the fate of former midwestern constituents who had migrated to the region. Southern Democrats, notably John C. Calhoun, insisted on protection for the peculiar institution through the insertion of a slave clause in the act organizing the territory and selection of a portion of the judiciary from "only southern men . . . who would maintain the southern view on the subject of slavery." Calhoun eventually retreated from both positions; he accepted "northern men in Oregon," but urged the president, in filling new judgeships in the Mexican Cession, to select only southern Democrats. Polk refused, but Calhoun's demurrer on the composition of the judiciary and the absence of a slave clause in the Oregon organic act eased southern demands on the president.[51]

According to provisional Governor George Abernathey, Polk initially intended "to fill the offices of [the] territory with the residents of Oregon."[52] The president was interested in territorial wishes, but he was more concerned with the demands of loyal congressional Democrats from states that provided the bulk of the Oregon population. Only two territorial applicants were serious contenders: J. Quinn Thornton and Peter H. Burnett. Ostensibly, Thornton had the advantage; his visit to Washington provided an opportunity to lobby personally. He won some backing among the influential Illinois and Missouri congressional delegates, who were impressed by his service on the provisional supreme court. The American faction denounced Thornton as a "Whig" and an "office seeker"; they charged that his longstanding connection with the English-controlled Hudson's Bay Company raised doubts about his ability to preside impartially over land suits.[53]

The American faction recommended Peter H. Burnett, a native of Tennessee, who had migrated first to Missouri and then, in 1843, to Oregon. A Benton Democrat in Missouri politics, Burnett received the unanimous endorsement of the Democratic congressional delegation from that state. Furthermore, Burnett's friend, Sheriff Joseph L. Meek, who "had the private ear of the President," urged Polk to select the Tennessee native. These political and personal pressures induced Polk to nominate Burnett an associate justice.[54]

Nonresidents received the other posts. The Pennsylvania, Ohio, and Iowa congressional delegations all pressed candidates upon the president, but Polk resisted; he selected Democrats from Indiana and Illinois.[55] Sen. Edward A. Hannegan, who had supported administration policy in Oregon, won the appointment of William Perkins Bryant of Rockville, Indiana, as chief justice. Bryant's varied legal and political career included service as a prosecuting attorney, state circuit judge, and a twice-elected member of the Indiana legislature. James Turney of Jo Davies County, Illinois, received the other associate justiceship. The basis of Turney's nomination remains unclear; the Illinois congressional delegation, including Stephen A. Douglas, supported other candidates. Turney, who was a former state legislator and attorney general of Illinois, may well have owed his nomination to his cousin, Tennessee Senator Hopkins L. Turney.[56]

Turney and Burnett, who knew nothing of their candidacies, refused to accept their commissions. The Illinois Democrat balked at the hazardous journey to Oregon and the $1,800 salary. Polk attempted to replace him by granting a recess commission to William A. Hall of Randolph County, Missouri, a brother of Congressman Willard P. Hall, a Democratic presidential elector in 1844 and a state circuit court judge. The Missouri congressional delegation mediated the selection, but William Hall preferred his state judicial post to the uncertainties of territorial service.[57]

With little time remaining before the inauguration of a new Whig president, Polk acted rapidly. The president wanted a guarantee that his next nominee would accept. Illinois Congressman John A. McLernand, who had been instrumental in supporting administration policy, assured Polk that twenty-nine-year-old Orville C. Pratt possessed the necessary judicial temperament, political beliefs, and a willingness to serve. Pratt was a protégé of Senator Douglas, a former resident of Jo Davies County, and a special agent sent by Secretary of War William L. Marcy to investigate the status of military posts in the Far West. Pratt immediately accepted.[58]

Polk had left office by the time Peter H. Burnett declined his commission. In the spring of 1849 he had moved from Oregon to California to prospect for gold. The hope of instant wealth was more alluring than the mediocre salary and drudgery of territorial service.[59]

Polk responded to judicial vacancies in Iowa and Oregon in significantly different ways. In the former he exploited an indigenous party structure and a Democratic territorial delegate to mediate the selection process. Of course, he had only to renominate the sitting Democratic judges.

The web of Democratic organization did not extend fully to distant Oregon territory. Polk could not rely upon a coherent party organization or a Democratic territorial delegate. The selection process was party-directed; congressional Democrats from the states, anxious to exploit the patronage, identified nominees. Nonetheless, nonpartisan pressures shaped the Oregon judiciary. Informal ties of kinship and instrumental friendship linked successful nominees to mediators, and, in the case of Burnett, these connections reached into the White House. While Polk rebuffed the demands of Calhoun, he accommodated sectional interests by allowing loyal midwestern congressional Democrats whose former constituents comprised most of the population of the territory to mediate the selection process. Throughout, however, low pay, the hazards of travel to Oregon, and slow communications frustrated Polk's attempt to fill the bench before the inauguration of his Whig successor.

IV

"Dead and gone," concluded a Pennsylvania Democrat in 1846, were "the old parties of individual personalities and faction[s]." They had been replaced by "new parties" possessed of a "galvanic animation" stimulated by the "law of spoils."[60] The acceptance of party legitimacy and the evolution of a competitive two-party system transformed the political culture of the nation and with it the federal judicial selection process. Polk and congressional Democrats embraced cooperation and party discipline. The president scrupulously attended to the wishes of loyal members of Congress; he just as systematically ignored the demands of party recalcitrants. This party-directed mode of selection was founded on the reciprocal commitment of the executive and legislative wings of the Democracy to further national and state party interests. Until 1848 those interests were sufficiently similar that cooperation was possible. A common party affiliation also bridged the administrative distance separating the president from the states and territories. Through collaboration with the legislative wing of the party, Polk attained what Jackson had sought through confrontation and cronyism. He selected candidates with previous judicial and public legal experience who were loyal to his vision of state rights, the Union, and limited national government. Ever conscious of the need to maintain the independence of his office, Polk bent but he did not break under congressional Democratic pressure.

The impersonal, party-directed symmetry of the selection process was partly transitory. Vestiges of a traditional patron-client mode of selection and party factionalism persisted; Democratic senators, representatives, and local party leaders promoted their kinsmen and friends for judicial office, although the tough-minded Polk usually considered candidates from an impersonal, partisan perspective. The decentralized and state-centered Democratic party abetted traditional patronage practices. As important, the relentless pace of territorial expansion kept the second party system in a constant state of becoming; it had no sooner defined its geographical boundaries than a new burst of expansion added politically undeveloped territories. By the end of the Mexican War the political culture was developed and developing. Polk, in this regard, was blessed with a bit of good fortune in making judicial selections; the territories acquired during earlier phases of expansion had coherent party organizations, and, except in Oregon, he never had to deal with the disruptive political consequences of his own imperial schemes. Difficulties in Oregon, however, were a portent of the future: territorial expansion, slavery, and the unattractiveness of judicial service in the territories carved from the Mexican Cession challenged the capacity of both political parties to persuade able nominees to accept commissions. Polk bequeathed to his successors the example of a disciplined, party-directed selection process, but he also left them to wrestle with the political and administrative problems of extending federal justice to his newly won empire.

COUNTRY FIRST AND FRIENDSHIP SECOND

I admit with sorrow that there has [*sic*] been some unfortunate appointments. . . . There is no portion of my duty that
I have been more solicitous about than making proper and
judicious appointments, and have . . . looked myself closely
into these matters.—Zachary Taylor, 1850[1]

Across the nation in 1848 Whigs were factionalists first and partisans
second. The Whig party was a bisectional coalition of loosely knit state
organizations plagued by internal divisions. Its leaders alleviated the
disruptive consequences of this factionalism and assured further
bisectional cooperation by offering Zachary Taylor as the party
standard-bearer. A party blessed with such imposing figures as Daniel
Webster and Henry Clay could capture the White House only by
nominating the politically inexperienced Taylor, who had devoted his
adult life to military service. The traits of a military leader could not,
in the developing political culture of the second party system, substi-
tute for the skills of effective party leaders. The southern wing of the
Whig party demanded Taylor's nomination, but his ultimate success
resulted from the support of two New York Whigs—William Henry
Seward and Thurlow Weed. Much as Clay had hoped to control William Henry Harrison, Seward and Weed expected to manipulate
Taylor. The military hero was a fish out of water; his lack of qualifications to direct the Whig party made him president.[2]

The inherent artificiality of the second American party system
produced the nomination of Zachary Taylor. Presidential election
victory in the constitutionally endorsed, majoritarian, two-party system required intraparty cooperation and compromise. The election
process tended to suppress divisive tensions among the leaders of the
coalitions that composed the Whig and Democratic parties. The party
system succeeded by evasion. The bisectional cords of cooperation
within the two decentralized and state-centered parties were maintained only so long as the disruptive slavery issue was excluded from
national politics. The rising antislavery critique of the two parties
combined with the fruits of the Mexican War to pierce the veil cloak-

ing the party system; the slavery issue insinuated itself into national politics in the guise of a constitutional and legal debate about the rights of slaveholders to take their property into the new American possessions. When joined with the cultural shock brought about by massive immigration, the slavery extension controversy provoked a fundamental realignment of the two-party system: the bisectional cords of cooperation within the two national parties snapped.[3]

The exigencies of this artificial party system affected the judicial selection process. With the exception of the bolt of Free-Soilers in 1848, Democratic and Whig leaders until 1852 operated within existing party structures. The tenacious commitment to party had a paradoxical effect; the parties in 1848 and 1852 selected presidential nominees capable of appealing to the divergent sectional wings within each party. Ultimately, the most able and articulate party spokesmen were excluded from the White House. This diminished the authority of the president as a party leader; the ability of Whig and Democratic chief executives to influence the congressional wings of their respective parties declined. This development gradually eroded the prerogative of the president and enhanced the authority of the Senate in the selection of lower court judges. Polk had cooperated with the congressional wing of his party while retaining discretionary power because he commanded his party and possessed a disciplined sense of public and political purpose. His Whig successors lacked these traits and suffered with a Democratic majority in the Senate. The weakened spring of presidential leadership, the sectional divisions within both parties, and the political and administrative hazards of organizing new and distant territories altered the institutional relationship of the president and the Senate. The transformation began with the brief presidency of Taylor, gained momentum under Millard Fillmore, and culminated during the adminstration of Democrat Franklin Pierce.

Taylor only reluctantly acquiesced to partisan demands for distribution of the federal patronage. In view of his political inexperience, the former general was undoubtedly sincere when he announced at his inauguration that dispensing federal offices was "a delicate and onerous" duty that made "honesty, capacity, and fidelity indispensable prerequisites to the bestowal of office."[4] He resurrected the patronage policy contemplated by Whig critics of Andrew Jackson two decades earlier; he promised to stand above party and faction and to nominate and remove officeholders on the basis of ability exclusively. Such pronouncements stirred dissension among veteran Whig politicians, who had long since abandoned self-righteous hostility toward partisan distribution of the patronage. Nicholas Dean of New York

City in April, 1849, commended Taylor's quest for "pure . . . princi-ples," but he warned that "in the new political circumstances of the era" a "political party can be sustained only by bestowing its patronage—*its whole patronage*—upon its supporters."[5] Under relent-less prodding by state Whig leaders, cabinet officers, and Seward and Weed, Taylor yielded. In the months following his inauguration speech, the new Whig president removed more officeholders than any of his predecessors.[6]

Taylor repudiated demands that he diminish the independence of the judiciary. His judicial nominations reflected the ascendancy of a new party; all ten of them were Whigs. He did not, however, extend his otherwise broad use of the removal power to the territorial judiciary. When Taylor assumed office there were two territories: Oregon and Minnesota. Polk had appointed Democratic judges to the former, but, since the latter was organized on the next-to-last day of his administration, he believed Taylor properly deserved to fill the posts. Taylor had only to remove the Oregon judges; however, he concluded that to do so would violate the privileged constitutional position of the judiciary. Reverting back to the precedent of Jackson's administration, the Whig president believed that territorial judges were susceptible to removal only on proof of malfeasance or incom-petence in office, and only when their commissions specified that they served at the pleasure of the president. This position complemented Taylor's public profession of support for preservation of the judiciary as an independent branch of government free from party strife.[7]

In addition to Whig demands, three other pressures affected Taylor. Frist, principal mediators boosted their kinsmen and instru-mental friends for judicial office; three of ten nominees had kinship ties to mediators responsible for their selection, and three others—all from Taylor's home state—were instrumental friends of the presi-dent. Second, the growing disparity between the rewards of private law practice or state judicial service and employment on the federal bench frustrated Taylor's quest for "capacity"; two nominees declined their commissions. Third, the Whig party was a minority in the Sen-ate.[8] The president dealt with the Senate opposition boldly; in six instances he filled vacancies during the congressional recess. The Democratic majority confirmed all of the Whig president's nominees, although three of these, originally recess appointees, awaited confir-mation for six months or longer. As had the Whigs, Democrats ac-cepted the right of the president from the opposition party to wield the patronage.

Taylor anticipated that Secretary of State John M. Clayton would provide the administration with political and administrative expertise. The secretary of state, like his predecessors, supervised the judicial patronage. A variety of Whigs criticized the choice of Clayton. Their doubts seem at least partially justified. To the overwhelming task of replacing one set of public officeholders with another, Clayton, a former leader of Senate Whigs, brought neither organizational talent nor previous administrative experience. His friends dubbed him "Atlas" in recognition of his tireless loyalty to the president. His critics were less generous. Seward, who objected to the secretary's ready access to the president, complained that Clayton was "impulsive and forgetful."[9] "There is amongst the Whig party," observed Whig Congressman David Outlaw of North Carolina, "strong feelings of dissatisfaction against . . . the Secretary of State. They say there is no truth in the man—that he promises every body, and even when he makes an appointment, it scarcely gives satisfaction."[10] More damaging than Clayton's administrative laxness was his failure to assist Taylor in formulating a coherent patronage policy. Neither the president nor his secretary of state paused to consider fully how the judicial, or any other, selections would affect the president or the party.[11]

II

During the Polk administration the Democratic "shrine of party" had united the majority congressional wing of the Democratic party and the president. A combination of cooperation and discipline had nourished partisan coherence and administrative cohesion. The new Whig president filled federal judgeships under a more limiting set of circumstances; Whigs were a minority in the Senate and in the four states to which Taylor made district court nominations. Congressional Whigs participated in the selection process, but Democrats from the affected states, the president, and, at least in Arkansas, a nominee's kinsman who was a friend of the president mediated the selection process. In filling four territorial posts, Taylor recognized the wishes of the congressional wing of the party, but his administrative laxness and that of Clayton dissipated the positive political effects of such cooperation. These selections tended, on the whole, to abet party factionalism and to weaken the national administration.

When Taylor took the oath of office, five judgeships were vacant. During the brief special session of Congress in March, 1849, he made nominations to all of these: one each for Alabama and the Western District of Louisiana, and three for Minnesota territory. The Senate confirmed them, but the faultily prepared commission for a Minnesota judge forced the president to issue him a recess commission. Taylor also during the recess granted commissions to four other judges: two for the Western District of Louisiana (the first two nominees declined), and one each for Arkansas and Oregon territory. He submitted to the first session of the Thirty-first Congress regular nominations for these interim appointees and for a judge for Illinois.

The president cooperated with the heavily Democratic Alabama congressional delegation to fill the district court judgeship in that state. The death of Judge William Crawford on February 28, 1849, created the vacancy in Alabama. It was the first judgeship filled by the new Whig administration.

Conflicting sectional interests in Alabama had historically tugged at the federal court. Crawford's death, after twenty-three years on the bench, furnished the north Alabama bar an opportunity to make the court more responsive to the needs of that section. Congress in 1819 had provided the new state of Alabama with one district court. This arrangement during the 1830s faltered under the dissimilar legal demands of the two sections of the state. In the south, planters, merchants, shippers, and insurers relied on the federal court to settle important admiralty and maritime questions arising from the cotton export business. In the north, the business of the court was different: civil suits, land litigation, and federal criminal violations filled the docket. To accommodate northern litigants, Congress directed Crawford, who resided at Mobile, to hold regular terms in the north. Poor transportation, bad weather, and pestilence repeatedly forced the judge to remain in Mobile; litigants who wanted federal justice had to go to him. In response to the explosion in federal litigation that accompanied the Panic of 1837, Congress divided the state into two judicial districts, one northern and the other southern, with a federal attorney and marshal in each. The penurious Congress declared an additional judge an extravagance; Crawford was assigned to preside over both districts. The cadence of criticism from the north Alabama bar quickened as advancing age and declining health restricted Crawford's judicial activity.[12]

The president completely ignored the wishes of north Alabama Whigs. By the time their demands reached Washington, Taylor, in concert with the Alabama Democratic congressional delegation, had already nominated a candidate from Mobile—retiring Whig Congressman John Gayle.[13] Henry W. Hilliard, one of the two Whig members of the House from Alabama, recommended George N. Stewart, a Montgomery Whig with an extensive admiralty and maritime practice before the federal court, as a candidate whose residence inland might assuage northern Whigs while providing the commercial interests of the south with a readily available judge.[14] Gayle, however, coveted the post as a financially stable and prestigious reward for a thirty-year career in politics which had taken him from pro-Union Jacksonian governor to Whig presidential elector, state supreme court judge, and congressman. Despite his break with the Democratic party, Gayle remained popular with the opposition; he won election to Congress in 1848 from a heavily Democratic district outside of Mobile.[15]

Congressional Democrats and Gayle triumphed over Hilliard and the interests of the Whig bar of north Alabama. The president did not even wait to consider the demands of disappointed Whigs in that section. In view of Gayle's party service and the forceful backing of Alabama Democrats on Capitol Hill, the president placed bipartisan cooperation ahead of the independence of his office and local party interests.

While Alabama Democrats mediated the selection of a district court judge, Taylor adhered to the wishes of Senate Whigs in filling the Minnesota judgeships. Despite his avowed intention to supervise closely the selection process, the president in making these nominations exercised slight administrative control. This precluded him from imposing standards of ability or belief on judicial nominees. Kinship and friendship connections, within a common Whig affiliation, prevailed over national party interests.

Personalities rather than organized parties dominated Minnesota politics. In his position as territorial delegate, Henry Hastings Sibley of St. Paul studiously avoided party identification; a Wisconsin Democrat complained that Sibley was "neither Whig nor Democrat."[16] The delegate believed that the politically dependent territory would benefit from a united political front. This strategy attempted to smother the clamorous demands of nonresidents for position in the new territory while promoting cooperation among "loose territorial alliances" that would eventually mature into a two-party system. Taylor granted to residents recommended by Sibley minor patronage posts, but he bowed to the demands of nonresident Whig leaders in filling the major offices.[17]

The three vacant Minnesota judgeships stirred conflict among New York Whigs. The party was already divided between the followers of Seward and Weed and the adherents of Vice-President Millard Fillmore. Both factions argued that the heavy migration of former New York residents to the territory gave New York Whigs a proprietary role in the judicial selection process. Although Taylor subsequently came under the influence of Seward, in early March the president was committed to neither faction. Instead of trying to reconcile the powerful leaders of the New York party by selecting candidates from both factions, the president and the secretary of state chose to ignore them.[18]

Whig Senators Truman Smith of Connecticut and John Bell of Tennessee dictated the composition of the Minnesota bench. They had orchestrated the pro-Taylor forces in their respective states; Smith had also organized the temporary National Whig Executive Committee that engineered the president's nomination and election. Taylor entrusted Smith to select both associate justices. He asked only that the senator inform the harried secretary of state of his choices. Clayton, in turn, made Smith promise to consult the Whig congressional delegations from the home states of his candidates.[19]

Smith disregarded his promises with humiliating consequences for the administration. He first conferred with Sen. James Cooper of Pennsylvania, a Clay Whig skeptical of Taylor, who was contending with Gov. William F. Johnston for mastery of the state Whig party. Secretary of State Clayton had pledged to Johnston full administration support; the governor was to clear all federal appointments involving Pennsylvania Whigs. Smith, however, recommended Cooper's brother, twenty-eight-year-old David Cooper of Lewiston, Pennsylvania, a member of the Whig state central committee. Whig members of the Pennsylvania congressional delegation aligned with Cooper endorsed his brother's nomination, but the other Whig congressman and Governor Johnston withheld approval. Smith designated his nephew, Bradley B. Meeker of Flemingsburg, Kentucky, for the other judgeship. The Connecticut senator completely ignored the Kentucky Whig congressional delegation; its members were unaware of Meeker and the intervention of his uncle in Kentucky party affairs. Smith "intimated," according to the secretary of state, that both candidates had the blessings of their respective Whig delegations. Taylor nominated them; the Senate confirmed them.[20]

Taylor's abdication of the presidential selection prerogative and Clayton's administrative laxity rankled Kentucky Whigs. Gov. John J. Crittenden and Sen. Henry Clay shared the leadership of the Whig party of that state. The two were longtime rivals; Crittenden's early declaration favoring Taylor had further annoyed the perennial presidential aspirant Clay. Nonetheless, both factions denounced Meeker and the intrusion of Smith into Kentucky party affairs. Crittenden informed the secretary of state that Smith's nephew was "positively *odious*" to all Whigs; Meeker did "not possess one single qualification for the station." The Kentucky governor hoped that "Taylor will not charge him to Kentucky—he ought to be set down as so much patronage bestowed on Connecticut."[21] The disapproval of Clay Whigs was equally animated.[22] Clayton replied sheepishly that the "sly old rascal Smith" had "duped" him.[23]

Clayton sought to rectify his blunder without admitting culpability. When news reached him in early May that Meeker was dead, Clayton seized the initiative; with the acquiescence of Crittenden, he planned to mend party fences in Kentucky by bestowing the allegedly vacant judgeship on Leslie Combs, a Clay Whig. When reports of Meeker's death proved false, the strategy collapsed; Combs never received further consideration.[24]

Clay during the first session of the Thirty-first Congress demanded Meeker's rejection. The Democratic-controlled Senate Committee on the Judiciary willingly investigated allegations that the judge had no formal legal training and had fled a bevy of outraged Kentucky creditors. The committee concluded the charges were mere fabrications; they favorably reported his nomination. In addition, Smith sprang to his nephew's defense.[25]

Taylor and Clayton in nominating associate justices for Minnesota squandered an opportunity to strengthen the administration and party cohesion. Party united the chief executive, Smith, and the nominees in the selection process, but traditional kinship connections took precedence over national party interests and the candidates' professional preparedness. Cooper and Meeker were legal mediocrities at best; the subsequent furor over their selection confirmed that Taylor and Clayton were politically and administratively inept. "I had supposed," complained a Seward-endorsed New York candidate, "that thirty years of exertion for the growth of Whig principles . . . would have insured me a judgeship at least, but in this I was mistaken."[26]

By allowing Whig senators to dictate the Minnesota selections, the president relinquished control over the quality and political impact of the nominations. Unlike Polk, the Mexican War hero Taylor lacked the political savvy and toughness to shape the actions of members of the upper house to his own purposes. Sen. John Bell of Tennessee, in designating the chief justice for the territory, acted with greater restraint and political acumen than had Smith or Cooper.

Tennessee between 1836 and 1852 was a Whig stronghold. As in Kentucky, the Whig party in Tennessee had splintered into Clay and anti-Clay factions, with Senator Bell a spokesman for the latter. The

senator in 1848 had to win reelection; Clay Whigs in the Tennessee
General Assembly attempted to unseat him. Bell prevailed only by
accumulating impressive political debts.[27]

Aaron Goodrich, a Dover, Tennessee, lawyer, Taylor presidential
elector, and state legislator, had voted for Bell's reelection. A native of
New York and a former political protagonist of Millard Fillmore,
Goodrich in 1838 settled in Dover, where he established a respectable
law practice in the courts of northwest Tennessee. He expected com-
pensation for his political loyalty. Bell reciprocated by advocating
Goodrich's appointment as collector of Detroit, but when Michigan
Whigs protested, he persuaded Clayton to submit the Tennessean's
name to the president for chief justice of Minnesota. On the same day
Bell recommended Goodrich, Taylor nominated him.[28]

Taylor needlessly forfeited much of the inherent power of the
president to direct the selection process. He allowed Clayton and
Whig senators to dictate—not just mediate—the selection process. He
fulfilled the limited task of ratifying their recommendations. The
president failed to define patronage goals; he neglected to establish
criteria for judicial nominees. More significantly, in contrast to Polk,
Taylor, through his submissiveness, diminished the productive reciprocal tensions between the president and the congressional wing of his
party. As a result, in Minnesota the president's promise to place the
national welfare above political and personal friendships was shat-
tered.

While Taylor allowed Senate Whigs to dictate the composition of
the Minnesota bench, he participated directly in the last judicial
nomination during the special session of the Thirty-first Congress.
This appointment was for the newly created Western District of
Louisiana, his home state. The president searched among his wealthy
Whig acquaintances for a nominee willing to serve on a salary of
$2,000 a year.

During the previous three decades the growth of population and
commercial activity in the hinterland above New Orleans had dou-
bled, then tripled the business of the federal court. Congress in 1831
attempted to alleviate the congested docket of the court by dividing
the state into eastern and western districts manned by a single judge
who resided in New Orleans. The bar of that city objected; the judge
spent valuable days hearing criminal and land cases in the western
district while the year-round admiralty and maritime business of the
port city accumulated. Western residents were also unhappy; the repeated failure of the judge to hold the designated terms of the court
forced them to travel to New Orleans. Congress, during the final days

of the Polk administration, attempted to rectify the problem by authorizing a separate judge for the western district.[29]

Taylor trusted his knowledge and that of personal friends to fill the vacant judgeship. He ignored altogether the heavily Democratic Louisiana congressional delegation. On March 16 he nominated James G. Campbell, a Natchitoches lawyer and former state circuit court judge who had campaigned for his election. The thirty-eight-year-old lawyer, who had no hint of Taylor's intentions, declined; he preferred his lucrative private law practice and planting to the inadequate federal judicial salary.[30] With encouragement from Campbell, Taylor then decided on John Kingsbury Elgee of Alexandria, a state circuit court judge and first generation Irish immigrant who had amassed a fortune through sugar planting and law practice. "Elgee," Campbell argued, was "one of the very best jurists in Louisiana"; as important, he possessed "an ample fortune which will enable him to accept the appointment, for with the salary attached to it, the Judge will have to support the office and not the office the Judge." The president on April 24 issued a recess commission to the Alexandria Whig, who promptly declined; he refused to exchange the duties of his better-paying but geographically smaller state circuit court for the extensive travel required to hold the federal court in the western district.[31]

The president issued a second recess appointment to a friend and wealthy Whig planter. He elevated the recently confirmed federal attorney for the western district, Henry Boyce of Rapides Parish, to the judgeship. Like Campbell and Elgee, Boyce knew nothing of his candidacy. He was a first generation Irish immigrant who had accumulated, through marriage, sugar planting, and land speculation, a massive fortune. The former state circuit court judge readily accepted his recess commission.[32]

The personal involvement of the president was critical to the selection of a judge for the western district of his home state. Taylor trusted his personal knowledge of the Whig planter-lawyers in the district. Whig affiliation alone did not insure nomination; instrumental friendship ties to the president and financial independence were prerequisites to selection.

Taylor during the recess following the special session also made interim appointments to Arkansas and Oregon territories. In both instances, Whigs from outside these heavily Democratic areas mediated the selection process.

Judge Benjamin Johnson of Arkansas died on October 2, 1849. The Arkansas Whig party at his death was even weaker than its

Alabama counterpart; Democrats occupied every Arkansas seat in Congress. Like the party in Alabama, the minority Whig party in Arkansas suffered sectional divisions stemming from differences in the economy of the state. Whigs from west Arkansas tended to be small farmers, while members of the party in east Arkansas engaged in planting and commercial activity generated by trade on the Mississippi River. Eastern residents coveted the vast tracts of undeveloped lands in the western section; they relied upon the bar of Little Rock to bring suits challenging the validity of titles, many dating back to the period of Spanish control, in west Arkansas.[33]

Whigs in the two sections wanted a new appointee sympathetic to their interests. Congress in 1836 had constituted the new state a single judicial district. The judge for the court resided at Little Rock but held terms throughout the state. Subsequently, Congress created two districts: one in the west and the other in the east; but Little Rock, in the eastern district, remained the judge's residence. Disgruntled small farmers in the western district complained that Judge Johnson often failed to hold the allotted terms of the court; they were forced to come to Little Rock, where the skilled bar of that city too frequently persuaded the judge and jurors to favor litigants from eastern Arkansas in controversial land cases. Johnson's death afforded these western Whigs—indeed, Democrats in the section as well—an opportunity to have a western lawyer appointed who would counteract the influence of the powerful Little Rock bar. They complained to Taylor that "the local interests and prejudices of Little Rock" invariably infected the judge who resided there.[34] They insisted that the selection of a Little Rock lawyer experienced in land suits to sit on the "most important court in the state" would constitute a "denial of justice" and give "great dissatisfaction."[35]

The president mixed friendship with politics in selecting the Arkansas judge. His long-time friend Fredrick Trapnall of Little Rock, an influential leader of the state party, recommended the appointment of his brother-in-law, Daniel Ringo of Little Rock, a former state supreme court judge and land law expert. Trapnall argued that since land cases constituted the major business before the court, the president had to select a lawyer skilled in that branch of the law and capable of commanding the confidence of the Little Rock bar. Trapnall also enlisted the aid of Sen. John Bell of Tennessee; Arkansas Whigs had "no representative at Washington to take care of their interests . . . they have of necessity to invoke the aid of Whig members from other states." The Arkansas leader also engaged the support of

Secretary of the Interior Thomas Ewing, whose influence was growing within the administration. In addition to the endorsements of these influential national figures, Trapnall made a personal appeal to the president; he traveled to Washington to assure Taylor of Ringo's willingness to serve. Pleas by western Whigs to the contrary, Taylor granted Ringo a recess commission.[36]

The final recess appointment was to Oregon territory. Polk had originally filled all of the Oregon judgeships, but Peter H. Burnett had declined to serve. On the recommendation of Thomas Ewing, Taylor appointed William Strong, a youthful Cleveland lawyer.[37]

When the first session of the Thirty-first Congress convened in December, 1849, Democrats attacked Taylor's removals and recess appointments. The president submitted regular nominations for all of his ad interim judicial appointees. Democratic Senators James Bradbury of Maine and Stephen A. Douglas of Illinois charged that through extensive removals and recess appointments Taylor had usurped the constitutional position of the Senate in the selection process. Democrats in the upper house intended to embarrass the administration; they delayed action on any nominee who had previously received a recess commission.[38]

While Senate Democrats procrastinated, the death on January 23, 1850, of Judge Nathaniel Pope of Illinois created another vacancy. Illinois was a Democratic state with a divided minority Whig party; Congressman Edward D. Baker of Galena was the sole Illinois Whig on Capitol Hill. Baker, who served as a brigadier general under Taylor in the Mexican War, enjoyed the president's respect and confidence.[39]

Baker's informal personal connection to the president disrupted the formal partisan connection between Taylor and Illinois Whigs. At least nine applicants sought the post; of these, state supreme court justice Samuel F. Lockwood of Jacksonville and state legislator Stephen T. Logan were the best supported. Lockwood had impressive support from outside the state: both of the senators from Kentucky believed he would respect the property rights of Kentuckians to have escaped slaves returned; and Supreme Court Justice John McLean, whose circuit included Illinois, thought Lockwood ideally suited by experience to share circuit court duties.[40] The president, however, heeded Baker's recommendations; he selected Thomas Drummond of the congressman's home town.[41] The supporters of Lockwood and Logan were thunderstruck. "Judge Drummond," complained one Whig, was "not well known in the state . . . and his nomination surprised and disappointed the friends of the administration in Illinois."[42] Taylor pleased his friend Baker at the expense of other loyal Illinois Whigs.

The Senate eventually confirmed all of the nominees. Drummond was approved three weeks after his nomination; the recess appointees were confirmed late in the first session, after Taylor's death. The Democratic majority engaged in partisan harassment of Taylor, but it accepted partisan distribution of the judicial patronage as a legitimate function of the new Whig president. "The Senate," observed Daniel Webster, did not "seem to be in a proscriptive mood."[43]

III

Zachary Taylor pledged in distributing the federal patronage to make "country first & friendship second."[44] He stressed his devotion to patronage matters; he praised partisan harmony; and he promised an able cadre of public officials. Political realities quickly loosened the president from his granitelike posture of disinterested public service. He responded, however, not as a modern, disciplined, and impersonal party leader. He wielded the judicial patronage in an outwardly party-directed fashion—all of his nominees were Whigs—but instead of quelling Whig factionalism, Taylor's judicial nominations exacerbated it; instead of strengthening the administration, his selections weakened it. Indeed, he seemed oblivious to the broader consequences of his actions. Taylor exercised erratic administrative control over the judicial patronage; he devoted personal attention to some vacancies while allowing congressional Whigs to dictate others. Secretary of State Clayton failed to inject administrative and partisan discipline into the process. Without a coherent patronage program, Taylor made judicial nominations on an essentially ad hoc basis. The personal ties he cursed as destructive of the public welfare figured significantly in the selection of judges for Minnesota, Arkansas, Louisiana, and Illinois. These appointments subordinated disinterested partisan goals to traditional personal politics. Taylor's political inexpereince and administrative laxity, the factionalism of the Whig party, and the minority position of Whigs in the Senate and the states eroded presidential independence. Under Millard Fillmore this disintegration quickened.

6

THE EVILS OF THESE
ENORMOUS ACQUISITIONS

In times like the present, when laws obnoxious to particular
sections of the country are opposed by violence, and the
authority of the courts openly set at defiance, no reasonable
effort should be spared to secure the services of judges who
have not only the ability to understand their duties, but the
firmness to discharge them with fidelity.—Millard Fillmore,
November 29, 1851[1]

President Millard Fillmore inherited a deepening political crisis over
the future of slavery. "If General Taylor had lived," concluded Secretary of State Daniel Webster, "we should have had civil war."[2]
Taylor had adopted a rigid anti–slavery extension posture; he vowed
to veto any legislation that secured the future of the peculiar institution in the American Southwest. Fillmore eased sectional tensions by
cooperating with congressional moderates of both parties. Assured
that the Whig president would promote sectional reconciliation in
organizing the Mexican Cession, Democratic Sen. Stephen A. Douglas
of Illinois formulated the Compromise of 1850. Its provisions included a harsh Fugitive Slave Law, the creation of Utah and New
Mexico territories without regard to slavery, and the admission of
California as a free state.[3]

The Compromise relied on the power and prestige of the law to
smother political controversy. It removed the slavery extension issue
from political debate (thereby preserving the artificial character of the
two-party system) by authorizing the presumably neutral judges of
Utah and New Mexico to decide the status of slavery in their respective territories. The composition of these three-man territorial
benches thus had potentially broad implications for critics and defen-
ders of the peculiar institution.[4]

The Compromise hastened the disintegration of the Whig party.
This frustrated the new president in organizing the selection process.
Conservative and moderate Union Whigs, such as Daniel Webster,
promoted the Compromise as the best hope of quieting agitation over
the slavery issue and preserving the Union; they insisted that fellow

Whigs accept it as the definitive solution to the slavery extension controversy. In the North, "Conscience" Whigs and other anti–slavery members of the party, such as Sen. William H. Seward, refused. In every state the national issue of slavery extension blended with local concerns to divide sectionally and factionally the already decentralized and state-centered Whig party. "Cliques and factions," Fillmore complained in 1851, threatened to "send the party in twain."[5]

Fillmore intended to fuse ability and political principle on the federal bench. He promised to enhance the quality of federal officeholders, including the judiciary, by "elevating the standards of official employment" and selecting "for places of importance . . . individuals fitted . . . by their known integrity, talents and virtues." He also expected to nominate only "Whigs" who agreed with his unionism and who combined "a vigorous constitution, with high moral and intellectual qualifications—a good judicial mind and such as gives a prospect of long service." He hoped to balance partisan necessity with administrative wisdom; he would remove public officers, including territorial judges, guilty of "neglect of duty and malfeasance of office."[6] Fillmore viewed Whig unity as essential to the future of the party; thus, he allowed many previous Taylor appointees to retain their offices. Nonetheless, he planned to solidify support in his home state against Seward and Thurlow Weed by bestowing vacant posts on Whigs committed to the Compromise.[7]

In seeking an able judiciary, Fillmore unsuccessfully sponsored substantial reforms in the administration of the federal lower courts, including increased judicial salaries. Two developments lent urgency to this cause. First, the meager and inequitable compensation allotted federal judges handicapped the selection of distinguished candidates. Beginning with Tyler's administration, low salaries and often arduous duties had prompted judicial appointees to decline commissions. Congress abetted this condition by treating the courts as separate local fiefdoms rather than components in an integrated system of federal jurisprudence; as a result, salaries varied from district to district and territory to territory. Congress only grudgingly acquiesced to increased salaries; members feared the subordination of their state judges to better-paid federal judges. "Men of distinguished ability and merit," Fillmore complained to Congress, "unless they are in affluent circumstances, cannot afford . . . to accept a judicial appointment." To remedy this the president proposed a uniform national judicial salary.[8]

Second, the hostile reaction in some quarters to the Compromise and territorial expansion required nationalization of the federal courts. Fillmore in 1851 worried that civil disorder might overwhelm the federal lower courts. Attempts to enforce the new Fugitive Slave Law culminated in a few sensational incidences of public defiance of federal authority. At the same time, in the distant territories, nonresident judges became embroiled in local controversies. "In order to obtain judges with the firmness to discharge" their duties "with fidelity," Fillmore concluded, a "just compensation must be paid." The Democratic majority in Congress and northern "Conscience" Whigs thoroughly frustrated this and other proposals. Congressmen from both parties were reluctant to cease their traditional administrative control over the lower courts; northern anti–slavery Whigs denounced all proposals to facilitate judicial enforcement of the controversial Fugitive Slave Act.[9]

Fillmore implemented change where he could. He chose Daniel Webster to fill the influential post of secretary of state. Fillmore admired Webster's pro-Compromise and unionist views, previous cabinet experience, and dedication to the federal courts. Under President John Tyler, Webster had exercised often decisive influence in the selection process; he promoted political friends for judicial office, and insisted that nominees possess previous judicial experience and sound legal reputations. In the Fillmore administration, Webster promulgated administrative reforms that enabled him to influence the selection process while disposing efficiently of swelling numbers of applications and recommendations. With the approval of Fillmore, Webster ordered his clerks to prepare detailed synopses of judicial candidates' supporters and attributes. The president usually acted only after reviewing these and the accompanying letters of recommendation. The procedure allowed Webster to register his own preference with the president. While the secretary of state gained additional administrative control over the selection process, Fillmore, unlike Tyler, tended to rely on his own judgment, to seek detailed information about potential nominees, and to listen to members of the congressional wing of the Whig party. Nonetheless, Webster frequently mediated the selection process, and Democrats exercised a veto over the selections of the minority president.[10]

II

Millard Fillmore made eight of twenty-three judicial nominations to the district courts. Six of these were to two districts in California; one each was to Maryland and the Northern District of New York.

Factional divisions among Whigs in these states and a Democratic majority in the Senate diminished the independence of the chief executive. Traditional patron-client relations, primarily in the form of instrumental friendships, imposed order on the selection process.

Fillmore in September, 1850, nominated judges to California. Congress had established two district courts, separated along the thirty-seventh parallel, with a single judge assigned to each. This division complemented regional differences within the state; it acknowledged that one judge could not preside over the federal legal business in such a vast area. In the lightly populated south, individual agriculturalists invariably owned their land. In northern California, however, the gold boom brought a dramatic influx of miners who leased their land. San Francisco blossomed into a bustling port to serve the flood of population. Congress recognized that leaseholding, gold, population, and commerce would create a special burden for the northern district judge; it provided him a salary of $3,500 a year, while his southern counterpart received $2,800.[11]

A two-party system developed rapidly. "It was curious," wrote Bayard Taylor of San Francisco in 1849, "how soon the American passion for party politics . . . emulated the excitement of . . . the older states."[12] The Democracy immediately controlled state government; it remained, with the exception of the 1855 Know-Nothing uprising, the majority party during the decade. The Chivalry, a faction of southern Democratic immigrants led by Sen. William M. Gwin, dominated party affairs. Even in his new surroundings the transplanted Mississippi physician remained loyal to the South and the peculiar institution. With a Democratic majority to sustain him, Gwin cultivated "an easy relationship with . . . Whig President Fillmore."[13]

The factionally divided California Whigs had limited influence with the administration. In 1851 Whigs in San Francisco—the only area of party strength—aligned with either Thomas Butler King, collector of the port, or James Carne, editor of the *California Courier*. Carne and King impugned each other's loyalty. The former cautioned Fillmore to nominate as judges "only Whigs true to the administration" and admonished him never to send "any man from the states with a commission in his pocket to hold office in California because he would meet with the bitterest kind of opposition." The editor warned the president to be "cautious of Gwin."[14] To assure confirmation of nominees, Fillmore chose to ignore this advice; he cooperated with the Democratic senator and the remainder of the solidly Democratic California congressional delegation.[15]

The California judgeships constantly occupied the president.

Between September, 1850, and February, 1852, Fillmore nominated six judges. Of these, two were rejected, two declined to serve, and one died before ever holding office. The pressure of eastern Whigs was intense; over one hundred out-of-state applicants clamored for the opportunity to dispense justice in the new American Eldorado.[16]

Fillmore relied on Webster to winnow these applications. The secretary adopted the same strategy he had pursued during Tyler's administration: he sought to forestall Senate opposition by selecting nominees of uncontested ability. Webster also believed that the administration, if it acted before the California congressional delegation arrived, could demonstrate its commitment to sectional cooperation and acceptance of the Compromise by appointing one judge from a northern state and the other from a southern state. The secretary dismissed the flood of Whig applicants as unfit; they had little legal reputation and most of them could not speak the Spanish language. Instead, he successfully recommended that Fillmore nominate two lawyers who had not even applied for the posts: Judah P. Benjamin of New Orleans and John Plummer Healy of Boston. The former had been a presidential elector, friend, and political advisor of Zachary Taylor. He was a nationally recognized expert in civil, admiralty, and maritime law, fluent in Spanish and French. Healy also spoke Spanish and, despite his youth, was considered one of the finest admiralty and maritme lawyers in New England. He was also the law partner and former student of the secretary of state. While Webster had pursued his political career, Healy had attended to the Boston law office. The Senate confirmed both nominees the same day California entered the Union.[17]

The appointees declined. They explained that the salaries offered inadequate compensation for extended family separations, the arduous journey to the Pacific Coast, and the responsibilities of a judgeship. The gold-induced price inflation of California meant that "no competent lawyer . . . would take the posts for less than $9,000." The declinations dismayed the administration. "I fear no fit men," observed Daniel Webster, "will take the offices at the salaries now provided."[18] Administrative circumstance frustrated the goal of appointing a competent and sectionally balanced judiciary before Gwin could intervene.

Fillmore and Webster altered their strategy. In December, 1850, they endorsed a proposal by Gwin to increase the judges' salaries to $5,000 in the Northern District and $4,000 in the Southern. Unable to secure suitable nominees outside of the state, the president restricted his search to "fit men without families" in California.[19]

The change in policy afforded California Whigs no additional voice in the selection process. The King and Carne factions endorsed different candidates for the northern judgeship.[20] The president ignored them; he exploited the vacant post to strengthen his position with New York Whigs. In December, 1850 he nominated John Currey of San Francisco, a native of New York, who in 1848 migrated to California without his wife. Currey was recommended by his legal mentor, Whig Congressman William Nelson of Peekskill, New York. Nelson was a maverick; he had unswervingly supported the Compromise measures, but he retained significant political contacts with the Seward and Weed faction. By rewarding Nelson's position on the Compromise, Fillmore hoped to draw the representative closer to the adminstration.[21]

The president also disregarded California Whigs in selecting the Southern District judge. Gwin failed to convince Fillmore to appoint a Democrat, but in mid-December the senator agreed to the nomination of twenty-seven-year-old James M. Jones of San Jose, the federal attorney for the Southern District. Gwin had established a friendship with the former Louisiana lawyer during the long voyage from New Orleans to California; subsequently, despite party differences, they had cooperated in the 1849 state constitutional convention. The president, and perhaps Gwin, was unaware that Jones suffered from chronic tuberculosis.[22]

Gwin and Senate Democrats further restricted Fillmore's independence. The Senate confirmed Jones; it rejected Currey. At the insistence of Gwin, the Senate Committee on the Judiciary, chaired by South Carolina Democrat Andrew Pickens Butler, investigated Currey's background. They discovered that Currey was a former New York Free-Soiler. Butler complained that the nominee's background mocked Fillmore's pledge to nourish sectional reconciliation. An embarrassed Congressman Nelson pleaded that Currey "was no abolitionist." The committee also received anonymous and unsubstantiated charges that Currey had fled to California to avoid a scandal stemming from misuse of clients' funds. Nelson once again defended his former student, but without result; the Senate voted thirty-five to eight against confirmation. Majorities from both parties, as well as Free-Soilers, joined with Gwin. The spurious charges of corruption combined with the suspicion of southern Democrats to defeat the nominee.[23]

With Currey's nomination doomed, Fillmore attempted to placate Gwin and New York City Whigs. The latter were especially anxious for the president to fill the northern judgeship. San Francisco had profited from booming ocean commerce by placing a tax on steam vessels using its port. Whig merchants and shippers in New York City, led by William H. Aspinwall, president of the Pacific Mail Steam Ship Company, denounced the tax as an unconstitutional interference with interstate commerce; they expected a federal judge, once appointed, to void the tax. Aspinwall enlisted Webster; together they recommended the nomination of twenty-nine-year-old Ogden Hoffman, Jr., the son of a redoubtable Webster supporter and prominent New York City Whig. The younger Hoffman was a bachelor, a graduate of the Harvard Law School, and a San Francisco resident.[24]

The president wanted Gwin's endorsement of the candidate. The senator objected to the former New Yorker's youth and inexperience, but Webster prodded him into agreement by arguing that the president would not appoint a Democrat and that no better Whig could be found. Fillmore immediately nominated Hoffman; the Senate on February 27 concurred.[25]

Six months elapsed between California statehood and Hoffman's appointment. The Senate Democratic majority, sectional tensions, and administrative difficulties forced Fillmore and Webster to alter their original strategy. Lacking the political resources to suppress Gwin's influence, the president sought accommodation at the expense of the divided California Whigs. Personal and informal patron-client relations rather than party organization bridged the physical isolation separating Fillmore from California.

The president subsequently challenged Gwin's mastery of the selection process with unfortunate results for the administration. When the chronically ill Jones died in December, 1851, without ever holding court, Fillmore nominated Currey to the Southern District. The once-rejected nominee was endorsed by his patron, Nelson, and, this time, by the Carne faction. The latter denounced previous charges that Currey was an abolitionist; to the contrary, the San Francisco lawyer was a "sound, conservative National Whig, loyal alike to the Constitution, the Union and the Compromise measures." Webster urged Fillmore to avoid further jeopardizing the presidential prerogative by nominating Currey; Gwin and Senate Judiciary Committee Chairman Butler were "opposed on the same grounds as before."[26]

Webster was correct. Butler protested that the nomination would disturb the balance of sectional interests in the federal courts; a native of the North already held one California judgeship, the other properly belonged to a slave state immigrant. When Butler's committee reported the nomination unfavorably six months later, the newly elected Democratic senator from California, John Weller, had the nomination tabled indefinitely. He joined with the disabused Gwin to further strip the president of his appointment prerogative. The senators rushed through Congress a measure that retained the Southern District but eliminated the judge; it assigned the over-worked Hoffman to preside over the entire state. The measure was entirely partisan; when President Franklin Pierce took office, the Democratic majority repealed it.[27]

Fillmore also contended with disruptive Whig factionalism. In filling the California judgeships, the wishes of Democratic Senator Gwin had made this a secondary problem. During the same first session of the Thirty-second Congress in which Currey's second nomination was tabled, the president successfully appointed district judges to Maryland and New York. In both states factionalism stemming from the Compromise of 1850 shook the Whig party.

"There is a wild spirit," observed prominent Maryland Whig John W. Crisfield in January, 1851, that "prevades all parties and persons. . . . In Maryland voting is wild and unaccountable." The old two-party system was in the throes of a profound transition; the once dominant Whigs splintered under a rising Democratic majority and an incipient native American party. The Baltimore "courthouse clique," a small but influential faction within the Whig party, was an alliance of commercial leaders and prominent lawyers in the city. "Orthodox Whigs" inside and outside Baltimore resented the clique's traditional dominance. They expected Fillmore to halt "the disbandonment of the Whig party in Maryland" by reducing the influence of the clique in patronage matters and rectifying Taylor's egregious failure to remove every Democratic officeholder. Sen. James A. Pearce, an old friend of the president and fervent advocate of the Compromise, straddled these divisions.[28]

Political regionalism induced by the geographic eccentricity of Maryland exacerbated party factionalism. When Judge Upton Scott Heath of Baltimore died on February 21, 1852, Pearce, of the Eastern Shore, recommended two orthodox Whigs from that region: former United States senator Ezekiel Chambers, and former circuit judge John W. Crisfield. Pearce emphasized their legal abilities and the necessity of recognizing through the patronage the contribution of Whigs from the Eastern Shore. "If forced to choose between them," Pearce concluded, "I would be in a fix. My choice would be Chambers first and Crisfield next."[29]

The Baltimore clique was equally insistent. "The City," Congressman Thomas Y. Walsh asserted, was "entitled to the appoint-

ment of a judge . . . because it embraces nearly all the commerce of
the state." Under the sponsorship of Reverdy Johnson and Sen.
Thomas Pratt, the clique recommended John Glenn, son of former
federal judge Elias Glenn, and the most successful admiralty lawyer in
the city. Democratic Supreme Court Justice Roger B. Taney, whose
circuit included Maryland, applauded the Whig candidate's legal
reputation, especially his knowledge of admiralty law.[30]

Whigs in western Maryland claimed the judgeship as compensation for previous unrewarded partisan loyalty. Their candidate was
Robert N. Martin of Hagerstown, who until January, 1852, was chief
justice of the Maryland Court of Appeals for the Western District.
Orthodox Whigs throughout the state praised him as an acceptable
compromise candidate; in the course of a long judicial career, he had
acquired "little political influence."[31]

The two factions of the party polarized over the appointment.
Orthodox Whigs, led by state party chairman George E. Langston,
charged that the nomination of Glenn would "give *great umbrage* to the
Whig party (what's left of them)." Langston warned that Glenn was
sympathetic to Winfield Scott's presidential ambitions; his nomination
to the bench "would be received with about the same feelings by the
party here, that the appointment of Thurlow Weed in Albany would
be received by the party there."[32]

Fillmore took the initiative. He established two criteria for selection: the nominee had to be a Whig sixty years of age or younger, and,
upon confirmation, he had to reside in Baltimore. The president
attempted to preclude further factional squabbling by offering the
post to forty-eight-year-old Senator Pearce, whose legal reputation
and respect by both Whig factions made him an ideal compromise
candidate. He reacted favorably: Democratic dominance of the state
legislature cast doubt on his reelection two years hence, and a steady
income from "the *only* life office in Maryland" was preferable to the
"declining yearly" trial law business in the state.[33] Reverdy Johnson
protested that Pearce's nomination would increase the Senate Democratic majority and deny the party a campaigner whose presence
during the forthcoming presidential election "might prevent the loss
of the state." Embarrassed at even seeming to have sought after office
and sensitive to the arguments of Johnson, Pearce on March 5 withdrew from consideration.[34]

This confounded Fillmore's compromise plan. Advanced age
eliminated Chambers; the residency requirement excluded Crisfield.
By the second week of March only Martin and Glenn remained. While
the president had refused Pearce's recommendations, he deferred to

the Maryland senator in choosing between the last two candidates. Pearce preferred Glenn: he was more experienced than Martin with admiralty litigation; he was acceptable to Taney; and he was "least obnoxious to other portions of the party than any of his associates of the Clique."[35]

When party factionalism narrowed his prerogative in the selection process, Fillmore resorted to traditional instrumental friendship connections. This technique failed in Maryland, but succeeded in the president's home state. Judge Alfred Conkling of the Northern District of New York in August, 1852, resigned his low-paying judgeship to become American minister to Mexico. By this time, the Whig party, as a result of the work of Seward and Weed, had embarrassed Fillmore by designating Winfield Scott as the party's presidential standard-bearer. Fillmore retaliated by dismissing demands by Seward and his equally dissident Whig colleague Hamilton Fish that they mediate the selection of Conkling's replacement; instead, he nominated his former law partner and politicial confidant, Postmaster General Nathan K. Hall. Seward and Fish asked the full Senate to reject Hall, but the Democratic majority, impressed by the nominee's excellent legal reputation and inclined out of political expediency to side with the lame-duck president, added its confirmation without a roll-call vote.[36]

Whig factionalism, a Democratic majority in the Senate, and, in California, inadequate salaries diminished presidential independence. Fillmore took a lively interest in district court nominations: he consulted frequently with his secretary of state; he enforced minimum selection criteria; and he nominated instrumental political friends in an attempt to circumvent party factionalism. He struggled to protect the prerogatives of his office, but, as an accidental president leading a divided party, he was unable to stem the flow of power over district court nominations to the Senate Democratic majority.

III

To Millard Fillmore fell the task of organizing the new American empire. This responsibility included the unique administrative and political problems of distributing the territorial judicial patronage. Of Fillmore's twenty-three judicial nominations, eighteen were to Utah, New Mexico, Oregon, and Minnesota territories. In filling vacancies in these territories, Fillmore had to overcome the isolation imposed by great distance and slow communications and transportation. Undeveloped or underdeveloped territorial Whig organizations compounded the problems of isolation and political dependency. The clash of personalities and cliques typified territorial politics. The administrative problem of attracting able candidates complemented this political handicap; the tenure during good behavior granted district judges did not include the territorial judiciary. In return for arduous travel, lengthy family separations, harsh living conditions, and meager salaries, the territorial judge was granted a four-year renewable term. By 1850 even this limited tenure was susceptible to challenge. Andrew Jackson had declined to fully extend his policy of rotation-in-office to the territorial bench, and his successors had acquiesced in this practice. Nonetheless, the *Canter* decision of two decades earlier was an available precedent by which to limit the independence of the territorial judiciary.

Religion and slavery figured prominently in the selection of judges for Utah and New Mexico. The Catholic population of New Mexico and the Mormon residents of Utah were the objects of suspicion and hostility. The organic acts of these territories contained two crucial provisions relating to slavery. On the one hand, they established the doctrine of popular sovereignty; residents of the territories, through their legislatures, could decide whether to recognize the peculiar institution. On the other hand, these same organic acts stipulated that residents were not, after all, to have the final word; instead, suits involving the status of slavery might be brought before the territorial supreme courts with subsequent direct appeal to the Supreme Court in Washington. The scheme provided the facade of popular participation while ultimately leaving the politically explosive slavery issue to a supposedly neutral judicial power. The selection of judges for these territories had fateful implications for religious liberty and the peculiar institution and significant ramifications for Fillmore's policy of seeking sectional harmony.[37]

In his dual capacity of administrator and party leader, Fillmore was frustrated in his selection of territorial judges. Of the chief executive's eighteen nominees, almost two-fifths never served: five appointees declined to accept office once confirmed, and the Democratic Senate claimed two more; it rejected one nominee and forced the withdrawal of another. Despite the unwillingness of appointees to serve, the president refused to select any candidate who was a territorial resident. He also encountered difficulties with judges who had accepted commissions; he broke with precedent by summarily removing two judges enmeshed in political controversy and administrative scandal.

Through the territorial judiciary Fillmore tried to reinforce his policy of sectional balance and the finality of the Compromise. He cooperated with Democrats: three of his nominees, all to Utah, were Democrats. As with the California appointments, administrative exigencies and the Senate Democratic majority limited his independence.

When Congress organized Utah in September, 1850, the president immediately submitted judicial nominations. These appointments consumed the president's energy and produced controversy. Only one of his eight Utah nominees served a full term; the others declined appointment, resigned, were removed, or died in office. This turnover, coupled with public suspicion of the Mormons, generated continuous turmoil.

The Mormons wanted political autonomy, religious freedom, and the benefits of participation in the Union. The crucial matter was the conditions of admittance. In August, 1846, Brigham Young concluded that establishment of a "territorial government . . . was one of the richest boons on earth." The strong-willed leader also warned that he would "rather retreat to . . . islands or mountain caves, than consent to be ruled by Governors and judges, . . . drenched in the blood of innocents, . . . who delight in injustice and oppression."[38]

Subsequent conflict during the 1850s between Mormons and the federal government has been attributed to "the selection of inferior men to fill the Territory's offices." The appointment of men deficient in ability and character, it has been charged, stemmed from the "common practice of using the Territory's posts as payment for political debts."[39] This moralizing and unsophisticated view of political patronage warrants reconsideration—not because the judges achieved better records than has heretofore been assumed, but because the selection process was a complex web of sectional, personal, administrative, and political pressures.

Fillmore agreed that sectional balance on the Utah and New Mexico benches was essential to preservation of the Compromise. Moderate anti–slavery northern Whigs urged the president to appoint only free-state judges "who want to see slavery excluded." At the worst, they suggested, Fillmore could recruit candidates from either "Delaware or Missouri where . . . a moderate feeling on slavery existed." Slave-state Whigs and Democrats favorable to the Compromise argued for balance; the president had to "be disposed to take the judges *from the different sections of our country*."[40]

Three different spokesmen in 1850 represented the provisional government of Deseret in Washington. Two were official emissaries: Dr. John M. Bernhisel, a Whig, Mormon convert, and close associate of Young; and Almon W. Babbitt, a Democrat and former gentile counselor to martyr Joseph Smith. A third, unofficial, spokesman was Thomas Leiper Kane of Philadelphia, a gentile with an intense personal commitment to the Saints.[41]

Together the three urged the president to remember the representative function of the judiciary. "The peculiar circumstances of the community of Deseret," Bernhisel argued, required the selection of Mormons, with whom the residents of the territory could unite "in their opinion and feeling." Fillmore was sympathetic. "The President," Bernhisel observed in August, 1850, was "quite friendly disposed" toward the Saints, as were Webster and Secretary of the Treasury Thomas Corwin. Nonetheless, the chief executive had to cooperate with "influential political friends" anxious to control the federal patronage in Utah.[42]

Fillmore personally directed the selection process. He announced that only candidates below fifty years of age, in good health, and committed to the Compromise would receive nominations. He agreed to Mormon representation on the bench, although not necessarily by Utah residents. To secure suitable nominees he solicited recommendations from free and slave–state congressmen of both parties and from the Mormon spokesmen.[43]

The church representatives divided. Bernhisel and Kane suggested three Mormons: Zerubbabel Snow of Canton, Ohio, a Democrat, for chief justice; and Newell K. Whitney, a bishop of the church, and Heber C. Kimball, the lieutenant governor of Deseret, for associate justices. Unlike the austere Bernhisel, the gregarious and crude Babbitt had courted members of Congress from both parties; he won the confidence of Fillmore by providing invaluable intelligence about Democratic attitudes toward the Mormons. At the urging of Democratic Congressman David K. Cartter, Babbitt joined his colleagues in recomminding Snow as chief justice. He designated Perry E. Brocchus, an Alabama native, Democrat, and law clerk in the office of the solicitor of the treasury during the Polk administration, for one associate justiceship. Alabama Senator William R. King praised Brocchus as a suitable representative of southern interests. Babbitt, on the recommendation of anti–slavery expansion congressional Whigs from western Pennsylvania, suggested Joseph Buffington of Kittanning, a former congressman opposed to the Mexican War and the extension of slavery, for the other associate justiceship.[44]

Fillmore decided to forestall controversy in Utah by combining sectional interests, Mormon representation, and bipartisan cooperation. He deviated from Babbitt's recommendations only in elevating

Buffington to the administratively important chief-justiceship; he afforded greatest visibility on the bench to gentile, Whig, and Union sympathies. Brocchus and Buffington balanced free and slave states. Mormons were represented by Snow. Secretary of State Webster and Ohio Whigs objected to the Canton Democrat, but Fillmore insisted the selection of a Mormon member of the opposition party would encourage bipartisan agreement on Utah policy. The Senate on September 28, 1851, confirmed the nominees.[45]

The rapid turnover on the Utah bench during the 1850s commenced before the first appointees reached the territory. Buffington declined because of "the smallness of the salary, the shortness of the tenure, and the fates and exposure of journeying to that distant region with a family." At the insistence of anti–slavery extension Whigs from western Pennsylvania, Fillmore perpetuated his orginial scheme by nominating Lemuel G. Brandebury of Carlisle, a lawyer of less distinction than Buffington. Brandebury was apprehensive over the demands of territorial service, but he eventually accepted his commission.[46]

The Utah nominations mirrored the complex pressures besetting the administration. The judgeships were not simply given away to faithful Whigs for past service; to the contrary, the president nominated two Democrats in the hope of accommodating religious and sectional pressures through bipartisan cooperation. Relieved of the demands of the Mormon Church, Fillmore selected the justices for New Mexico in a more party-directed fashion.

The ambiguous legal precedents for slavery in New Mexico made the selection of judges especially important. The Spanish civil law inheritance of the territory did not recognize the American institution of chattel slavery. If the territorial judges accepted this view, then slavery was certain to be excluded. Experience in neighboring Texas suggested that American law might simply displace the Spanish civil law tradition. The Texas judiciary had preserved the peculiar institution by subordinating Spanish civil law to American common law and statutory enactments. In view of the predominantly southern migration into the territory, the same development was possible in New Mexico.[47]

As he did with the Mormons in Utah, Fillmore solicited the advice of Whig spokesmen in New Mexico. Loosely organized personal factions, divided between Protestant Americans and Catholic Mexicans, competed to control the new territorial government. Santa Fe lawyer John W. Folger led the Whiggish minority of Protestant American immigrants. He admonished Fillmore that with religious tension "running so high" and with disputed Spanish land titles creating "such bitter animosity," it would be "better for both the territory and the President" if the judges were "entire strangers."[48]

In appointing nonresidents, Fillmore was attentive to two matters. He persisted in his commitment to sectional balance, but he reversed the pattern of representation established in Utah. The important post of chief justice went to a southerner; the two associate-justiceships were bestowed on free-state candidates. He also expected his nominees to meet the administrative criteria he established in Utah and to sustain the Union and the Compromise of 1850.

By January, 1851, the search for a chief justice had narrowed to James H. Peters of Charleston, South Carolina, and Grafton Baker of Jackson, Mississippi. Secretary of the Treasury Thomas Corwin recommended Peters. Despite his residence in a slave state, the thirty-eight-year-old Whig was a thoroughgoing unionist opposed to the spread of slavery but disposed to implement fully the Fugitive Slave Law. The candidate "firmly believed" that the "good results" of the Compromise were "incomplete; the appointment of . . . Judges . . . for New Mexico will have a vast influence upon the future destiny of our beloved country." Peters asserted that the "Spanish law" forbade "involuntary servitude . . . as we know it in the United States . . . save for offenses against the state. . . . The Mexican courts have so determined it repeatedly." "Unless the courts *judicially legislate* it," Peters concluded, "slavery will be kept from New Mexico."[49]

Grafton Baker was a Whig unionist who benefited from Democratic support. Democratic Senator Henry S. Foote of Mississippi, a proponent of the Compromise and a leader of the southern "Nationals" during the Senate debate, joined Democratic Senator William M. Gwin of California and the leadership of the Mississippi Whig party in urging Baker. In reply to inquiries, they assured the president that during the debates in the Mississippi legislature over Taylor's plan to exclude slavery from the Mexican Cession, Baker had "heroically and patriotically" battled "with Disunion"; he viewed "secessionists and disunionists as the grave diggers of our glorious Union." Baker's candidacy was also boosted by the unhappiness of southern "Nationals" with Peters's hostility toward the legal extension of slavery and the president's mistaken belief, propounded by Baker's advocates, that the South Carolinian "was a man of between 50 and 60 years of age—decrepit—and in very bad health."[50] Baker won the post.

The president also successfully insisted on the conservative unionism of the two free-state associate justices. Indiana Whigs, with bipartisan support from the Indiana Democratic congressional delegation, assured Fillmore that John S. Watts of Bloomington, Indiana, who the year before had lost a bid for Congress, was a "radical National Whig."[51] The other post went to Horace Mower, the "most prominent Whig in western Michigan." Mower's former law partner and the only Whig from Michigan in the Congress, William D. Sprague of Kalamazoo, joined Justice John McLean to secure the nomination of a "national Whig . . . sound on all constitutional questions."[52]

Fillmore nominated judges for New Mexico faithful to the administration. The president wished to do nothing to encourage the spread of slavery; his conservative national nominees were unlikely to disappoint him. He cooperated with "National" Democrats determined to make the Compromise a success. This facilitated confirmation of his nominees and fulfilled his pledge to make the Compromise the final solution to the slavery extension controversy. Under difficult circumstances, Fillmore retained a modicum of independence. The Democratic Senate majority confirmed the nominees without incident.[53]

The controversial behavior of some territorial justices renewed demands for the president to invoke the removal power. In each territory residents expected the president to discipline and remove judges they charged with malfeasance and partisanship. The potential collapse in public confidence in the judiciaries of Minnesota, Utah, New Mexico, and Oregon led Fillmore to reexamine the constitutional bases of the presidential removal power. When he broke with precedent and used it, the Whig president discovered that potential nominees were reluctant to accept office for fear that an incoming Democratic administration would quickly remove them.

Conflict between rival political factions engulfed the Minnesota bench. The "Fur Company" faction was led by Gov. Alexander Ramsey, Chief Justice Aaron Goodrich, and territorial delegate Henry H. Sibley. All of them shared an economic stake in the American Fur Company. Henry M. Rice, a St. Paul lawyer and independent fur trader, headed the opposition. The Sibley and Rice factions by 1852 matured into the Whig and Democratic parties respectively, but this process of party alignment was uneven. Sibley adopted a neutral position in national politics; he eventually joined Rice in the Democratic party. In 1850 and 1851, however, the two factions split over the removal of Chief Justice Goodrich, who, in cases involving trapping rights and land claims, had consistently found in favor of the Fur Company faction. The independent fur traders charged the chief justice with conflict of interest, "undisguised despotism," "want of qualification as a lawyer," "drunkenness," and "adultery." "Goodrich," they informed the president, "would be a disgrace . . . in any civilized society."[54] The chief justice's often arbitrary judicial manner and his favoritism lent credence if not substance to these allegations. The specter of moral turpitude distressed Fillmore; he informed Webster in January, 1851, that "we must appoint a new chief justice."[55]

The president delayed for two reasons. First, Sibley successfully argued that the attack on Goodrich was factually erroneous and politically motivated.[56] Second, Fillmore was uncertain about the scope of his removal power.

The president in January, 1851, requested Attorney General Crittenden and Webster to submit opinions on the constitutionality of removing Goodrich. On the basis of John Marshall's *Canter* decision, Crittenden concluded that the president could remove the chief justice "for any cause that may . . . require it." Webster extended this to the entire territorial judiciary. He dismissed as a "mistaken idea" the argument that territorial judges were immune from removal; they were mere civil officers unprotected by Article III and, therefore, susceptible, regardless of the wording of their commissions, to discharge at the president's discretion. Since Congress could not impeach negligent territorial judges, the president, Webster concluded, had the constitutional obligation to eliminate them. The secretary of state warned that such action might stir congressional protests that the president had violated the traditional independence of the judiciary. "The removal of a judge," the secretary concluded, "would be seen with pain." He urged Fillmore to soften the blow by seeking Senate cooperation.[57]

Fillmore ended the tradition of extraconstitutional independence afforded territorial judges. On October 22, with the Senate safely in recess, he replaced Goodrich with Jerome Fuller of Albany, New York, his only interim judicial appointee. Fillmore rewarded an instrumental political friend, who, during the previous two years as editor of the proadministration *Albany State Register,* had denounced the Seward wing of the party for refusing to accept the finality of the Compromise of 1850. Burdened with financial losses from his editorship, Fuller welcomed the appointment. Both factions in Minnesota rebuked the president for selecting still another nonresident.[58]

While Fillmore had pondered the fate of Goodrich, he also heard complaints lodged against other judges. Oregon Whigs demanded the removal of the remaining Democratic judge, Orville C. Pratt, who had broken with his two Whig colleagues over the location of the territorial capital. Pratt established a separate court in the same city as the

Democratic rump of the legislature; he proceeded to declare its act the law of the territory. In New Mexico, Chief Justice Grafton Baker became mired in controversy as a result of his anti-Catholic statements, excessive absences from the territory, and his decisions in disputed land title cases.[59]

The most serious crisis erupted in Utah. Associate Justice Perry E. Brocchus in September, 1851, after less than one month in the territory, enraged the Saints: he denounced them as disloyal, rebuked them for practicing polygamy, and tactlessly defamed Governor Young. As a result of their self-induced crisis, Brocchus and his defender, Chief Justice Brandebury, deserted their judicial stations and fled to Washington. Their allegations of Mormon immorality further titillated public and congressional imaginations already primed by a decade of anti-Mormon literature. By the spring of 1852 the glaring inaccuracies in the judges' recitation of events shifted sentiment toward the Mormons.[60]

Congress in early 1852 inconclusively debated the crisis of territorial justice. With bipartisan support it required judges to obtain the president's consent before leaving their duties. Congress rejected as unconstitutional a proposal by territorial delegates Sibley and Bernhisel that residents elect the judges. The Senate Democratic majority also refused either to approve or reject resolutions of support for the Whig president's removal power. While unwilling to endorse Fillmore's specific actions, Senate Democrats tacitly accepted them as necessary to halt judicial chaos in the territories and circumvent the unwieldy impeachment process.[61]

Armed with the opinions of Webster and Crittenden, the president acted with dispatch. He used the threat of certain removal to extract resignations from Brandebury and Pratt. Grafton Baker, who had hurried to Washington, narrowly escaped the president's wrath. In allowing the New Mexico justice to retain his post, the president observed that he was governed "more by my sympathy as a man and less by my judgement as a magistrate." Fillmore had no compassion for the intransigent Brocchus; when the judge refused to resign, the president removed him.[62]

Administrative chaos in the territories prompted Fillmore to extend the removal power to the judiciary. Paradoxically, while sectional pressures, a Democratic majority, and the unattractiveness of judicial service diminished presidential discretion in the selection process, Fillmore asserted a power that the strong-willed Jackson had disdained as unconstitutional. As a lame-duck president rejected by his party for renomination, Fillmore was unable to make political capital out of his new-won administrative power. Near the end of his term, he made eight separate nominations to fill four judicial vacancies; only two appointees accepted, both in Utah.

Brocchus's debacle made Fillmore all the more sensitive to Mormon wishes. "The President," John Bernhisel reported in May, 1852, "honestly and sincerely desires to do what is right toward us. . . . He is a noble high minded accomplished gentleman" who "believes that all have the right to worship God according to the dictate of their conscience."[63] Fillmore decided to restore a viable judicial presence in Utah by establishing a Mormon majority on the court. To join Mormon Zerubbabel Snow as associate justice, he nominated, with Bernhisel's enthusiastic recommendation, Orson Hyde, a Mormon newspaper editor from Kanesville, Iowa. He bestowed the chief-justiceship on Samuel Stokely of Steubenville, Ohio, a friend and supporter of Secretary of the Treasury Thomas Corwin, who mediated his selection. Neither nominee served. Senate Democrats refused to confirm Hyde; they claimed his selection would leave the South without a representative on the bench and that he had perpetuated election frauds amongst the Mormons in Iowa. Stokely thought a position in Washington better suited to his talents and ambitions.[64]

Fillmore capitulated to Senate Democrats. On May 13, 1852, he nominated two nonresident gentiles: Lazarus H. Read, a Whig of Bath, New York, to be chief justice and Leonidas Shaver, a Democrat of Lexington, Missouri, to be associate justice. Bernhisel and Congressman Reuben Robie of Bath recommended Read as sympathetic to the Mormons. When the president, who did not know Read, inquired about the candidate, friends of the administration in Steuben County reported that he was a "sound National Whig," who had "failed to reach the position of esteem he should have" because "he was somewhat deficient in perseverance and enterprise."[65] Shaver was an equally undistinguished lawyer. Missouri Democratic Senator David R. Atchison recommended him as a "bright young man," "from a southern state," who was "sound on the Wilmot Proviso and slavery questions." Sectional priorities and Mormon interests converged in the nomination of these political opposites. Bernhisel was satisfied; the nominees were "personally known for integrity and moral character" and "very different from their fugitive predecessors."[66]

Fillmore was unable to secure judges for either Oregon or Minnesota. The president first offered the Oregon post to Charles Train of Framingham, Massachusetts. Daniel Webster mediated the nomination of Train, whose father was a longtime friend. When Train declined, the president accepted Webster's second recommendation.

John P. Sanderson, editor of the *Philadelphia News,* had performed
"good services for the administration." Like Train, Sanderson declined: the pay was too low, the distance too great, and removal by the
incoming Democratic president too certain.[67]

The Senate, on August 30, 1852, administered Fillmore a bitter
defeat by rejecting his old friend Jerome Fuller as chief justice of
Minnesota. While Fuller had fulfilled his judicial duties under a recess
commission, his nomination had languished in the Senate. New York
Whig Senators Hamilton Fish and William H. Seward denounced the
nomination as an act of political cronyism. They failed, with the same
argument, to secure the rejection of Fillmore's friend Nathan K. Hall
to be judge of the Northern District of New York, but they gained the
support of the Senate Democratic majority to table indefinitely Fuller's nomination. "Within five minutes," a triumphant Hamilton Fish
gloated, "the business was concluded and Jerome was a 'dead cock in
the pit.'"[68]

IV

"The evils of these enormous acquisitions," concluded Daniel
Webster in 1851, only "now begin to be felt."[69] Political sectionalism,
Whig factionalism, and unprecedented administrative burdens accompanied the extension of federal authority to the vast new trans-
Mississippi empire. Under these pressures the Whig party lacked the
energy to perform the administrative task of identifying potential
nominees. Fillmore attempted, without the benefit of party unity or a
Senate majority, to appoint able judges to fill hazardous and low-
paying judicial offices. His frustrations stemmed from limited party
resources rather than administrative or political ineptitude. The
president actively supervised the selection process; indeed, he frequently searched, as had Jackson, for candidates with proper administrative qualifications and acceptable political views. He sought to
maintain the presidential prerogative: he resisted the encroachment
of the congressional wings of both parties, and he responded to administrative necessity by breathing life into the dormant presidential
removal power. He conscientiously endeavored to elevate the unique
interests of the Mormons above crass party concerns.

Ultimately, power flowed away from the presidency. The accident
of Fillmore's residence in the White House, a Democratic Senate
majority, and Whig factionalism combined to cancel the president's
initiatives. He implemented his pledge to settle the slavery extension
controversy by cooperating with Senate Democrats in selecting judges

for California and for the territories carved from the Mexican Cession. Under the Whig administration, Democrats prominently mediated the selection of judges whose decisions might have shaped the legal future of slavery. This cooperation, coupled with Fillmore's policy of appointing only proadministration Whigs to the federal bench in other areas, further separated the president from the Seward-Weed faction. Both southern Democrats and antiadministration Whigs in the Senate defeated judicial nominees.

Contradictory currents of modernization and tradition transfused the selection process. It remained predominantly, but not exclusively, party-directed; the majority of Fillmore's nominees were Whigs, as were the mediators who recommended them. The national Whig party, however, remained decentralized and state-centered; it had only the barest rudiments of a national party organization. This institutional weakness and the unattractiveness of judicial service prompted Fillmore and Webster to resort to instrumental friendship connections; personal ties fostered an administrative coherence in the decentralized and factionally divided minority Whig party. Senate Democrats took a modern posture toward the president's judicial candidates, his use of the removal power, and the party-directed character of his nominations—regarding them as wholly legitimate, although susceptible to Democratic supervision. The interparty character of the selection process and the growing strength of the Senate were corollary developments precipitated in the artificial party system by the sectionalism and Whig factionalism unleashed by the Mexican War. The president claimed greater administrative control over the courts; the Senate gained increased discretion in the selection process. Under Fillmore's Democratic successor, the Senate Democratic majority bent the selection process to its will.

7

A TALISMANIC POWER

An effort will be made to procure the rejection of many
appointments. . . . To prevent the Senate from being
afflicted, it is all important that in those states whence come
Democratic Senators, their wishes should be consulted.—
Samuel Treat to Caleb Cushing, August 26, 1853[1]

The Democracy in 1852 was a coalition of antagonistic sectional interests. On the right wing of the party, southern state rights advocates
paradoxically demanded limits on national power while insisting the
federal government protect slaveholders in the territories and enforce strictly the Fugitive Slave Act of 1850. On the opposite wing,
northern Free-Soil Democrats, many of whom had bolted the party in
1848, denounced federal efforts either to protect slavery in the territories or to implement the Fugitive Slave Act. Most Democratic
leaders stood between these extremes. James Buchanan of Pennsylvania and William L. Marcy of New York sympathized with the southern wing and believed its cooperation essential to Democratic success.
Southern Democratic Unionists, such as Howell Cobb of Georgia,
nourished bisectional cooperation to blunt the thrust at home of ardent state rights Democrats. Sen. Stephen A. Douglas of Illinois was
the most important moderate; his ambiguous scheme of popular
sovereignty was a common ground upon which all Democrats might
conceivably unite.[2]

Democrats reclaimed the White House by adopting a nominee
acceptable to all sectional interests. Franklin Pierce of New Hampshire threatened no major Democratic leader nor any sectional interests. A pledge to sustain the Compromise of 1850, an able Mexican
War record, and long party service enabled Pierce to win the nomination and subsequently defeat Winfield Scott. Once in office the New
Hampshire Democrat expected through the patronage "to build up a
strong party organization which would not only insure continued
Democratic success" but would also facilitate his reelection. In systematically replacing Whigs, the president promised to follow a policy
of equality; all factions were to share equally in the patronage, even
former Free-Soilers.[3]

Pierce nominated the largest number of judges of any antebellum president. Of the more than fifteen hundred nominations he submitted, fifty-three were to the lower federal courts. This surge in the judicial patronage resulted from several developments. The president created ten vacancies by extending the concept of rotation-in-office to the territorial judiciary. The organization of Washington, Kansas, and Nebraska territories added nine new judgeships. The Congress authorized five new judgeships in districts with crowded court dockets. It also organized two new courts: a circuit court with a single judge for the Northern District of California and a three-man Court of Claims.

Significant administrative reform in the selection process accompanied expansion of the judicial patronage. Secretary of State William L. Marcy wanted to diminish his already overwhelming patronage responsibilities. Attorney General Caleb Cushing was equally anxious to fortify his position within the cabinet by taking command of a single facet of the patronage. On their mutual recommendation, Pierce in 1853 entrusted Cushing with supervision of the judicial patronage. The attorney general assigned one of his two clerks to prepare detailed, annotated lists of applicants by judgeship, their supporters, and the bases of their claims. Cushing indicated his preference by placing the candidate's name at the top of the memorandum he forwarded to the president. The attorney general exercised administrative control over selections, but Pierce retained discretionary authority to accept or reject recommendations.[4]

The attorney general possessed an integrated view of the relationship among the structure of the lower federal courts, the selection process, and public policy. Federal court reform and the selection of competent and politically sound judges was essential to enforcement of the Fugitive Slave Act, maintenance of the Compromise of 1850 as the definitive settlement of the slavery expansion controversy, and restoration of calm to the troubled territories. Cushing unsuccessfully argued for the same kind of centralized authority over the legal business of the United States earlier proposed by Andrew Jackson and Millard Fillmore. The lower federal courts were capable of assuming additional tasks; Cushing planned to relieve Supreme Court justices of circuit riding and to assign their duties to district court judges. The attorney general also argued that, if the federal government expected to attract the best judicial talent, the salaries of territorial and district judges had to be increased and equalized. A penurious spirit and lingering distrust of the federal courts by Congress defeated these proposals.[5]

Cushing did persuade Pierce to base the selection process on general administrative and political criteria. He recommended the president appoint "only Democrats well qualified by experience" and "properly trained so as to meet the duties of the office." He also advised the president to consider, in filling free-state district court vacancies, whether a candidate would sustain the Fugitive Slave Act. "It is necessary," Cushing observed, that the president select judges "whose past course promises the most unqualified guarantee of their fidelity in all cases which may arise under the Fugitive Slave Act."[6] In every instance, the president should select "National Democrats" independent of either sectional extreme. Cushing rejected the promotion of Free-Soilers and ardent state rights advocates to the bench. The attorney general insisted that Pierce nominate candidates "schooled in political experience," ideally, members of Congress whose political views were known before appointment. "Jackson and Polk," Cushing counseled, "had erred in proscribing from judicial positions members of Congress." The administration's success hinged on cooperation with congressional Democrats.[7]

As the compromise choice of his party, Pierce could ill afford to ignore the congressional Democratic majority. Democrats in the Thirty-third Congress controlled both houses; the sectional wings of the party were evenly balanced. The party suffered heavy losses in the 1854 congressional elections following passage of the Kansas-Nebraska Act, but Democrats did retain a twenty-vote Senate majority. Sectional balance in the Thirty-fourth Congress collapsed; southern Democrats had a seven-vote majority—twenty-two to fifteen—over northern party members.[8] Throughout, influential Senator Andrew Pickens Butler of South Carolina presided over the Senate Committee on the Judiciary.

Pierce heeded Cushing's advice. All of his nominees were Democrats. The executive and legislative wings of the party worked harmoniously; only one nomination was tabled, another was withdrawn under protest.

Less visible pressures also molded this stable and party-directed selection process. Traditional patron-client relations persisted; 22 percent of the nominees had kinship connections to principal mediators. Although to a lesser extent than Fillmore, Pierce had difficulty persuading appointees to serve; 22 percent of them refused their commissions. Pierce successfully asserted his independence by extending rotation-in-office to the territorial judiciary, but congressional Democrats seized the initiative in the selection of district court judges. Throughout, Pierce fruitlessly attempted to maintain his party, his policies, and his administration by balancing sectional interests.

II

"We need a change of administration," complained an Oregon Democrat in 1852, "and a thorough overhauling of the officers receiving their appointments from the Federal Government. Our Territory has been thrown into a state of anarchy and confusion." Prominent New Mexico Democrats were also dissatisfied. They denounced Chief Justice Grafton Baker as "a drunkard and a lout," who preferred, on the few occasions he was in the territory, "gambling to presiding over his court." Minnesota territorial delegate Henry H. Sibley advised Pierce that "the Whig judges . . . were a disgrace to the territory, as well as to those who appointed them."[9] Only in Utah were territorial residents satisfied with their sitting judges.[10] The brittle surface of factional politics in these territories heightened the storm of protest raised against the judges. More than personal political careers were at stake, however; there was genuine dissatisfaction with the quality of the judges and the justice they dispensed.

These complaints smoothed the way for the president's political decision to remove all of the Whig judges. Pierce was the first president to extend systematically rotation-in-office to the territorial judiciary. His disposed of the judges either by refusing to renew expired commissions or, when the judges' terms extended beyond the president's inauguration, by removing them.

Bipartisan support for Pierce's removals emphasized the severity of the crisis over territorial justice. On March 16, 1853, Whig Senator George E. Badger of North Carolina, a respected constitutional authority, introduced a resolution concurring in the president's "power under the Constitution and laws of the United States to remove a Territorial judge from office before the end of his four year term and without the presence of a clause in the territorial enabling act granting him such power." By a vote of twenty-five to nine, the upper house adopted the resolution.[11] After two decades of uncertainty, the Senate acknowledged the constitutional position set forth by John Marshal in *Canter:* territorial judges were not protected under Article III, and executive removal, rather than legislative impeachment, was the proper means by which to deal with judicial incompetence. Administrative necessity prodded the Senate to subordinate the independence of the territorial judiciary to party interests and presidential discretion.

As a result of this removal power and the organization of three new territories, Pierce made the majority of his nominations to the territorial courts. He nominated resident candidates only to Oregon and Minnesota. In both instances, territorial delegates mediated the selection process.

Two-party competition in the spring of 1853 displaced the personal factionalism of early Oregon politics. Controversy over the territorial judiciary had spurred this party development. Whig Justices Thomas Nelson and William Strong during the preceding two years had struggled with the heavily Democratic legislature and with Justice Orville C. Pratt over the location of the territorial capital. Nelson and Strong invalidated the decison of the legislature; Pratt sustained it. Oregon Democrats expected Pierce to remedy the difficulty by removing Nelson and Strong and reappointing Pratt, whom Fillmore had forced to resign.[12]

Democratic territorial delegate Joseph Lane persuaded the president to replace the Whig justices with Oregon residents. Lane was concerned with Pierce's policy of equality; it was "an awful mistake" that threatened to abolitionize the Oregon bench. The chief executive disagreed, but their Mexican War friendship and Lane's support of the administration surmounted this barrier. Pierce accepted the delegate's recommendations without questions: Orville C. Pratt to be chief justice and Matthew P. Deady and Cyrus Olney to be associate justices. The nominees, Lane observed, were "National Democrats" who disdained "the treachery of the Free-Soilers."[13]

The new administrative machinery for supervising the selection process immediately produced turmoil. Sen. Stephen Douglas of Illinois complained that Cushing had neglected to consult him about the nomination of Pratt, a former Illinois resident. Douglas objected to the nomination; Pierce cooperated by replacing Pratt with the senator's "close friend," George Williams of Iowa.[14]

Cushing also enabled Oregon Whigs to circumvent temporarily the appointment of Matthew P. Deady. They opposed his selection because he had orchestrated the attack against Strong and Nelson during the location controversy. Amory Holbrook, a former resident of Massachusetts, communicated these sentiments to his old friend Cushing. Holbrook explained that an error in Deady's commission (the judge's Christian name had been spelled Mordecai) afforded the president an opportunity to select "a better candidate." The Oregon Whig asserted incorrectly that Deady was "so utterly obscure that even Lane did not know his name." Cushing accepted the advice of his old friend; he refused Deady's request for a new commission.[15]

The decision provided the administration with a short-term opportunity that eventually became a political embarrassment. On the recommendation of Cushing, Pierce, on August 4, 1853, issued a recess commission to Obadiah B. McFadden of Washington County, Pennsylvania. The selection of McFadden accommodated Postmaster General James Campbell, a Philadelphia Catholic and member of the Buchanan faction of the Pennsylvania Democracy. Pierce expected the inclusion of Campbell in the cabinet to foster cooperation with the Buchanan wing and to demonstrate administration disdain of the rising nativist movement. The president had earlier passed over McFadden for a judgeship in Minnesota; the mistake in Deady's commission created an opportunity to pacify Campbell.[16]

McFadden's unexpected arrival in Oregon ignited a storm of protest by territorial Democrats. When Lane demanded an explanation, Cushing quickly reversed his position; he claimed disingenuously that an administrative error had occurred. The attorney general in mid-January, 1854, with Campbell's consent, settled on a compromise: Deady assumed his old post, and McFadden was dispatched to a recently vacated associate-justiceship in Washington Territory. The clumsy handling of the Deady and Pratt appointments dissipated any political benefits the president hoped to reap from the Oregon patronage. "Pierce," concluded a territorial Democrat, was "small Potatoes" and not "up to being President."[17]

Minnesota Whigs protested Pierce's reconstruction of the judiciary. The chief executive removed Henry Z. Hayner and Bradley B. Meeker; he failed to reappoint David Cooper. Although Hayner never reached the territory and Meeker was frequently absent on personal business, the Whig press charged Pierce with "executive usurpation" that "threatened the independence of the territorial judiciary." It argued that by invoking the removal power, the Democratic president had assured a lessening of the quality of the judiciary; "no man of spirit, of a decent self respect, would accept an office . . . held on such a tenure." Minnesota Democrats praised the removals as a "proper means to the efficient administration of justice."[18]

Outgoing territorial delegate Henry H. Sibley mediated the selection process. By 1853 Sibley and Henry M. Rice, the incoming delegate, were competing for leadership of the emerging Minnesota Democracy. They differed over the conduct of the fur trade, railroad development, and Sibley's partisan neutrality during the previous Whig administration. Pierce, however, favored Sibley. The former delegate attempted to strike a middle ground between territorial interests and the wishes of nonresident office seekers. Aware that factional divisions in the Minnesota Democracy and intense pressures from state party leaders precluded Pierce from appointing only territorial residents, Sibley submitted on March 30 a list of four candidates, only one of them a territorial resident. Pierce deleted Free-Soil Democrat Jefferson P. Kidder of Vermont and sent the three remaining names to the Senate. The important post of chief justice went to a territorial resident and political ally of Sibley's, William H. Welch of St. Paul. Two nonresident "National Democrats" were appointed associate justices: Moses Sherburn of Phillips, Maine, and Andrew G. Chatfield of Kenosha, Wisconsin, a native of New York. Sibley was pleased that the backgrounds of the nominees complemented the New England and New York origins of the territorial population.[19]

Pierce and Cushing also applied the representative principle to New Mexico territory. They attended to balance free-, slave-, and border-state Democrats. Supporters of slavery extension, argued Alfred O. P. Nicholson of Tennessee, expected the president to nominate judges for New Mexico "of the right grit from the South."[20] Secretary of War Jefferson Davis propounded this view in the cabinet; he insisted Pierce replace Whig Chief Justice Grafton Baker of Mississippi with a Democrat from the state. The secretary successfully recommended the appointment of James J. Deavenport of Okalona, a member of the Mississippi Democratic Central Committee. The free-state position went, at the insistence of Stephen A. Douglas, to Kirby Benedict of Edgar County, Illinois. The other associate-justiceship was bestowed on a border-state resident, Perry E. Brocchus of Maryland. The former Utah judge was a kinsman of two influential Alabama Democrats: Jeremiah Clemens and Sen. Clement C. Clay, Jr. They argued that the appointment would exonerate Brocchus of charges of dereliction of duty made when Fillmore removed him from the Utah bench. Pierce was persuaded; he transferred majority control of the New Mexico bench from northern unionist Whigs to southern state rights Democrats.[21]

The sectionally significant issue of popular sovereignty was imbedded in the religious controversy over the Mormons in Utah. Whig territorial delegate John M. Bernhisel, who appreciated that "strong forces" in the Democratic party were "at work to injure the Utah people," believed the administration would hesitate to impose reforms upon the Saints for fear of the broader political consequences. "If the principle [of popular sovereignty] were once violated," Bernhisel observed, "it would apply everywhere, to all religions and slavery." Popular sovereignty, he argued, would aid the Saints in obtaining "judges of their own choice."[22]

Democratic Governor Brigham Young wanted the incumbents retained. He and the Mormon legal community praised their legal abilities and accommodative spirits. Their retention, the governor asserted, made "administrative sense." "No sooner would new appointees arrive," he informed Pierce, than they would begin "to make . . . arrangements to leave, and then another year would elapse before another arrives, only to act the same farce over again."[23] Despite Young's arguments and Bernhisel's vision of popular sovereignty, Pierce succumbed to the deep and politically volatile pressures stirred by polygamy and religious enthusiasm. He believed less accommodation and more disciplined justice were in order for troubled Utah; he removed the judges, two of them Democrats.

Apostate Mormon Almon W. Babbitt and congressional Democrats mediated the selection process. Whig delegate Bernhisel, on the instructions of Young, repeatedly proffered names of Utah residents for the posts, but Cushing ignored him. Pierce had appointed Babbitt, a Democrat, secretary of the territory. On his recommendation, the president nominated Babbitt's former law partner, George Edmunds, Jr., of Carthage, Illinois, one of the associate justices. The thirty-one-year-old Edmunds was an obscure lawyer who had once acted as legal counsel for the Saints during their residence in Nauvoo. Babbitt joined with the Iowa Democratic congressional delegation to recommend successfully the appointment of John F. Kinney as chief justice. As a member of the Iowa Supreme Court, Kinney in 1849 won praise for his forthright investigation of alleged Mormon election frauds. The expectation of financial gain by selling goods to the Mormons and a wish to succeed where others had failed motivated him to relinquish his seat on the Iowa Supreme Court.[24]

The president, through the other Utah associate-justiceship, promoted his policy of factional equality. On the recommendation of Cushing and prominent Georgia Union Democrats, he nominated John W. H. Underwood of Rome. Georgia unionists stressed that Underwood's appointment would enhance their ascendancy over state rights Democrats; Cushing insisted the appointment would balance the state rights composition of the New Mexico bench.[25]

Administrative difficulties frustrated Pierce's Utah patronage policy. Both associate justices declined because of the low pay, arduous travel, and extended family separations that accompanied the posts. Young and Bernhisel immediately reiterated the foolishness of appointing nonresidents, but the administration recognized that the selection of residents would precipitate a storm of Democratic congressional protests. Appointees willing to serve, however, often had less than disinterested motives. On the recommendation of Babbitt, Pierce selected another of the secretary's former law partners, an apostate Mormon, George P. Stiles of Council Bluffs, Iowa, who accepted in order to further his already prosperous overland trading business with Utah. Stephen A. Douglas mediated the selection of the southern representative on the court; he persuaded Pierce to appoint William Wormer Drummond of Oquakwa, Illinois, a native of Virginia. Before reaching the territory, Drummond gathered most of his slaves from his home state and a prostitute from the District of Columbia whom, despite the presence of Mormon kinsmen in Utah, he intended to pass off as his sister.[26] While the administration acted in good faith, the twin stones of political and administrative necessity ground into insignificance its commitment to impartial justice.

"The Federal Judiciary," observed a Minnesota Whig newspaper in 1854, "has entered a new age. It vacillates and fluctuates with the fluctuations and vacillations of the parties and factions of the country."[27] On the one hand, Pierce, by extending the concept of rotation-in-office to the territorial judiciary, subordinated the independence of the judiciary to partisan values of the political culture. On the other hand, as bipartisan Senate approval of the Badger resolution revealed, the presidential removal power was rooted in administrative necessity. Uncertain tenure and the unattractiveness of territorial service converged to further politicize the courts rather than insure efficient and impartial justice.

Pierce gained little from his enhanced power. As a compromise president, he had to accommodate the sectional and factional demands of congressional Democrats. Pierce adopted Cushing's advice: he chose to remake the territorial judiciary from the center and right wings of the party and to ignore Free-Soil Democrats.

III

Pierce also nominated judges for the Court of Claims and the new territories of Washington, Kansas, and Nebraska. The president and the attorney general avoided selection of Free-Soil Democrats, but they were attentive to demands for sectional representation. These demands were of two kinds. The first came from free- and slave-state Democrats, who held different views about the relationship of the judiciary to the peculiar institution; the second, from the traditional pressures asserted by the South, East, and West for a voice in any national political institution. The former affected the composition of the territorial benches of Kansas and Nebraska; the latter had an impact on the selection of judges for the Court of Claims.[28]

Powerless to resist passage of the Kansas-Nebraska Act, Pierce expected to blunt its impact by insuring that the always troublesome process of territorial organization proceeded smoothly. He and Cushing appreciated that free- and slave-state Democrats differed over the role of the judges. The president intended to appoint "western and Southern men" to the courts of Kansas and Nebraska "because they were better acquainted with the habits and customs of the people."[29] A three-man bench ruled by majority vote did not lend itself to a simple division between free- and slave-state representatives. The governorships were easy enough; he appointed a slave-state Democrat to Nebraska and a free-state party member to Kansas. Pierce fatefully reversed the pattern for the judiciaries; slave-state Democrats were to hold a majority on the Kansas bench, while free-state appointees were to dominate the Nebraska court. The policy of sectional balance succeeded in Nebraska, where slavery was never at issue, but it failed disastrously in Kansas.[30]

Pierce divided the Kansas associate justiceships between free- and slave-state Democrats. On June 22, 1854, he nominated two veteran officers of the Mexican War: Rush Elmore of Montgomery, Alabama, and Saunders W. Johnston of Georgetown, Ohio. Supreme Court Justice John A. Campbell recommended Elmore as a suitable representative of southern state rights and slave interests.[31] Douglas and Congressman Alfred P. Edgerton of Ohio recommended Johnston. The appointee had the confidence of the president and the attorney general: he had served under Pierce in the Mexican War, organized veterans in support of the president's candidacy, and had voted for Pierce in the Democratic National Convention.[32]

The president genuinely believed that he could satisfy southern Democrats without antagonizing northern moderates by appointing a border-state Democrat chief justice. He rejected overtures by Missouri Democrats; residents of that state were too deeply involved in Kansas affairs. Instead, on the recommendation of Congressman Henry F. May of Baltimore and with the concurrence of Cushing, Pierce nominated Madison Brown of Cambridge, Maryland. Brown accepted, then declined. The post was too controversial.[33]

Pierce in October, 1854, issued a recess commission to Samuel Dexter Lecompte of Cambridge, Maryland. Once again, May successfully intervened. The new chief justice was a strong proslavery Democrat who in 1852 stumped Maryland for Pierce. His legal career had been uneventful; "pecuniary embarrassment" and a sense of "having slept too long under the branches" propelled him into the crisis atmosphere of Kansas.[34]

Pierce and Cushing anticipated that an honest and efficient judiciary would facilitate the peaceful and speedy organization of the territory. The judges repeatedly frustrated these goals. When Elmore and Johnston reached Kansas in October, 1854, they immediately plunged into speculation in valuable Indian lands. Their behavior was typical of many territorial judges who compensated for low pay by using their public positions for private gain. But in volatile Kansas the hint of impropriety threatened to discredit the judiciary before increasingly contentious free- and slave-state settlers. The judges further damaged Pierce's Kansas policy by declaring that the fraudulently elected proslavery legislature could assemble wherever it wished. The decision clashed with the position of the embattled governor, Andrew Reeder, and hopelessly stalemated territorial government.[35]

Pierce attempted to cut the knot. With the judges' speculative land dealings as the ostensible reason, on August 7, 1855, he removed Elmore and Johnston. The attorney general advised the action; the judges had become an "embarrassment to the administration."[36] Elmore objected to the decision; his removal was "unconstitutional" and a manifestation of a "political policy which would not be successful without the removal of an equal number of territorial officers from the North and the South."[37] Armed with the Badger resolution, Pierce and Cushing brushed aside the constitutional arguments.

The administration persisted in its scheme of sectional representation. The attorney general forwarded to Pierce separate lists of slave- and free-state condidates. Cushing joined with Supreme Court Justice John A. Campbell and Alabama Senator Clement C. Clay, Jr., to endorse Sterling G. Cato of Eufaula, Alabama, as the southern representative. Campbell reiterated the arguments he had earlier made in behalf of Elmore: Cato's selection would insure a voice on the Kansas bench for "State Right Democracy and strict construction of the Constitution."[38]

Cushing recommended Jeremiah Murray Burrell of Greensburgh, Pennsylvania, for the free-state post. Like his predecessor, Burrell was a "National Democrat" sympathetic to Douglas's doctrine of popular sovereignty. Postmaster General Campbell, who intervened with the president and the attorney general, argued persuasively that the presence of a "proven judge" would enhance the credibility of the administration and the court. Pierce on September 13, 1855, granted Burrell and Cato recess commissions.[39]

The sectional commitments of the slave-state appointees further undermined Pierce's policies. Free- and slave-state supporters in May, 1856, clashed in a civil uprising that shook the territory. In hearing suits arising from the crisis, Cato and Lecompte consistently favored proslavery litigants. The free-state presence was reduced in June, 1856, when Burrell left the territory; three months later, he died at his Pennsylvania home.[40]

As a lame-duck president Pierce labored under enormous disadvantages during the waning days of his administration. Not the least of his problems was winning the cooperation of the southern Democrats he had originally intended to mollify. He clung to his policy of sectional balance. Postmaster General Campbell in September, 1856, persuaded him to replace Burrell with Thomas Cunningham of Beaver, Pennsylvania, another northern "National Democrat" favorable to popular sovereignty.[41]

The southern judges were more troublesome. Gov. John W. Geary in September, 1856, pleaded with the president to remove the slave-state judges in order to restore free-state confidence. After fruitless cabinet discussions, Pierce in mid-November decided to remove Lecompte but to retain Cato. On the recommendation of Secretary of the Treasury James Guthrie, the president proposed to issue a recess commission to James O. Harrison, a slaveholder and prominent Lexington, Kentucky, lawyer. Pierce hoped to circumvent the hostility of southern Senate Democrats, who applauded the zeal with which Lecompte fitted law to the interests of the proslavery faction. Word of Harrison's willingness to serve arrived too late; the president on December 10 was forced to submit a regular nomination. Southern Democrats, already angered over Pierce's alleged free-state bias and equipped with Lecompte's detailed refutation of the charges against him, refused to confirm Harrison. Unable to qualify a successor, Pierce could not remove Lecompte. Southern Democratic senators stripped the hapless Pierce of his removal power.[42]

Pierce and Cushing pursued a judicial selection policy intended to foster sectional balance and limited factional equality. Although the president excluded Free-Soil Democrats, most of whom had deserted the party after the Kansas-Nebraska Act, he did select territorial judges from both the center and right wings of the party. The free- and slave-state majorities on the benches of Kansas and Nebraska were intended to represent the divergent sectional interests of the

Democracy. The rise of southern control of the Senate wing of the Democratic party and the proslavery bias of the southern appointees frustrated Pierce's plan to organize Kansas quickly and without incident. The president became the victim of the southern Democratic majority he originally expected to control.

IV

The dominance of the congressional wing of the Democratic party also affected the selection of judges for the constitutional courts. Senators of the president's party had sporadically mediated the selection process. During the previous Whig administrations, the Senate Democratic majority had gradually encroached on the presidential appointment prerogative, but the presence of a weak Democrat in the White House hastened this process. Pierce's political future and his program of party harmony dictated cooperation rather than confrontation.

The congressional wing of the Democratic party actively mediated the selection process. Of the one-term presidents during the second party system, Pierce nominated the greatest number of judges to the constitutional courts. Of his sixteen nominees, three were to the District of Columbia, one to a special circuit court for northern California, and twelve to the district courts. Only in three states—Ohio, Tennessee, and Vermont—with district vacancies did the party lack a Democratic senator. In these instances, the president relied on House Democrats and state party leaders. Within this common party affiliation, however, personal connections typical of a traditional political order persisted. These patron-client relations, at least in the selection of a district judge for Tennessee in 1853, further exacerbated Democratic factionalism.

The Mexican War and the slavery extension controversy split the Tennessee Democratic party. Moderate party leaders from mountainous east Tennessee opposed the extreme state rights views of party leaders from slaveholding middle and west Tennessee. Congressman Andrew Johnson and state central committeeman J. G. M. Ramsey led the more moderate eastern faction. Former governor Aaron V. Brown and his brother-in-law, Gideon Pillow, both of middle Tennessee, directed the state rights Nashville Clique. The moderate Alfred O. P. Nicholson, whom Pierce had selected public printer, stood between these factions.[43]

The death of Judge Morgan W. Brown on March 7, 1853, raised the broad issue of whether the administration would sustain moderate southern Democrats. On the day of Brown's death, moderate Democrats in the Tennessee congressional delegation recommended the immediate nomination of George W. Churchwell of Knoxville, the father of Congressman William W. Churchwell. The elder Churchwell was a moderate and a former United States attorney for east Tennessee. Nicholson joined in support of the Knoxville lawyer; his appointment would demonstrate in Tennessee and throughout the South that the president was committed to the moderates.[44]

Only quick action by Supreme Court Justice John Catron of Tennessee prevented Churchwell's nomination. Catron, the brother-in-law of the deceased judge, ridiculed the hasty action; he intended to share circuit duties only with a judge who possessed "a fair record" as a lawyer. The justice insured Pierce's cooperation by persuading Andrew P. Butler, the chairman of the Senate Committee on the Judiciary, to delay confirmation of any nomination until "the claims of all the competent lawyers should be considered."[45]

Aaron Brown and Gideon Pillow exploited the delay to muster support for their brother-in-law, West Hughes Humphreys of Nashville. During the previous twelve years Humphreys, an ardent state rights spokesman, had served as attorney general and reporter of the decisions of the Tennessee Supreme Court. To facilitate the selection, Brown hurried to Washington while Pillow milked his old military connections. The Tennessean had been Pierce's commanding officer during the Mexican War; he had subsequently organized the Democratic war veterans in behalf of Pierce. Nomination of his brother-in-law, Pillow informed his old friend the attorney general, would place him "under lasting obligation."[46]

State rights Democracy and patron-client relations fused the selection process. Cushing endorsed Humphreys's candidacy; Pierce promptly nominated the Nashville lawyer. Moderate Democrats were bitter and apprehensive. The appointment, Nicholson concluded, further enhanced Brown's influence, "threw [the president] into the arms of the states right wing of the party," and discredited "throughout the South" Pierce's policy of factional equality.[47]

Instrumental friendship connections and anxiety over enforcement of the Fugitive Slave Act influenced one of Pierce's two other district court nominations to states without Democratic senators. When Congress in early 1855 established a new district court for northern Ohio, the Democratic party of that state divided over a judicial nominee. With Cushing's endorsement and the approval of Ohio House Democrats from the northern district, the president nominated Hiram V. Willson of Cleveland, a well-known defender of the Fugitive Slave Act. Willson was a boyhood friend and law partner of Henry B. Payne of Cleveland, a longtime friend and supporter of Pierce. "There is no favor," Payne confided to the president, "in my power to ask, or in your power to grant, which would be so gratifying to my feeling as [his appointment]."[48]

Most of Pierce's district court nominations were to states with at least one Democratic senator. Previous presidents had acknowledged the peculiar interests of senators of their party in these patronage decisions, but under Pierce a privilege became a prerogative. Within this party-directed selection process, senators sometimes promoted instrumental friends.

Pierce's nominations of judges to slave states with Democratic senators occurred during the Thirty-fourth Congress between March, 1855, and March, 1857. The president appointed judges for the Northern District of Florida, South Carolina, and the Western District of Texas. The Democratic parties in these states were not monolithic; indeed, they divided between moderate and state rights factions. State rights Democrats had a crucial advantage: they controlled the Senate seats.

The selection in 1855 of a judge for the Northern District of Florida typified the intraparty tensions that accompanied these slave-state appointments. The moderates were represented in the Senate by Stephen A. Mallory of Key West and the state rights faction by David L. Yulee of Homasassa. The latter was a bitter opponent of the Compromise of 1850 and a leader of the "southern movement" in the Senate.[49]

The immense area embraced by the Northern District of Florida encouraged geographic rivalries over the judgeship. The jurisdiction of the court stretched from Pensacola in the western panhandle eastward to Jacksonville on the Atlantic and then south to the Everglades. Spanish land titles and admiralty suits arising in ports along the Gulf of Mexico and at Jacksonville on the Atlantic crowded the court docket. Since statehood in 1845, the business and legal interests of west Florida had sought a greater presence on the federal court. They objected to Judge Isaac H. Bronson's residence at Palatka in the east; irregular transportation across north Florida frequently delayed litigation, especially admiralty and maritime suits. The legal community of Jacksonville was equally anxious following Bronson's death on August 13, 1855, to have the new judge retain the seat of the court in the east.[50]

The vacancy occurred during the recess between the Thirty-third and Thirty-fourth Congresses. Mallory successfully urged the president not to make an interim appointment; delay would allow time to learn the "wishes and feelings of Florida's best Democrats." It was important, the senator explained, to have an "appointee acceptable to all"; otherwise the party could "not be expected to hold the power which it does at present."[51]

Mallory and Yulee divided over Bronson's replacement. The former endorsed George S. Hawkins of Apalachicola. Hawkins had migrated in 1835 from New York City; subsequently, he was United States attorney, state supreme court justice, member of the legislature, and from 1851 to 1855 a circuit court judge. Mallory, who often spoke for the interests of west Florida, insisted that that region was due to receive the judgeship; the extensive previous judicial experience of Hawkins made the selection all the more appropriate.[52]

Yulee boosted twenty-eight-year-old McQueen McIntosh of Jacksonville. More than two decades younger than Hawkins, McIntosh was a radical state rights Democrat. In addition to holding a common political philosophy, he was deeply involved with Yulee as a director of the Florida Railroad Company, an enterprise disdained by Mallory and west Florida residents.[53]

The attorney general broke the deadlock. Cushing's motivation in recommending McIntosh remains unclear, but when he submitted the candidates' names to the president, he ranked the Jacksonville lawyer as his first choice. Pierce on February 27 nominated the youthful McIntosh instead of the more experienced Hawkins. The appointment was the product of senatorial prerogative, instrumental friendship connections, and the new influence of the attorney general in the selection process.[54]

Democratic senators in the free states exercised a prerogative similar to that of their slave-state counterparts. Pierce made four free-state nominations: one each to the Southern District of California, Connecticut, the Southern District of Illinois, and Iowa.[55] As in the southern states, the new judges' factional alignments and ideological predispositions reflected the propensities of the Democratic senators. The convergence of factional, personal, and ideological interests in the January, 1854, selection of a judge for the Southern District of California typified the broader pattern of free-state appointments.

During the Fillmore administration, Democrats had averted the nomination of a Whig judge for the Southern District by abolishing the judgeship. Democratic Senator William M. Gwin in 1852 successfully sponsored legislation which eliminated the Southern District judge and assigned his duties to the judge in the Northern District. When Pierce entered the White House, Gwin and fellow Democratic Senator John B. Weller persuaded the Democratic majority in Congress to reinstate the southern judgeship.[56]

The California Democratic party in the 1850s was a diverse coalition of immigrants from every section of the Union. The decline of Whiggery following the 1852 election heightened conflict between the Chivalry, or proslavery wing, and antislavery Free-Soil Democrats. Under the tutelage of Gwin, the Chivalry drew on the South for rhetoric and members; it advocated the spread of slavery into the trans-Mississippi West and the enhancement of southern power. Gwin during the Fillmore administration had mediated the selection of many California federal officials; he expected to exercise greater influence over Pierce. The Free-Soilers' principal leader was Lt. Gov. David Broderick of San Francisco. Without a Senate spokesman, they were unable to counter Gwin's influence.[57]

By January, 1854, three contenders emerged for the judgeship. Benjamin Hayes, a state district court judge from Los Angeles, and Harry Lee, a lawyer who resided in the Northern District city of Benecia, were moderate Democrats; Isaac Stockton Keith Ogier, the federal attorney for the Southern District, belonged to the Chivalry. Hayes was endorsed by the principal state officers and by Democrats in Los Angeles who resented the Chivalry's dominance. Milton S. Lathan and James A. McDougall, the two Democratic congressmen from California, recommended Lee. Unlike the other two candidates, Ogier was originally from a slave state; he had been raised in Charleston and had practiced law in New Orleans before migrating in 1849 to California. As a member of the First California General Assembly, he had helped to elect Gwin to the United States Senate.[58]

Ogier's vigorous campaign to win nomination reflected the changed character of the selection process. Previously, candidates who came to Washington to promote their selection had concentrated on the White House, but Ogier spent his energies consulting with Gwin, Weller, and Cushing. He strengthened his position with Cushing by submitting statements from Democrats in Los Angeles who applauded his familiarity with the Spanish language and the civil law issues raised by Spanish land titles. On January 19, 1854, a day after receiving recommendations from Weller and Gwin, Pierce nominated Ogier. He was quickly confirmed.[59]

During the Pierce administration senators of the president's party mediated the selection of district court judges. Senatorial control of the district court appointment in California was paralleled in the other free states.[60] The new role for the senators came at the expense of the president; the legislative wing of the party assumed the power to initiate the selection process. Democrats promoted to the federal bench reflected the beliefs and commitments of the senators who mediated their selection, and this handicapped the president's implementation of his policy of factional equality. Within this party-directed selection process, informal ties of instrumental friendship persisted.

V

"Party ties," concluded Whig Congressman David Outlaw of North Carolina, were "among the strongest associations which bind men together. . . . The very name of party has a talismanic power."[61] The judicial selection process corroborated Outlaw's observation. Democrats alone decided who would occupy the federal bench. The president nominated only Democrats; the Senate Democratic majority quickly confirmed them. The concept of rotation-in-office was finally extended on a systematic basis to the territorial judiciary; Democratic senators emerged as the principal mediators of district court appointments.

The rise of senatorial courtesy and the application of rotation-in-office to the territorial judiciary were significant, if somewhat belated, modernizing developments. Along with the new role of the attorney general, they institutionalized the selection process by integrating the needs of the executive and legislative wings of the party and by regularizing the method of selection and removal. Nonetheless, the Democratic party remained a loosely knit, factionalized, and state-centered coalition of diverse interests. Traditional patron-client relations, within the context of a shared party affiliation, remained significant. The rise of senatorial courtesy enhanced the relative power of individual senators, but it restricted the president's freedom in using judgeships to attract wavering partisans, to discipline recalcitrant senators, or to expand administration influence. Unlike Jackson, Pierce was unable to build political strength through the selection of his friends.[62]

Heightened institutionalization of the selection process coincided with the disintegration of the second party system. Parties were less tenacious than Outlaw supposed. During the Pierce administration, the Whig party collapsed; a northern Republican party emerged; and Democratic bisectional unity faltered. The slavery expansion issue and accompanying sectional tensions insinuated themselves into the political culture. In the judicial selection process, Pierce and Cushing sought sectional balance; they selected judges to enforce the Fugitive Slave Act in the free states while affording each section representation on territorial courts likely to hear litigation involving the peculiar institution. The threat posed by the southern Democratic majority in the Senate made a sham of their scheme; sectional balance came to be equated with border state neutrality. Especially in filling the Kansas judgeships, Pierce was restrained by southern Democratic strength in the upper house. Not only did he fail to establish impartial and efficient justice, but at the same time the advent of the Republican party added political fervor to the notion that in a society paradoxically committed to slavery and human freedom, moral obligation derived from the individual's, rather than the state's, understanding of the law. As Pierce's successor discovered, the "strongest associations which bind men together" crumbled when the concepts of impartial and efficient justice became relative.

8

NO MASTER BUT THE LAW

When considering judicial nominees, the President must remember this simple rule: the wolf of abolitionism is pitted against the lamb of African subordination and that wolf either has to forego his appetite or . . . he must expect that the good shepherd will move his flock to safety.—Jefferson Buford to James Buchanan, September 17, 1856[1]

After more than a century the scholarly condemnation of James Buchanan has only begun to subside. He was, concluded Allan Nevins, "weak-nerved," "pliable," "self-seeking," "deceitful," and "too timid to be a fighter." The fifteenth president, Nevins complained, was "unswerving" in his "alignment with the southern proslavery wing of his party."[2] These criticisms have a special meaning—indeed, almost a sinister quality—in view of Buchanan's failure to save the Union. However, as the president's most thoughtful biographer warns, the secession crisis is a tortured perspective from which to generalize about Buchanan or the politics of the late 1850s. To be sure, Buchanan was committed to the maintenance of slavery and the property rights of slaveholders in the territories, but he also believed that strict adherence to the law offered the best hope of diminishing sectional tensions. Buchanan actually practiced little law, but he was an acknowledged authority on the Constitution; his early legal training remained with him throughout his public life. The new president had a reflexive habit of seeing most issues, even those with enormous moral implications, in narrow legal terms.[3]

Northern antislavery spokesmen and southern proslavery extremists doubted the legal and constitutional authority on which Buchanan founded his administration. While the president "cheerfully" submitted to the proposition enunciated by Chief Justice Roger B. Taney in *Dred Scott* that Negroes were inherently inferior and that masters could take their property wherever they went, angry Republicans denounced the court and the legal-constitutional system as an agent of the Slavepower. These attacks on the high court were symptomatic of a broader assault upon federal authority that plagued the administration. Defiant antislavery mobs resorted to physical

131

coercion when the surreptitious methods of the underground railroad failed.[4]

Contempt of federal authority also surfaced outside the free
states. Proslavery advocates propounded a contradictory theory of
state rights and federal power. They threatened to dissolve the Union
to preserve state rights, but they demanded the federal government
guarantee the property rights of masters by coercing territorial residents to accept the peculiar institution. Southern filibusters flouted
federal neutrality laws; a small but persistent band of smugglers continued to import slaves. In the distant territories law and order were
strained. Free- and slave-state men in "Bleeding Kansas," as well as
persons who cared little for the fate of slavery but a great deal for the
preservation of the main chance, substituted violence for the rule of
law. The Latter-Day Saints in Utah, animated by a paranoia produced
by persecution and a self-certainty fostered by isolation, defied the
gentile officers of the central government.[5]

The realignment of the antebellum party system affected Buchanan's ability to meet these crises. Following the Kansas-Nebraska Act,
Democrats suffered extensive defections. Buchanan, unlike his predecessor, confronted an animated northern Republican party blessed
with astute leaders, a sense of purpose, and congressional strength. In
the Senate, Republicans held twenty seats in the Thirty-fifth Congress
and twenty-six seats in the Thirty-sixth. Republican gains came at the
expense of the northern wing of the Democratic party; control of the
legislative wing of the party shifted to the slave states. Southern Democrats in 1857 were "no mere wing of the party but almost the party
itself." Of thirty-seven Democratic senators in the Thirty-fifth and
Thirty-sixth Congresses, twenty-five were from slave states. Southern
Democrats held a veto over administration patronage decisions.[6]

The political landscape in 1857 contained not only sectional cleav-
ages but fault lines in each state which separated regular and opposition factions of the Democracy. In the North administration dissidents followed Sen. Stephen A. Douglas. In the South no single leader
of Douglas's stature challenged Buchanan, but in every state party the
administration suffered its detractors.[7]

The status of slavery in the territories posed the most significant
threat to Democratic unity. Buchanan and the delegates to the 1856
Cincinnati convention pledged themselves to halt further sectional
division by adhering to the doctrine of popular sovereignty. Democrats disagreed over its meaning. Douglas argued that territorial residents, through popularly elected legislators, could decide on the
peculiar institution at any time. Democratic conservatives, North and

South, adopted a different position. They insisted that, since the territories were the property of all of the citizens of the nation, territorial residents could decide on slavery only in a constitutional convention.[8] The conservative position, of course, enabled slavery to gain a foothold that might not be easily loosened.

Buchanan anticipated that the federal lower judiciary would sustain his conservative view of popular sovereignty. "The soundness of the Judiciary," he informed Sen. Joseph Lane of Oregon in 1858, "was of the utmost importance to the future of the country."[9] The president held an eminently practical view of the future of slavery in the territories: climate and geography would prevent the peculiar institution from flourishing in most territories; thus, it made no practical political sense to alienate the majority southern wing of the party by denying slaveholders property rights in territories to which they were unlikely to go. With *Dred Scott* as precedent, Buchanan wanted to insure that federal authority prevented an antislavery majority in any territorial legislature from abrogating the property rights of masters. "Non-intervention on the part of Congress with the question of slavery is the true as it is the actual policy of the Democratic party," he wrote two years after *Dred Scott*. "Neither is intervention necessary," he continued, "because the Federal Judiciary is capable of maintaining the rights of slave property in the Territories."[10] Buchanan expected his judicial nominees to possess political and legal views compatible with his, to uphold federal authority, to avoid legal innovation in matters relating to the sectional controversy, and to sustain the rights of the states.[11]

Attorney General Jeremiah Sullivan Black, as the president's most important advisor on the judicial patronage, reinforced Buchanan's legalistic predilections. "In mental outlook," wrote Black's biographer, the former chief justice of the Pennsylvania Supreme Court "was a lawyer and a lawyer only. Every question of life he saw from a legal view. Problems of statesmanship and politics were not excepted. In them he saw the legal issues, applied the legal remedy." The attorney general was determined to enforce the Fugitive Slave Act, the neutrality laws, and the ban against the slave trade. He also expected the rule of law to prevail over territorial violence and disorder.[12]

Buchanan directed Black to identify candidates with specific attributes. Since a federal judgeship was "of . . . the greatest dignity, and of the greatest importance to the country," the new chief executive proposed to nominate candidates of "eminent respectability." Ideally, he wanted lawyers with previous judicial service. "A man, by study, may become a profound lawyer, in theory," he observed, "but nothing except practice can make him an able judge." Despite this emphasis on experience, he also favored youth. "Old judges should not be appointed," the president explained, because they usually did not live long enough to benefit the public, and territorial service quickly sapped their strength.[13] Whatever the experience or age of the candidate, Buchanan refused to nominate anyone "related to me, either by blood or marriage."[14]

Administrative and partisan difficulties impeded the president's quest for an ideologically acceptable and legally respectable judiciary. Meager salaries and the hardships of territorial service remained; neither Buchanan nor Black sought legislative relief. Democratic factionalism and sectional conflict were formidable obstacles. "The pressure for office," noted the president-elect in 1856, "will be as great as though I had succeeded a Whig administration."[15] Buchanan was sensitive to the condition of the party in each state and territory. Unlike Pierce, he exercised the removal power with restraint; only four judges (three appointed by Pierce and one by Buchanan) were removed, three of these in Utah. The president preferred to enhance party harmony by allowing Pierce appointees to hold office until their commissions expired.[16] Judicial vacancies created special tensions, however; judges possessed the potential to sustain through legal means the political policies of the administration.

II

The most politically sensitive of Buchanan's thirty territorial nominations were for Utah and Kansas. Defiance of federal authority in these territories menaced the president's goals of restoring party harmony and fostering sectional unity through faithful execution of the laws. Republicans heaped moral ridicule on the Democrats for their policies; judically supervised popular sovereignty perpetuated "the twin relics of barbarism"—slavery and polygamy.[17]

By 1857 the Mormons and the federal judges had plunged into another crisis. Associate Justices William Wormer Drummond and George Parker Stiles were at the center of the storm. The former was a caricature of the inept territorial official. When not absent to oversee commercial and mining ventures in California, he zealously campaigned against the alleged moral decadence of high church officials. His public preachings contradicted his private behavior. The judge, who had abandoned his wife in Illinois, maintained a mistress he clumsily identified as his sister. Impulsive and hot-tempered, Drummond ran afoul of the Mormons after he and his Negro slave beat a

Jewish horse-trader whom the judge accused of fraud. An angry Mormon grand jury indicted the judge for attempted murder and unsuccessfully ordered him tried before a local probate court. Drummond retaliated by submitting to Congress charges that the Mormons were guilty of treason, moral depravity, and plotting the murders of federal military officers. Subsequently, he fled the territory; "constant harassment by the Mormons" made it impossible to hold court.[18]

The Saints' treatment of George P. Stiles lent credibility to Drummond's generally dubious charges. The Mormons resented the presence on the bench of an excommunicated church member. A Mormon mob on the night of December 29, 1856, broke into the judge's office and absconded with the federal court records. The thieves undertook an elaborate ruse: they pretended to burn the records unceremoniously in a back-yard outhouse, while actually storing the purloined documents in a place of safekeeping. The judge, who assumed the records had perished in the flames, joined Drummond in Washington to urge the administration to halt "the Mormons . . . treasonable doings against the Government."[19]

The judges' allegations ignited a politically destructive national debate about polygamy and popular sovereignty that Buchanan wanted halted. In the spring of 1857 he launched the "Mormon War" in an attempt to quell Republican attacks and to restore civil authority. "I do not wish to interfere with the Mormon religion," Buchanan informed territorial delegate John M. Bernhisel, "but the laws must be enforced." The president also realized that Drummond and Stiles had contributed to the collapse of territorial justice. "The President acknowledged," Bernhisel observed, that the previous administration had appointed "some very bad men." Buchanan and Black assured the Utah delegate that they would replace them with "the best men they could find in the country."[20]

Buchanan cited the collapse of civil authority in Utah to justify the invocation of his seldom-used removal power. Drummond resigned rather than accept removal, but Chief Justice Kinney and Associate Justice Stiles clung to their commissions. The president and the attorney general concluded that only new judges sensitive to the administration and capable of winning the respect of the Mormons would suffice.[21]

Buchanan and Black wanted a chief justice who would restore the appearance of popular sovereignty and win Mormon confidence without threatening the property rights of southern masters.[22] Delana R. Eckles, a former circuit court judge from Greencastle, Indiana, emerged as the candidate with the necessary experience and political beliefs. He was recommended by Indiana Senator Jesse D. Bright, an early backer of Buchanan at the Cincinnati convention, a stalwart defender of the president's Kansas policy, and a bitter rival of Stephen A. Douglas. The president demanded assurances from Eckles about his constitutional views. "I am," the applicant replied through cabinet members, "for state rights, against the Wilmot proviso, for the Fugitive Slave Law and against abolitionism." "I wish there were not a slave on earth," he concluded, "but . . . I am for the Union—the Constitution. I love the state right doctrine as understood in Virginia." Buchanan on July 13, 1857, issued him a recess commission.[23]

The president sought similar qualities in the associate justices. On the same day he appointed the chief justice, Buchanan issued recess commissions to Emery D. Potter of Toledo, Ohio, and Charles Sinclair of Culpepper Courthouse, Virginia. Potter was a former congressman who had supported the Fugitive Slave Act and the Kansas-Nebraska Act. He was an experienced circuit court judge and one of the few Democrats in northern Ohio aligned with the pro-Buchanan faction of William Allen. When Potter declined the commission because of family problems, the post was given to another Allen adherent, John Cradlebaugh, a one-eyed lawyer from Circleville, Ohio. Secretary of War John B. Floyd mediated the selection of his fellow Virginian, the twenty-nine-year-old Sinclair.[24]

Despite his caution in the selection process, Buchanan was unsuccessful in predicting the courtroom behavior of his appointees. New Utah Governor Alfred Cumming complained that the president's failure to appoint "an intelligent, and impartial bench" had "contributed to the pains and difficulties" of restoring order. Eckles and Cradlebaugh were rabid anti-Mormons; they rejected the proposition that under popular sovereignty the Saints could regulate the domestic institution of polygamy unimpaired by the national government. Sinclair was impartial, but ineffectual in restoring Mormon confidence in the judiciary.[25]

Buchanan sought through circumvention what he had failed to attain directly. Attorney General Black ordered new United States District Attorney Alexander Wilson to cease bringing any polygamy indictments. "There is no reason to believe," the attorney general argued, "that the act of polygamy applies to the territory as an offense punishable in the courts." These "criminal matters," Black concluded, with an eye to popular sovereignty, were cognizable only under "local laws passed by the territorial legislature."[26] When the judges went out of their way to seek indictments for polygamy, the president in December, 1859, delivered an ultimatum: resign or face removal. Sinclair and Eckles accepted; Cradlebaugh refused. In the spring of 1860 Buchanan nominated three new judges. "The President," recently elected Democratic territorial delegate William H. Hooper observed, "was anxious for peace, quiet and happiness to reign in Utah."[27]

Buchanan delegated to the attorney general the task of filling the judgeships. He instructed Black, in keeping with previous practices, to maintain sectional representation. Despite the pleas of Governor Cumming and territorial delegate Hooper, he also directed that only gentiles were to receive consideration; "the Senate would not ratify the nomination of any man . . . who had a plurality of wives."[28]

Black heeded these instructions and Mormon interests. "Attorney General Black," territorial delegate Hooper concluded, was a "good friend" of the Church.[29] On the basis of the attorney general's recommendations, the president on April 9, 1850, nominated Alexander Wilson chief justice and Robert Patterson Flenniken and Edward Harden associate justices. "The judges," Black explained, "were selected with a careful view to their moral as well as their intellectual qualities." Wilson was a Mormon favorite; the selection had been pressed by Wilson's Philadelphia patron Thomas L. Kane and Brigham Young. As United States attorney for Utah, the youthful Wilson had faithfully cooperated with Black's instructions to invoke popular sovereignty as a legal barrier to further prosecution of polygamists. Flenniken was a Pittsburgh lawyer and an "intimate friend" of the attorney general. This personal knowledge and Flenniken's untiring support of the Buchanan faction in Pennsylvania politics prompted the appointment. "If there be a man in this nation," Black wrote assuringly to Young, "who hold the scales [of justice] scrupulously even and execute the judgements in righteousness and truth, I may safely claim that he is the man."[30] Harden of Georgia was the southern representative. His brother-in-law, Supreme Court Justice James Moore Wayne, and Howell Cobb applauded his distinguished record on the Nebraska territorial bench. "The new judges," Young concluded, were "very acceptable to the citizens of our Territory."[31]

Party factionalism and the rigors of territorial service thwarted Black's attempt to accommodate the Mormons. In the Senate, Douglas Democrats and Republicans united to defeat Wilson. The former opposed the district attorney's cooperation with the administration; the latter objected to his friendship with Mormon leaders. Buchanan then reappointed John F. Kinney, whom he had removed two years earlier. When Edward Harden declined to make the long journey to Utah, the president selected Henry Roberjot Crosbie, an obscure Oregon lawyer with southern and proslavery sentiments.[32] Throughout his administration, Buchanan failed to restore coherence to the Utah bench.

The Kansas judiciary was also enmeshed in controversy. Chief Justice Samuel D. Lecompte and Associate Justice Sterling G. Cato were southerners with a predilection to favor the legal position of the proslavery minority. Free-state Democrats in Kansas warned that party harmony and reconciliation of the divided territory required that "all parties . . . stand on an equal footing" before a "good judiciary . . . willing to enforce even-handed justice."[33]

Buchanan continued the two controversial judges in office. As a matter of policy he refused to become embroiled in the factional struggles of any territorial Democratic party. Moreover, he was restrained by southern Democrats in the Senate who had previously foiled Pierce's attempted removal of Lecompte.[34]

Shortly after entering office Buchanan did fill a Kansas vacancy. Thomas Cunningham, appointed by Pierce as the free-state representative on the court, resigned on June 3, 1857, to exchange the continuous turmoil in Kansas for the security of a law practice in his native Pennsylvania.[35]

The president and the attorney general relied on the certainty of instrumental friendship to guarantee support of administration policies. Black persuaded his schoolboy friend and fellow law student, Joseph Williams of Dubuque, Iowa, to accept the associate judgeship. Previously, Black and Buchanan had prevailed on President Martin Van Buren to appoint Williams associate justice of Iowa territory. After statehood he became a justice of the supreme court. A defender of the Fugitive Slave Act, a strong-willed judge, an exponent of narrow construction of legislative enactments, and a "firm supporter of the Kansas-Nebraska Act," Williams had been "badly abused by Black Republicans."[36] The administration wanted his loyalty, his judicial experience, and his conservative jurisprudence on the Kansas bench.

The personal political interests involved in the selection of Williams undermined the efforts of Kansas Governor Robert J. Walker to fashion party harmony. Buchanan entrusted Walker to build a united Democratic party, to restore order, and to quiet agitation over the slavery extension issue through speedy admission of Kansas to statehood. Walker expected to have a voice in all patronage decisions, but he was disappointed. "The appointment of Judge Williams," he explained to the president, "has done a great injury in Kansas." The governor had succeeded in attaining agreement between the moderate proslavery and free-state leaders to support territorial resident William Stevens for the vacant judgeship. Walker appreciated that the president "no doubt reasoned that Williams was a good Democrat and a warm friend . . . from old Somerset"; however, the appointment had only caused "chagrin among our friends and . . . rejoicing among the black republicans and violent proslavery disunion leaders," who concluded that the new governor "had no influence in Washington."[37]

Buchanan filled the two other judgeships in the wake of congressional rejection on August 2, 1858, of the Lecompton constitution. He expected the judiciary to protect administration policy by preventing the local free-state majority in Kansas from threatening the property rights of slaveholders. "Neither Congress, nor a territorial legislature, nor any human power," the chief executive concluded, "has any authority to annul or impair this vested right." The Supreme Court in *Dred Scott*, he argued, had authorized masters "to hold such property there under the guardianship of the federal constitution, so long as the territorial condition shall remain." The territorial "judiciary would doubtless" afford "an adequate remedy" should a territorial legislature in Kansas or elsewhere violate this right.[38]

Buchanan appointed judges committed to administration policy. On August 13, 1858, Associate Justice Cato, convinced of the future success of free-state Democrats, returned to Alabama. Buchanan in March, 1859, declined to renew the commission of controversial Chief Justice Lecompte. To replace Cato, he issued a recess commission to Rush Elmore, a native of Alabama, whom Pierce in 1855 had removed from the bench for speculation in Indian lands. Elmore subsequently emerged as an influential moderate within the proslavery wing of the Kansas Democracy. The largest slaveholder in the territory, he doubted that slavery would ever flourish; further agitation would only strengthen the ascendancy of the Republican minority over the Democratic majority. As a delegate to the Lecompton convention, Elmore urged the adoption of a constitutional provision that would guarantee only the property rights of masters already in the territory. Elmore's brother-in-law, Alabama Senator Benjamin Fitzpatrick, and Kansas Governor James W. Denver recommended him as a "moderate man" who had "incurred the ill will of extremists." Buchanan was fully aware of his new judge's views; Elmore in 1858 had personally pleaded with the president not to submit the Lecompton constitution to Congress.[39]

Buchanan secured an equally sound administration adherent in John Pettit of Indiana, a former United States senator and representative, a state circuit court judge, and a Buchanan delegate to the 1856 Cincinnati convention. Powerful Indiana Senator Jesse D. Bright, whose influence had grown with Stephen A. Douglas's estrangement from the administration, mediated the selection. Southern Democratic senators added their endorsement; they believed Pettit's "conservative stance on public issues" would complement administration policy. The president struck a bargain: Pettit pledged "not to repeal . . . by judicial action . . . the existing laws effecting Kansas"; Buchanan promised to nominate Pettit district judge when Kansas entered the Union.[40]

Republicans charged the administration with subverting judicial integrity in order to perpetuate slavery. "The notorious Lecompte," Horace Greeley complained, had "found a successor in . . . John Pettit, . . . so that the change cannot be called an interruption of the strict continuity and congruity heretofore characteristic of the federal courts in that territory." The remaining northern Democrats in the Senate chose to support the administration and the southern Democratic majority; a unified Democracy sustained Pettit against solid Republican opposition.[41]

Buchanan carefully selected judges for Utah and Kansas whose political and constitutional views accorded with administration policy. He breached the traditional independence of the judiciary and the doctrine of popular sovereignty. The administration expected Utah judges to declare polygamy a domestic institution unassailable except by local legislative action. Slavery in Kansas pushed the president to contradiction; he explicitly recruited a judiciary predisposed to subvert popular sovereignty.

Through a party-directed selection process the administration harnessed its political goals to the judicial power. Buchanan and Black rewarded candidates and mediators from the administration factions of the state parties; they removed uncooperative judges and ignored party dissidents. Proadministration territorial delegates Joseph Lane of Oregon, Henry M. Rice of Minnesota, Isaac I. Stevens of Washington, and Miguel A. Otero of New Mexico had significant latitude in designating judicial nominees. Bird B. Chapman of Nebraska, a questionable ally of the administration, had no influence.[42]

Enervation of the Democracy heightened the importance of personal connections. Under attack from without by the Republican party and hammered by factional and sectional dissent from within, the administration became a party within a party in which informal personal ties had greater significance than formal organizational commitments. Forty percent of Buchanan's nominees had kinship connections to principal mediators; still others owed their posts to instrumental friendships. These informal ties assured a modicum of political loyalty and legal competence that Democratic affiliation could no longer guarantee; thus, the president and the attorney general recruited Flenniken and Williams to serve in the troubled territories of Utah and Kansas. These were not isolated examples. Buchanan nominated Samuel W. Black, a protégé of the attorney general and the son-in-law of District Judge Thomas Irwin of the Western District of Pennsylvania, to be associate justice of Nebraska. In four other instances, Buchanan appointed kinsmen of prominent mediators loyal to the administration: William G. Blackwood, associate justice of New Mexico, was the brother-in-law of territorial delegate Miguel A. Otero; Rush Elmore, associate justice of Kansas, was the brother-in-law of Sen. Benjamin Fitzpatrick of Alabama; Rensselaer Russell Nelson, associate justice of Minnesota, was the son of Supreme Court Justice Samuel Nelson; and Edward Randolph Harden, associate justice of Utah territory, was the brother-in-law of Supreme Court Justice James Moore Wayne.[43] Like Jackson, Buchanan resorted to a traditional mode of selection to cope with the pressures of party realignment.

III

"I know the relations which necessarily exist," Buchanan wrote to Sen. William M. Gwin, "between a Senator and his constituents must counsel his actions."[44] The president inherited from Pierce the precedent of senatorial dictation of district court selections. But he also had to contend, in making eight district court and two Court of Claims nominations, with a Senate Republican opposition that could embarras the administration and, after southern Democratic senators fled to the Confederacy, impair the president's appointment prerogative. The Republicans forced roll-call votes on three of the ten nominees, but they succeeded only in preventing the confirmation of John Pettit to Kansas.

Republican senators and the president disagreed over the role of the federal courts in the sectional crisis. Radical Republicans denounced the district court judiciary for punishing violators of the Fugitive Slave Act. Buchanan insisted the judges sustain federal authority. In the South, he expected them to encourage energetic enforcement of the neutrality laws and the federal prohibition against

further importation of slaves. In the North, he wanted district judges
who would vigorously punish persons abetting escaped slaves.[45]
Buchanan pursued this policy in Pennsylvania, his home state.

"We are in the midst of a division of party here," wrote Buchanan
Democrat Richard Vaux of Philadelphia in 1857, "and it is to a great
measure beyond human control." "If we are to survive," explained
Robert Tyler, another administration loyalist, "a judicious arrangement of the patronage in favor of the government is needed."[46] These
concerns stemmed from the growing opposition of former vice-
president George M. Dallas, former postmaster general James
Campbell, and erstwhile administration supporters Gov. William F.
Packer and newspaperman John W. Forney, who wanted to control
the Democracy in eastern Pennsylvania. They resented the administration's identification with the South, its determination to enforce the
unpopular Fugitive Slave Act, and its insistence on congressional
ratification of the fraudulently conceived Lecompton constitution. In
the spring of 1858 these antiadministration Democrats and the Republican opposition converged when the administration nominated a
replacement for deceased Judge John K. Kane of the Eastern District
of Pennsylvania.[47]

Two unrelated events insinuated the sectional controversy into the
selection of Kane's successor. First, Kane had drawn national attention for his strict enforcement of the Fugitive Slave Act. In 1855 the
judge had imprisoned Passmore Williamson, the secretary of the
Pennsylvania Antislavery Society, for contempt of court after he refused to cooperate in the return of the "kidnapped" slave Jane
Johnson, and Republicans had retaliated with an unsuccessful attempt to impeach the judge. Second, the vacancy coincided with the
prolonged debate over the Lecompton constitution. Buchanan mus-
tered the complete energies of his administration to win congressional
adoption; he expected the Democrats in his home state to sustain his
position.[48]

By late February of 1858, four candidates contended for the vacant judgeship. Douglas Democrats in Philadelphia, with the backing
of the only Democratic senator from Pennsylvania, William Bigler,
urged the nomination of James Campbell, Pierce's postmaster general. Bigler asserted that the nomination of the former Pierce cabinet
official "would tend to strengthen the present administration" in
Pennsylvania and "conciliate many minds now elevated in every party
of the Union."[49] District Attorney James C. Van Dyke claimed the
judgeship in recognition of his familiarity with court procedures and
his loyalty to Buchanan during the 1856 election. Van Dyke was his

own best advocate; Democrats of all stripes resented his record of political inconsistency, and the Philadelphia bar alleged that he had misappropriated government funds. Democratic lawyers in the city urged the appointment of George Sharswood, a neutral in party factionalism with a record of outstanding judicial service.[50]

The fourth candidate was John C. Cadwalader, a friend and political advisor of the president. While in the House of Representatives, Cadwalader defended the Fugitive Slave Act and exhorted northern Democrats to conciliate southern partisans on the Kansas issue. Buchanan's old friend wanted the appointment; through the president's private secretary, James Buchanan Henry, whom Cadwalader had trained as a lawyer, he indicated his willingness to serve. Robert Tyler and Collector of the Port Joseph B. Baker, both leading administration spokesmen in the city, added their endorsements.[51]

Buchanan waited two months to act, hoping that unhappiness with Cadwalader would dissipate. Van Dyke denounced his political and legal rival as politically inept and professionally unqualified. If the president appointed Cadwalader, Van Dyke threatened, he would embarrass the administration by resigning as district attorney. The Philadelphia bar criticized Cadwalader as a "prolix and impenetrable . . . lawyer" who "lacked proper temperament and habits."[52] The Republican and Douglas Democratic press denounced Cadwalader's position on the Fugitive Slave Law, his prosouthern and Lecompton views, and his connection as the son-in-law of Horace Binney, a former Whig and leader of the Philadelphia bar. Even Cadwalader's most enthusiastic supporter, Collector Baker, realized that nomination of the socially prominent and diffident Cadwalader "would not . . . be popular with the bar or the public." Nonetheless, he encouraged the nomination; it would demonstrate that Buchanan "would not tolerate open and violent opposition."[53]

The president wanted most a loyal judge he could trust not to embarrass the administration. Cadwalader was the only choice. When Buchanan nominated him on April 19, he explained that because he had "been on terms of personal friendship . . . for many years" with Cadwalader, he knew the judge would perpetuate "sound political principles."[54]

Republicans blasted the nomination. The *New York Tribune* denounced the nominee as "one of the old school of 'black-letter lawyers' " who placed "precedent" ahead of "the genial soul of Democracy . . . and Christianity." Cadwalader, it concluded, was more likely "to confirm an empire of . . . slaves . . . than freemen." A knot of Senate Republicans objected, but the president prevailed.[55]

Buchanan also blended instrumental friendship with political necessity in filling another vacant judgeship in Pennsylvania. On January 26, 1859, Judge Thomas Irwin of the western district chose to resign rather than accept impeachment on well-supported charges that he had supplemented his income and that of his son, who was the clerk of the court, by holding needless court sessions and requiring the marshal to hand over a quarter of his yearly salary. The scandal was a source of discomfort to the administration; Irwin was a Buchanan loyalist tied by marriage to prominent Democrats in western Pennsylvania.[56] Collector Baker in Philadelphia urged Buchanan to select quickly a replacement in order to deny "the opposition press" and "other enemies . . . an opportunity to further malign" the administration. The president could not act precipitously; the legal profession of Pittsburgh, which had devoted nearly a decade to forcing Irwin's resignation, pledged to scrutinize closely the next nominee.[57]

Buchanan resolved the impasse by tapping a political crony. Wilson McCandless of Pittsburgh was a successful lawyer, a consistent adherent of the president's Kansas program, an influential party advisor, and a Buchanan delegate to the Cincinnati convention. Attorney General Black and the Pittsburgh bar added endorsements. The president ignored Sen. William Bigler, who recommended George R. Barrett, a Douglas Democrat and respected state district court judge from Clearfield. One week after Irwin's resignation, the Senate confirmed McCandless.[58]

In the other northern states, Buchanan cooperated with Democratic senators loyal to the administration. When Minnesota entered the Union in 1858, he acceded to the wishes of Sen. Henry M. Rice, the leading administration spokesman in the new state, and Supreme Court Justice Samuel Nelson, by appointing the latter's son, Rensselaer Russell Nelson. One year later, Sen. Joseph Lane of Oregon successfully mediated the selection of Matthew P. Deady, who, like Lane, had played a decisive role in the Oregon convention that wrote slavery into the constitution of the new state. For Lane the nomination eliminated a potential rival; for Deady, despite constant involvement in politics, the office guaranteed the reliable income to which he had grown accustomed as an associate justice of the territorial supreme court. The Oregon senator responded to Buchanan's queries about the political and constitutional soundness of Deady with newspaper clippings of essays by Deady which lauded the president's Kansas policy. "The president," Lane confided to the new judge, "was very much pleased."[59]

Buchanan cooperated with loyal Democratic senators, but he refused to be, as Pierce had been, completely hamstrung by senatorial courtesy. The president manifested his independence following the death on July 28, 1859, of Judge John Gayle of Alabama. In selecting a successor, he rejected the advice of both Alabama Democratic senators, his attorney general, and a Supreme Court justice.

The vacant Alabama judgeship stimulated old regional rivalries within the state Democratic party. From the time of the admission of Alabama to the Union a single judge drawn from the Mobile bar had presided over the district court. This domination reflected the predominance of admiralty and maritime cases on the court docket; only two cities—New York and New Orleans—exceeded Mobile in the value of foreign exports. Democratic lawyers in north and central Alabama pleaded with the Buchanan administration for representation on the federal bench.[60]

The need to maintain federal authority in the midst of the growing sectional crisis intertwined with these regional rivalries. Buchanan pledged to quell sectional rancor through prosecution of violators of the federal neutrality and slave trade laws. Supreme Court Justice John A. Campbell, whose circuit included his home state of Alabama, sustained Buchanan's policy by encouraging vigorous prosecution of offenders. Campbell believed that his judicial integrity and the success of the administration policy depended on the character of the new district judge. "There are tens of thousands," he wrote in describing potential federal court jurors, "who do not appreciate the moral and religious arguments against the slave trade" and who "believe that the importation of Africans is . . . a missionary enterprise." "The district judge conducts most of the federal legal business in Alabama," Campbell warned the attorney general, and, therefore, the president "should not select a candidate who supports the measures that I have condemned."[61]

This same issue divided the Alabama Democratic congressional delegation. Sen. Clement C. Clay, Jr., spoke for radical state rights Democrats and his north Alabama constituents in recommending Leroy P. Walker, a successful Huntsville attorney, former circuit court judge, and "thoroughgoing State Rights Democrat." Walker had earlier denounced as an "unconstitutional exercise of federal power" prosecutions of suspected violators of the slave trade and neutrality laws.[62] Attorney General Black, however, opposed Walker; he had "put himself out of the race" by "his absurd opinion on the subject of the slave trade." Furthermore, Black counseled the president to "take no man from the northern district . . . because the northern district had no judicial business in the federal courts."[63]

Conservative Democratic Senator Benjamin F. Fitzpatrick endorsed Montgomery lawyer George W. Goldthwaite. A native of New Hampshire, Goldthwaite immigrated to Alabama, where he married Justice Campbell's sister and rose to the chief-justiceship of the state supreme court. He was, argued Fitzpatrick, a "sound Democrat" and "one of the leading lawyers of Alabama."[64]

Justice Campbell and Attorney General Black also endorsed Goldthwaite. Campbell dismissed Clay's charges that appointment of his brother-in-law would lead to one-family control of the Alabama federal courts; instead, Campbell felt, the appointment promised to harmonize legal ability and political necessity. Campbell believed that Goldthwaite, as "the most able lawyer in Alabama," would bring enormous prestige to bear in sustaining his earlier decisions. Black, who had suffered repeated frustrations in seeking prosecutions in southern federal courts, urged Goldthwaite as the only nominee with sufficient legal stature to awe juries with the authority of the federal government.[65]

William Giles Jones of Mobile emerged as the compromise candidate. A former Whig legislator turned Democrat, Jones applauded Buchanan's pledge to defuse the sectional crisis through a strict rule of law. "No man," observed Jones's brother-in-law and principal mediator, Congressman Sydenham Moore, had "labored more zealously or actively for Mr. Buchanan in the last election."[66] The Mobile bar and business community, anxious to retain the federal judgeship in their city, recommended Jones as the foremost authority in Alabama on admiralty, maritime, and insurance law. Campbell and Fitzpatrick ranked Jones only behind Goldthwaite as "a lawyer of reputation and ability . . . unobjectionable to the public and the bar generally."[67]

Buchanan chose selectively. He rejected Goldthwaite because of his family ties to Campbell; he eliminated Walker because of his unacceptable constitutional views. "I selected Mr. Jones," Buchanan revealed, shortly after granting him a recess commission on September 29, "because he enjoyed an eminent reputation as a lawyer, and resided at Mobile where nearly all the business of the court must be dispatched."[68]

Campbell and Fitzpatrick accepted the appointment with equanimity, but Senator Clay was "surprised and chagrined." "If the President requires exact conformity with his own political opinions of all who seek federal patronage," Clay asserted, "he will scarcely find an honest man in Alabama to take an office at his hands."[69] Buchanan was self-assured. "Senator Clay," he observed, "was one of the best men in the Senate," but "a little too imperious" in attempting to dictate patronage decisions. "I must," Buchanan explained, "uphold the independence of my office."[70]

Democratic factionalism and Republican strength in the Senate limited the president's discretionary power. These factors surfaced in Buchanan's most controversial nominations: Edward Greeley Loring to be chief justice of the Court of Claims and John Pettit to be district judge of Kansas.

The furor over the chief-justiceship of the Court of Claims had its roots in Franklin Pierce's decision to adopt a policy of sectional representation. The death of Chief Justice John J. Gilchrist on April 29, 1858, left the eastern seat vacant. This coincided with the termination of a three-year-old dispute over enforcement of the Fugitive Slave Law in Massachusetts. Boston in 1854 was the scene of the controversial Anthony Burns rendition case. United States Commissioner Edward Greeley Loring ordered Burns returned to Virginia and slavery. Incensed antislavery and Republican spokesmen in Boston could not distrub Loring in his federal office, but they could subject him as probate judge of Suffolk County to "address" by the state legislature and removal by the governor. In 1855 the antislavery majority in the legislature passed resolutions condemning Loring's conduct and insisting on his removal, but the Democratic governor refused to cooperate. Republicans in 1858 passed new resolutions, and newly elected Republican Governor Nathaniel P. Banks completed the ostracization.[71]

The repercussions from Loring's removal spread beyond the Bay State. Proadministration Democratic senators, most of them from the South, seized on the vacant Court of Claims post as a vehicle to register disfavor with Republican opposition to the Fugitive Slave Law. They urged Buchanan to demonstrate his commitment to the "integrity of the Constitution and laws" by appointing Loring.[72]

The president agreed to transform the selection process into a symbolic sectional struggle. With the concurrence of Attorney General Black, Buchanan on May 3, 1858, nominated Loring. The Republican *New York Tribune* condemned the selection as a "reward at the hands of the Slave Power now governing the Union." The president and the attorney general applauded Loring's devotion to federal authority, but they appreciated even more the irresistible force of overwhelming Senate Democratic support. Republicans forced a vote, but party lines held; every Democrat present voted to confirm.[73]

Buchanan thwarted the Republican opposition only as long as Senate Democrats remained a unified majority. By early 1861, how-

ever, southern Democratic senators had literally deserted the administration; twelve of them resigned to join the Confederacy. This produced virtual equality between Republicans and Democrats; a shift of
one vote meant administration defeat. The result was Senate defeat
for the president's nomination on January 30, 1861, of John Pettit to
be district judge of the new state of Kansas.[74]

Buchanan selected the most controversial but ideologically acceptable of the three candidates for the judgeship. In addition to Pettit,
both the associate justices, Rush Elmore and Joseph Williams, sought
the post. Buchanan, however, had agreed, when he originally persuaded Pettit to accept the chief-justiceship, to nominate him district
judge should Kansas achieve statehood. The president may have believed himself bound by this agreement (certainly Pettit did), but, as
important, he acted in concert with the nearly unanimous recommendation of the remaining Senate Democrats. Pettit had fulfilled
Buchanan's policy of using the territorial bench to sustain slaveholders' property rights. In February of 1860, the Republican-dominated
territorial legislature, in direct violation of the *Dred Scott* decision, had
abolished the peculiar institution. Buchanan had publicly speculated
that "such an act . . . plainly violating the rights of property . . . will
surely be decided void by the judiciary." Ten months later, on December 30, Chief Justice Pettit, relying on *Dred Scott,* declared the
statute unconstitutional.[75]

In the midst of the secession crisis, the diminished Democratic
party remained nearly united. The Senate debated the nomination of
Pettit at the same time it considered Buchanan's selection of Black to
be an associate justice of the Supreme Court. "The senators had an
exciting time," the *New York Times* reported on February 22, 1861, "in
the course of which Messrs. Black and Pettit were handled without
gloves." Separate votes six days later on whether to vote on the two
nominations went against the administration twenty-six to twenty-
five, with a single Democrat breaking party lines. The defector was
Stephen A. Douglas, who accused Buchanan of relying on the territorial judiciary to frustrate popular sovereignty. Incoming Republican
President Abraham Lincoln filled the Kansas judgeship.[76]

The sectional controversy was insinuated into the selection of district court judges. Democratic senators anxious to guarantee the
property rights of slaveholders responded warmly to Buchanan's
pledge to maintain law, order, and the Union through proper district
court appointments. Only Democrats loyal to the administration
mediated the selection process or reached the federal bench.
Buchanan did not use these judgeships to woo factional opponents;

indeed, the president was so insistent on loyalty and proper constitutional views that, when afforded the opportunity in Pennsylvania, he entrusted the federal courts to instrumental friends rather than to more judicially experienced factional opponents. Buchanan persistently maneuvered within the shrinking confines of the Democratic party to sustain his policy of sectional harmony by exploiting the image of a disinterested judiciary. District court nominees in the free states would enforce the Fugitive Slave Law; their slave-state counterparts would supervise prosecutions of violators of the neutrality and slave trade laws. Buchanan diligently pursued the policy, but the turnover in the federal judiciary was so slow that he enshrined his constitutional and political philosophy in only a small percentage of the district court benches.

IV

"I acknowledge no master but the law," James Buchanan proclaimed defiantly during the struggle over the Lecompton constitution.[77] He reiterated this theme throughout his administration; an unalloyed commitment to the letter of the law would harmonize political and sectional discord. Beneath this policy loomed a powerful and eventually fatal contradiction: equal federal enforcement of the laws did not mean equal justice. The legal perpetuation of slavery compromised the legal institutions of the nation to such a degree that the doctrine of judicial impartiality came to be seen as a violation of the moral imperatives of the more radical element of the Republican party. The president's collusive role in the *Dred Scott* decision was only his most blatant attempt to yoke the judiciary to the political fortunes of the administration. This same conscious effort animated the judicial selection process. Buchanan promised more than he could ever deliver through the participatory political process: he could not simultaneously sustain popular sovereignty and guarantee the absolute property right of slaveholders in the territories. He expected to partially bridge this chasm by relying on the territorial judiciary to suppress majority will while district judges carefully balanced prosecutions under the fugitive slave, neutrality, and slave trade laws. Buchanan and Black wanted only judges with safe constitutional views. The judgeships were instruments of political power too important to bestow on factional opponents who, once on the bench, might loosen the constitutional underpinnings of administration policy.

A resurgence of patron-client relations accompanied this quest for ideological purity. The selection process remained party-directed: Buchanan nominated only Democrats and, with more independence than his predecessor, relied on Democratic senators. Despite growing sectional division, the Democracy remained almost united on judicial nominees. Within this Democratic shrine of party, kinship and instrumental friendship connections assumed an importance unmatched since Jackson's administration. This traditional mode of selection reflected and reinforced the increasingly narrow base of the Democratic party, particularly in the North. The Democracy, in every state and territory, developed separate patronage or "regular" party organizations united to the administration in a bond of reciprocal loyalty. The chain of commitment in these insular and self-perpetuating organizations was short; as a result, they were susceptible to the pressures of kinship and friendship.

Buchanan dispensed the judicial patronage with purpose, authority, a modicum of independence, and caution. He was manipulative and decidedly prosouthern, but hardly timid or weak-nerved, as some historians have charged. He took the initiative to secure the judiciary he needed to sustain administration policy. The president realized the destructive potential of sectionalism and slavery; he myopically believed that resort to the law and the federal judiciary would stem the threat. The strategy failed and with it Buchanan, the Democracy, and the Union.

9

A NEW BREED OF POLITICAL JUDGE

It is as hard for a rich man's son to obtain the honors of the
bar, as it is for the rich man himself to enter the kingdom of
heaven. They come from the farm and the workshop, from
that condition of life to which the great majority belong. . . .
Thus it happens that the children of the cabins come up
and occupy the palaces of the Republic.—Archibald
Caruthers, Professor of Law, Cumberland University,
1851[1]

Presidents, senators, and a host of other mediators molded the antebellum lower federal judiciary. Our knowledge of the individual
and institutional roles they fulfilled, while central to an understanding of the how and why of the subterranean judicial selection process,
only partially illuminates its relationship to the broader political culture. When institutions such as the lower federal courts persist over
time, the extent of continuity and change in the social, political, and
professional backgrounds of nominees indicates the persistence of
institutional values.[2] What were the social bases of the selection process? Did Whig and Democratic administrations consistently nominate
judges of different social-class origins and positions? The social bases
of the selection process are related to fundamental assumptions about
the modernizing impact of the second party system. Was the gradual
institutionalization of the selection process accompanied by increased
dispersion of power through society? Were traditional elites replaced
by modernizing elites of professional politicians and technical legal
experts?[3] The nominees' backgrounds also reveal the extent to which
the differing institutional characteristics of the constitutional and
legislative courts affected the composition of the judiciary. Did district
and territorial judges differ in their relative social status, legal training, formal academic education, political experience, and preappointment public legal and judicial service?

Between 1829 and 1861, eight presidents nominated two hundred
lower court judges. In addition, forty judges appointed by previous
administrations held their posts during at least part of the era of the
second party system; thus, it is possible to speculate in a general way

about the extent to which judicial nominees during the era differed
from their predecessors.[4]

II

"The only feature in American society . . . indicative of the equality they profess," wrote the English traveler Frances Trollope in 1832,
"is that any man's son may become the equal of any other man's son."[5]
Other foreign visitors reiterated the theme of equal opportunity in
America; men of talent, regardless of their beginnings, might rise to
positions of power and influence by dint of hard work. The legal
profession received particular attention; the sons of the humble could
acquire a profession that would lead to wealth, political prominence,
and, perhaps, the accolade of a judgeship. Lillian C. Tuthill's *Success
in Life: The Lawyer* was a home-grown elaboration of the conjunction
of social mobility, the legal profession, and political and judicial
power. Tuthill's expansive and positive theme dotted the popular and
legal literature of the pre–Civil War era.[6]

The relationship between occupational and political success on the
one hand, and social origins and achieved social-class positions on the
other hand, has repeatedly stirred debate. Two decades ago, students
of the era believed that substantive differences existed in the social
composition of the leaders and followers of the two parties. Simultaneously, legal historians, usually relying on the conventional wisdom of political history and enticed by the claims of Tuthill and
others, held that a crass vulgarization of the legal profession coincided
with Andrew Jackson's presidency. The standards of bar admittance
dropped; state judges were elected rather than appointed; and the
competence and social origins of the profession declined.[7] More recently, historians concluded that men of wealth and social prominence were as likely to be Democrats as Whigs.[8] While access to the
profession became easier, this change was neither as devastating as
earlier scholars presumed nor as sweeping as contemporaries reported. The legal profession provided opportunity to greater numbers, but not every lawyer was equally successful. The most eminent
practitioners usually achieved distinction through the advantages of
inherited wealth, social prominence, and family connections.[9]

The concepts of social-class origin and social-class position em-
body the most elusive of historical phenomena. Social origin indicates
a nominee's inherited position in the social order. It divides into three
levels: elite, prominent, and modest. These categories constitute gra-
dations in the upper three-quarters of the antebellum social order;

men from the humblest and most deprived family backgrounds did not reach the federal bench. Nominees of modest origins compared most closely with the mythical common man of the era, who possessed neither great wealth nor social prestige, but who was damned neither to perpetual poverty nor to social ignominy. Social-class position refers to a nominee's achieved adult status before nomination. As with social origin, social position divides into elite, prominent, and modest.[10]

The path to the lower federal bench most typically began in the security of homes which offered exposure to politics and the advantages of wealth. Most nominees (table 1) emerged from either elite or prominent social origins. At a time when approximately 80 percent of the male labor force engaged in agricultural activity, only 35 percent of the judges had fathers who were farmers or planters; indeed, slightly more (38 percent) had professional as opposed to agricultural callings. The future nominees deviated from their fathers' career paths; only 16 percent of all fathers were lawyers.[11]

TABLE 1

NOMINATING PRESIDENT BY NOMINEES' SOCIAL ORIGINS

(Adjusted Percentage)

| President | % in Category | Origins | | | Total % |
		Elite I	Prominent II	Modest III	
John Q. Adams and Before	18.7	21.4	64.3	14.3	100.0
Jackson	16.7	28.0	48.0	24.0	100.0
Van Buren	6.7	—	70.0	30.0	100.0
Harrison-Tyler	5.3	25.0	75.0	—	100.0
Polk	5.3	25.0	50.0	25.0	100.0
Taylor	4.7	—	57.1	42.9	100.0
Fillmore	7.3	18.2	54.5	27.3	100.0
Pierce	20.7	22.6	51.6	25.8	100.0
Buchanan	14.6	22.7	54.5	22.8	100.0
% in Origin		20.7	55.3	24.0	100.0
Total Number	(150)	(31)	(83)	(36)	
Total Missing Cases	(90)				

*Missing cases have been excluded from all percentages in tables labeled "adjusted percentage."

Exposure to politics was a far more common experience. While few of the fathers bequeathed a tradition of legal service to their offspring, they did set an example of active political participation; 60 percent were elected or appointed to public offices. This exposure to politics only reinforced a connection widely acknowledged during the early nineteenth century between legal and political careers. It certainly impressed John Glenn, whom Millard Fillmore appointed district judge of Maryland. As a young law student, Glenn wrote to his father, who was himself an active political figure in Maryland, that after studying law in the office of prominent Philadelphia attorney Charles J. Ingersoll, he looked forward to a career of "excitement and political activity denied the merchant and banker."[12]

Family wealth undoubtedly assisted nominees from prominent and elite origins who aspired to political prominence and legal stature. A sharp cleavage existed between the fathers' highest known wealth and estimates of the wealth holdings of the total population. Estimates of wealth for the pre-1850 period are sketchy at best, but studies of the years 1850 and 1860 indicate that the national average for adult white males was about $2,580. The mean wealth of those judges' fathers for whom wealth data were available was nearly five times that amount—$10,490. At a time when approximately 10 percent of the adult male population held $5,000 or more in real and personal wealth, 53 percent of the nominees' fathers possessed wealth of $5,000 or more, and 21 percent had holdings of between $25,000 and $50,000.[13] A few fathers accumulated significant wealth. David McCaleb, the father of Judge Theodore Howard McCaleb of Louisiana, Charles Biddle, a prominent Philadelphia merchant and father of a Jackson nominee of the same name to the Florida territorial bench, and General Thomas Cadwalader, father of Judge John Cadwalader of Philadelphia, were all worth $100,000.[14] Such wealth, however, was extraordinary; 3 percent of the nominees' fathers possessed wealth greater than $100,000, but 8 percent had highest known holdings of less than $1,000. While the sons of the rich may have succeeded disproportionately at the bar, they had no special claim on the federal judiciary.

There was continuity and incremental change in the nominees' social origins. Democratic and Whig presidents selected nominees of similar social origins. Throughout the era, Democrats dominated the selection process, but despite a rhetorical commitment to the common man, they elevated to the federal bench few lawyers of modest social origins. Since nominees almost uniformly shared the party preference of the chief executive who selected them, the data indicate no connection between their party preferences and their social origins. Martin Van Buren, a Democrat, failed to nominate a judge from elite origins, but so did Zachary Taylor, a Whig. Presidents Jackson and Polk, both Democrats, made respectively 76 and 75 percent of their nominations from candidates with elite or prominent social origins, hardly evidence that the selection process reflected sweeping social change.

In comparison with earlier presidents, modest change occurred in the social origins of nominees selected by Jackson and later presidents. During the era of the second party system, the percentage of nominees with modest origins increased by 10 percent, while the percentage of elite nominees remained constant. The change was incremental and limited (again, the humblest members of the social order were not included), but at least in the judicial selection process, a tendency toward dispersion of power in society coincided with the advent of the new party system.

Social origin provides only one indication of the social bases of the selection process. Adult status did not necessarily correspond to social origin; mobility up or down the social hierarchy was possible.[15] The relationship between social-class position and nominating presidents (table 2) was more complex than that between social origin and

TABLE 2

NOMINATING PRESIDENT BY NOMINEES' SOCIAL-CLASS POSITIONS
AT NOMINATION
(Adjusted Percentage)

President	% in Category	SOCIAL-CLASS POSITION			Total %
		Elite I	Prominent II	Modest III	
J. Q. Adams(and before)	18.2	27.8	58.3	13.9	100.0
Jackson	14.6	17.2	58.7	24.1	100.0
Van Buren	6.1	16.7	66.7	16.6	100.0
Harrison-Tyler	6.1	25.0	58.3	16.7	100.0
Polk	6.1	8.3	83.4	8.3	100.0
Taylor	4.0	25.0	37.5	37.5	100.0
Fillmore	7.6	6.7	53.3	40.0	100.0
Pierce	22.2	4.5	72.8	22.7	100.0
Buchanan	15.1	10.0	80.0	10.0	100.0
% in Position		14.6	65.7	19.7	100.0
Total Number	(198)	(29)	(130)	(39)	
Total Missing Cases	(42)				

nominating presidents. Typically, nominees' social-class positions and social origins were similar; 80 percent of the nominees had elite or prominent social-class positions compared with 76 percent who had the same social origins. However, Whig administration had the largest percentages of nominees from modest social-class positions; Taylor and Fillmore selected respectively 37 percent and 40 percent of their nominees from this category. Furthermore, a far greater percentage (70 percent versus 30 percent) of elite judges were Democrats than were Whigs.[16] Contrary to accepted wisdom, at least in the judical selection process, Whig presidents nominated men of modest social-class positions more frequently than did Democratic presidents.

When compared with the pre-Jackson era, the selection process during the second party system drew from a modestly expanded social base. The percentage of nominees with elite social-class positions dropped by almost one-half (28 percent to 15 percent), while there was a small rise (6 percent) in the percentage of candidates from modest origins. This was a limited rearrangement of the social bases of the federal courts, but it lends credence to the notion that, in a small way, power was more broadly dispersed.

During the era of the second party system the judicial selection process incorporated limited social diversity. Modest differences appeared in the nominees' social origins and social-class positions and a slightly greater percentage of post-Adams nominees with modest social-class positions reached the federal bench. Neither Democratic nor Whig presidents systematically nourished this social openness. The social democratization of American politics, so frequently ascribed to the era of the second party system and the Democratic party particularly, was strictly limited. For a handful of nominees the decision to enter the legal profession resulted in upward social mobility, but for the overwhelming majority a life in law maintained and preserved their ascribed status. The preponderance of nominees with elite and prominent backgrounds leads inescapably to the conclusion that advantage begat advantage.

III

Precise and immutable criteria by which to establish qualification for judicial office do not exist, nor did they exist during the pre–Civil War era. Alexis de Tocqueville believed that in the United States the inherent ambiguity in the judicial role would frustrate any method of selection. "In a democratic regime," the French visitor observed, a judge "must be at once upright and subtle," possessed of "legal education, civic rectitude, and political adroitness."[17] As the preceding chapters suggest, most antebellum presidents wished not only to nominate lower federal judges who would subscribe to their political and constitutional views, but whose strength of character, moral probity, and tact would sustain and enhance the judicial application of those views. Chief executives believed that candidates' technical legal proficiency and prior public legal and judicial service could insure subsequent success on the federal bench. While it is impossible to assess collectively the moral courage and honesty of nominees, it is possible to analyze the extent of their preappointment education, judicial and public legal service, and professional prominence.

These criteria are especially applicable to the territorial judiciary. Lawrence Friedman and others have characterized these judges as a "mixed, controversial breed . . . [of] political hacks . . . ill-prepared for their jobs."[18] These assertions, however, have relied on a few descriptive studies which have stressed as much the crass and demeaning aspects of patronage politics as the unattractiveness of territorial service.[19]

The two judiciaries were similar in social origins and academic and legal educations. An equal percentage (table 3) of judges from elite origins served on the district and territorial benches, although about 10 percent more (31 percent versus 21 percent) of the territorial judges were from modest origins. This is a suggestive but slight difference; the hardships of territorial service were not so severe that

TABLE 3

NATURE OF JUDICIAL SERVICE BY NOMINEES' SOCIAL ORIGINS,
1829–61
(Adjusted Percentage)

Type of Judge	Number in Category	ORIGINS			Total %
		Elite I	Prominent II	Modest III	
District	57	22.8	56.2	21.0	100.0
Territorial	61	23.1	45.8	31.1	100.0
Court of Claims	4	—	75.0	25.0	100.0
% in Origin		20.5	53.3	26.2	100.0
Total Number	(122)	(25)	(65)	(32)	
Total Missing Cases	(78)				

men from the best social circumstances left these difficult posts to the sons of the less socially prominent. At least at the inception of their careers, the future judges shared many of, but not quite all, the same advantages.

The similarity of social origins was paralleled by the nominees' educational attainments. The lower federal judiciary was an educated elite (table 4); 53 percent of the nominees had graduated from (40 percent) or attended (13 percent) a college or university. Throughout the era no more than 1 percent of the population ever attended college.[20] Of those judges with college experience, 16 percent had been to prestigious Ivy League schools. District court nominees were slightly more likely (58 percent versus 52 percent) to have attended college. There was a more significant difference among the judges: while one-half had attended college, the other half had not. Federal judicial selection did not rest on an educational meritocracy; a college education was not essential to the pursuit of a federal judicial career.

The judges' varied educational backgrounds converged in their common decision to pursue a legal career. Throughout most of the nineteenth century, would-be lawyers acquired their training by reading law or clerking in the office of a practicing attorney or judge.[21] Nominees to the antebellum lower federal courts were typical; 88 percent of them learned the law from another lawyer or judge. The remainder either enrolled in one of the few law schools or read privately. All of the nominees had some legal training; territorial and district court nominees achieved the same level and kind of legal education.

While nominees shared similar social origins, academic education, and legal training, they diverged in social-class position at nomination. As a group, nominees to both courts were drawn from social-class positions similar to their social origins; 79 percent (table 5) of them were from elite or prominent social-class positions compared with 74 percent from the same social origins. Differences existed, however, between territorial and district court nominees; 33 percent of the territorial judiciary were from modest social-class positions compared with 8 percent of the district court nominees. While district court nominees of modest origins had raised their social status (21 percent of modest social origins compared with 8 percent of modest social-class positions), territorial nominees of similar origins had not done so. Thus, 31 percent of the territorial nominees had modest social origins and 33 percent had modest social-class positions. Territorial and district court nominees of elite origins both suffered a decline in status, but the drop was more precipitous (17 percent com-

TABLE 4
NATURE OF JUDICIAL SERVICE BY NOMINEES' HIGHEST LEVELS OF KNOWN EDUCATION, 1829–61
(Adjusted Percentage)

Judicial Service	Number in Category	HIGHEST LEVEL OF EDUCATION					
		College Graduate	Attended College	Academy	Common School	Tutor	Total Percent
District	72	45.8	11.1	22.2	16.7	4.2	100.0
Territorial	82	36.5	15.8	24.6	21.9	1.2	100.0
Court of Claims	5	80.0	20.0	—	—	—	100.0
Percent in Category		39.6	13.2	23.3	18.8	5.1	100.0
Total Number	(159)	(63)	(21)	(37)	(30)	(8)	
Total Missing Cases	(41)						

TABLE 5
NATURE OF JUDICIAL SERVICE BY NOMINEES' SOCIAL-CLASS POSITION
AT NOMINATION, 1829–61
(Adjusted Percentage)

| Type of Judge | Number in Category | SOCIAL-CLASS POSITION | | | Total % |
		Elite I	Prominent II	Modest III	
District	71	18.3	73.3	8.4	100.0
Territorial	84	6.0	60.7	33.3	100.0
Court of Claims	6	16.7	83.3	—	100.0
% in Category		11.8	67.1	21.1	100.0
Total Number	(161)	(19)	(108)	(34)	
Total Missing Cases	(38)				

pared to 4 percent) for the territorial nominees. Further, a smaller percentage (6 percent compared to 18 percent) of the territorial judiciary was drawn from elite social-class positions. As a group, the territorial nominees were less successful than their district court counterparts in maintaining their ascribed social status, although they enjoyed, as a group, the same advantages as district court nominees at the inception of their careers.

The two groups diverged even more sharply in their prenomination status within the legal profession. The notion persisted in the popular literature of the era that lawyers were an undifferentiated elite within the social order which, according to an essay in the *Yale Literary Magazine* in 1840, was "responsible for conducting the whole operations of society."[22] While Tocqueville may well have correctly characterized the bench and bar as America's only true "aristocracy," the profession embraced frontier barristers, pettifoggers, and Philadelphia lawyers.[23]

The selection process brought lawyers of differing professional stature (table 6) to the territorial and district courts.[24] The latter were of greater legal reputation: 5 percent had national legal reputations before nomination and 74 percent engaged in law practices or occupied judicial posts that afforded statewide recognition. Territorial court nominees were less prestigious; 61 percent either had no legal reputation or were known only in the immediate communities they served. While not necessarily indicative of future judicial performance, the professional prominence of the territorial nominees con-

TABLE 6

NATURE OF JUDICIAL SERVICE BY NOMINEES' PROMINENCE IN
LEGAL PROFESSION, 1829–61
(Adjusted Percentage)

Judicial Service	Number in Category	LEVEL OF PROMINENCE AT NOMINATION				Total %
		National	State	Local	None	
District	77	5.2	74.0	19.5	1.3	100.0
Territorial	98	—	38.7	56.2	5.1	100.0
Court of Claims	6	33.3	66.7	—	—	100.0
% in Category		3.4	54.7	38.7	3.2	100.0
Total Number	(181)	(6)	(99)	(70)	(6)	
Total Missing Cases	(19)					

firms charges by contemporary critics that too frequently nominees arrived at their posts lacking the stature to command confidence and respect.

Territorial spokesmen frequently complained that judicial nominees lacked sufficient experience to conduct court operations efficiently. These were not idle charges (table 7); fully 70 percent of the nominees had never presided over a court and 57 percent had never functioned in the capacity of a public legal officer. The territorial nominees' limited judicial experience and indifferent professional reputations resulted directly from the baneful effects of limited tenure, the threat of executive removal, low pay, and the physical harshness of the territories. When these handicaps were diminished or eliminated, as was the case in most district courts and the Court of Claims, legal prominence and prior judicial experience increased; 43 percent of the district court and all of the Court of Claims nominees had prior judicial experience.

This disparity between the district and territorial nominees was relative. The majority (57 percent) of the former were without prior judicial service, and only 5 percent were lawyers of national reputation. Of the four nationally prominent district court nominees, only Philip P. Barbour of the Eastern District of Virginia and Isaac H. Bronson of the Northern District of Florida accepted commissions. Horace Binney and Judah P. Benjamin, two distinguished nineteenth-century lawyers, declined their commissions. Their moti-

TABLE 7

NATURE OF JUDICIAL SERVICE BY NOMINEES' PREVIOUS JUDICIAL AND PUBLIC SERVICE, 1829–61
(Adjusted Percentage)

Type of Judge	NATURE OF SERVICE							
	Judical				Public—Legal			
	Number in Category	Yes	No	Total %	Number in Category	Yes	No	Total %
District	77	42.8	57.2	100.0	89	41.6	58.4	100.0
Territorial	97	29.8	70.2	100.0	97	43.3	56.7	100.0
Court of Claims	6	100.0	—	100.0	6	16.7	83.3	100.0
% in Category		37.7	62.3	100.0		41.7	58.3	100.0
Total Number	(180)	(68)	(112)		(192)	(80)	(112)	
Total Missing Cases	(20)				(28)			

vation in doing so involved financial, personal, and political considerations, but the case of Horace Binney disclosed a more fundamental problem. He rejected a commission for the Eastern District of Pennsylvania with the candid explanation that the post "was not equal to" his "professional merits."[25] The constitutional courts attracted more experienced and well-known lawyers than did the territorial bench, but district nominees were not, at appointment, among the most distinguished of antebellum lawyers or judges.

A significant age differential explains the divergence in the social-class positions, professional prominence, and legal and judicial experience of territorial and district court nominees. When nominated, they were in different career phases. Territorial nominees were significantly younger (table 8) than their district court counterparts; 61 percent of all territorial nominees were age forty or younger compared with 30 percent of the district court nominees. At nomination, a territorial judge, on the average, was 35.1 years of age, while district court nominees averaged 46.2 years. District court nominees had had a decade more than their territorial counterparts to enhance their social-class positions, to gain judicial or public legal experience, and to win professional prominence.[26]

Territorial and district nominees aspired to judicial service for different reasons. To the youthful territorial nominee, the prospect of federal service, despite the hazards and inconveniences, afforded an opportunity for advancement not otherwise immediately available. Edward Harden of Georgia, whom Franklin Pierce nominated associate justice of Nebraska territory in 1854, viewed his selection as a divine stroke of good fortune. "As now is my time," the ambitious Harden wrote to his mother on learning of the nomination, "if not taken at its flood—I will not rise. Many of my prominent friends, who write to congratulate me, give it as their opinion that if I now accept, in a few years I may be in the Senate."[27] For district court nominees, however, the judgeship was typically the culmination of a career and a welcome respite from the competitive rigors of politics and the often fluctuating income of a day-to-day practice.[28]

Presidents had varying success in bringing experienced nominees to the bench. The surviving written evidence provides only a patchwork of incomplete statements about the emphasis chief executives gave to prior judicial experience. Table 9 suggests three conclusions. First, not every administration stressed prior service; Jackson, Van Buren, and Fillmore had other priorities. Second, in every administration the matter of technical judicial competence, as manifested in prior service, was seldom an overriding consideration; instead, it was

TABLE 8
NATURE OF JUDICIAL SERVICE BY NOMINEES' AGE AT NOMINATION, 1829–61
(Adjusted Percentage)

Type of Judge	Number in Category	AGE AT APPOINTMENT							Total %
		Below 30	30–35	36–40	41–45	46–50	51–55	56 and Above	
District	79	1.3	12.6	16.5	21.5	16.5	20.2	11.4	100.0
Territorial	102	9.8	20.6	30.4	21.6	7.8	4.9	4.9	100.0
Court of Claims	6	—	—	16.7	—	33.3	—	50.0	100.0
% in Category		5.9	16.6	24.1	20.8	12.3	11.2	9.1	100.0
Total Number	(187)	(11)	(31)	(45)	(39)	(23)	(21)	(17)	
Total Missing Cases	(13)								

TABLE 9

NOMINATING PRESIDENT BY NOMINEES'
PREVIOUS JUDICIAL AND PUBLIC LEGAL SERVICE
(Adjusted Percentage)

President	Judicial Experience	Legal Experience	Both	Either
Jackson	28.1	43.8	12.5	59.4
Van Buren	23.5	52.9	11.8	64.7
Harrison-Tyler	50.0	44.4	22.2	60.0
Polk	58.3	75.0	33.3	100.0
Taylor	55.6	37.5	37.5	55.6
Fillmore	11.8	29.4	5.9	29.4
Pierce	42.0	41.3	19.6	58.0
Buchanan	45.5	54.8	19.4	78.8
% in Category	39.4	47.4	20.8	63.2
Total Number in Category	(68)	(80)	(31)	(141)

balanced against the partisan, sectional, and personal pressures which impinged on the selection process. Third, the majority (63 percent) of nominees had previous experience as either judges or public legal officers. In certain instances such experience benefited a candidate, but it was not essential.

Presidents controlled to a limited extent the quality of the judiciary. James K. Polk consistently nominated experienced candidates. This reflected his intense interest in the judiciary and, perhaps, a realization that he might better serve the public interest, while at the same time securing ideologically acceptable judges, by nominating experienced candidates.

Such presidential discretion could also have an opposite effect. Publicly, Millard Fillmore was as committed as Polk to securing able and experienced nominees, but he was markedly less successful. Unlike Polk, Fillmore had to recruit judges willing to serve in the distant territories carved from the Mexican Cession and in the new state of California. When older and more prestigious lawyers balked, Fillmore intentionally nominated younger men anxious to further their careers through federal appointment and able to endure the rigors of territorial service. The president consciously sacrificed experience and legal stature. Twenty-seven-year-old James McHall Jones accepted the judgeship of the Southern District of California because he believed that his salary, when invested in California lands, promised to "secure a competence in one fourth the time" it would have taken practicing law in his native New Orleans.[29] Fillmore's decision to nominate young candidates resulted in a large percentage of nominees with modest social-class positions and little prior judicial service.

A common bond of political activism united the divergent social-class positions, legal reputations, and judicial experiences of the lower court nominees. The judges were neither a traditional functional elite that served out of a sense of social responsibility nor a modern technical elite that commanded selection as a consequence of judicial experience and professional prestige. Rather, they were a unique slice of the legal subculture of the era—that part most notable for its political activism. The nominees' political and partisan careers offer the most dramatic evidence of the modernizing impact of the second party system on the lower federal courts.

Throughout American history the legal profession has offered access to politics. A heritage of politically active fathers further accentuated this tendency in judicial nominees. They adopted and expanded (table 10) on this inheritance; 78 percent held elective public office before nomination.[30] This incidence of elective political activity was an increase (78 percent compared to 65 percent) over that of pre-Jackson nominees. The selection process fashioned a lower federal judiciary intimately familiar with the participatory political culture of the second party system.

Partisan activism complemented political involvement. While party was accepted as a legitimate means by which to organize electoral and legislative activity and to distribute the public patronage, its influence on the judiciary was viewed with suspicion. In 1837 Sen. Alexander Porter of Louisiana complained that "the greatest evil which flows from party spirit is the selection of incompetent and unworthy judges."[31] Legal periodicals echoed these sentiments. The condemnation of the Supreme Court following *Dred Scott* derived partly from a belief that the justices had submitted to "party clamour."[32] These criticisms were a symptomatic reaction to the buoyant partisanship of the era. Presidents overwhelmingly selected nominees who did more than subscribe to party in name only. Their careers almost uniformly included significant labor on behalf of their party; fully 83 percent (table 11) had served as local or state organizers, as delegates to national nominating conventions, or as presidential electors. This was, moreover, a significant increase (83 percent compared to 55 percent) from the pre-Jackson era. The judicial selection process confirmed the legitimacy in the political culture of party activism.

TABLE 10
NATURE OF JUDICIAL SERVICE BY NOMINEES' PREVIOUS ELECTIVE EXPERIENCE
(Adjusted Percentage)

Type of Judge	Number in Category	ELECTIVE EXPERIENCE					Total % with Experience	
		Legislative	Judicial-Legal	Executive	Multiple Elective Experience	None	1829–61	Pre-1829
District	77	49.3	7.9	1.3	22.1	19.5	80.5	72.0
Territorial	96	35.4	11.4	—	30.3	22.9	77.1	50.0
Court of Claims	6	33.3	—	—	33.3	33.3	66.6	—
% in Category		41.3	9.5	.6	26.8	21.8	78.2	64.9
Total Number	(179)	(74)	(17)	(1)	(48)	(39)	(140)	(37)
Total Missing Cases	(21)							(3)

TABLE 11
NATURE OF JUDICIAL SERVICE BY NOMINEES' HIGHEST LEVEL OF PARTISAN ACTIVITIES
(Adjusted Percentage)

Type of Judge	Number in Category	HIGHEST LEVEL OF PARTY ACTIVITY			Total % Involved in Party Activity	
		Local Party Organizer	Presidential Elector or National Convention Delegate	None	1829–61	Pre-1829
District	71	54.9	18.3	26.8	73.2	60.0
Territorial	85	75.3	17.6	7.1	92.9	44.4
Court of Claims	6	33.3	16.7	50.0	50.0	—
Percent in Category		64.8	17.9	17.3	82.7	55.2
Total Number	(162)	(105)	(29)	(28)	(134)	(34)
Total Missing Cases	(38)					(6)

Territorial and district nominees differed modestly in the extent of their party involvement. Critics repeatedly charged that territorial nominees were mere party hacks—failed politicians unable to succeed in their home states who were crassly rewarded for their efforts by a grateful national administration. That they won nomination in part through party activism seems indisputable; fully 93 percent had served their party. This intense activity was the unique product of the second party system; these territorial nominees were more than twice (93 percent compared to 44 percent) as active in party affairs as were their pre-Jacksonian counterparts.[33] It makes little sense to dismiss the judges as hacks; indeed, the combination of youth, success in elective politics, and involvement in party affairs indicates that they were remarkably energetic. They gained political and party advancement at the expense of their legal careers; the price of early political success was retarded professional growth.

District nominees were only slightly less active in party affairs. Mediators of the process tacitly acknowledged that district nominees had to possess established professional as well as party credentials. The security of life tenure and the greater prestige of district service undoubtedly attracted candidates who would not have considered a territorial post. The more prestigious district posts attracted older party activists with established legal careers; thus, not only did 73 percent of the nominees have prior party activity but they also possessed more judicial experience and greater professional prominence than territorial nominees. In either instance party activity was rewarded; the new political men who worked within the participatory and party-directed political culture of the era gradually filled the lower federal bench.

Nominees of differing qualifications emerged from the judicial selection process. Although they began with similar social origins, academic education, and legal training, the territorial and district nominees diverged significantly in the length and content of their prenomination careers. The unattractiveness of territorial service posed a barrier that divided nominees into two streams; younger, less experienced, and less professionally prestigious nominees went to the territorial courts. As a whole, however, the political and party activism of all the nominees distinguished them from their predecessors.

IV

"A new breed of political judge," complained Timothy Walker, editor of the *Western Law Review*, "has been promoted to the bench,

less by reasons of merit, than . . . service to the party."[34] "Party organizations," he explained, were "but a conspiracy of wolves to hunt
in packs, to run down game and divide the conquest."[35] Walker's
hyperbole was a manifestation of his own deeply held fears about the
baneful influences of party on the professional standards of the bar.
The collective backgrounds of federal court nominees suggest that,
for all of his self-serving denunciations, the law editor correctly perceived a fundamental change in the subterranean selection process.
Partisan activism was an integral feature of the nominees'
backgrounds, more so than it had been during the pre-Jacksonian
years. While the infusion of partisanship underscored the modernizing impact of the second party system, the social bases of the selection
process remained only slightly altered. The change was glacial; a
slightly greater percentage of lawyers with modest social-class origins
obtained federal judicial nominations. A legal career may have allowed the "children of the cabins" to gain prominence, but few of
them reached the federal bench. The nominees were neither a traditional elite nor a modern technical elite; instead, they were, as Walker
suggested, a new breed of "political judge," with social origins similar
to those of their predecessors but with partisan attributes which
stamped them the products of their political culture.

10

THE POLITICS OF JUSTICE

The thirteenth rule . . . contemplates the exclusion of party
or personal influences. . . . Judges will . . . be selected from
the party in power; and as to personal influence, there is no
particular reason to believe it less important with Presidents
and Governors, than . . . with the crowned vice-regents of
Heaven. The rule thus far is purely Utopian.—Theodore
Sedgewick, January, 1846[1]

Between 1829 and 1861 the rise of mass national parties, the surge in
voter turnout, the acceptance of party as a legitimate means of organizing as well as opposing government, and the emergence of well-
articulated local party organizations altered the political landscape
inherited from a previous generation. In these changes, some historians have discovered a profound and rapid shift from a traditional to
a modern political culture; that is, politics became open to greater
numbers and it also became more formally structured by the impersonal bonds of party affiliation and the imposed discipline of party
organization. The emphasis on parties and political modernization
has diminished the political salience and moral dissonance raised by
slavery and the sectional controversy. The conduct and evolution of
the judicial selection process suggests that the political culture of the
era was in the midst of transition from traditional to modern, and that
slavery and sectionalism were indeed significant.

The process became more modern in the sense that it became
more institutionalized, but this occurred only gradually. More than
twenty years elapsed between Andrew Jackson's call for a fuller
cabinet role for the attorney general and Franklin Pierce's decision to
formalize the supervisory role of the attorney general in the selection
process. The systematic involvement of senators of a president's party
in the selection of district judges in their home states was further
evidence of institutionalization, but this attribute of a modern, party-
directed selection process developed slowly and incompletely. Not
until the Pierce administration could senators from the president's
party dictate judicial nominations. Nor was the practice fully established even then. Throughout the era senators failed to invoke

amongst their colleagues an absolute privilege to reject a nominee because he was personally obnoxious. In its most complete sense, senatorial courtesy was a post–Civil War phenomenon.

In the matter of patronage, Leonard White concluded that by 1861 "the legislative branch stood relatively the victor . . . even though the executive still held the high ground."[2] This applied to the judicial selection process. Members of the legislative wing of the president's party emerged as the most important mediators of the process, but chief executives retained the power to initiate the process and they claimed successfully the authority summarily to remove sitting territorial judges. Historians frequently claim that Andrew Jackson modernized the national political culture by implementing an impersonal system of party-directed rotation-in-office, but he was not responsible for the extension of that principle to the territorial judiciary. The presidential removal power emerged in response to the administrative and sectional crises produced by territorial expansion during and following the Mexican War; the judiciary became an instrument of the political goals of subsequent administrations. The traditional independence accorded the territorial judiciary was one of the silent victims of the war.

Limited institutionalization of the selection process was also evident in the influence exerted by various noncongressional mediators. Supreme Court justices, local, state, and territorial party leaders, cabinet members, and the bar had an impact. Lawyers were the least significant. The legal profession was unorganized, fragmented, and decentralized; lawyers, as a collective entity, lacked an effective institutional forum from which to impose professional criteria on the process. Judgments about nominees hinged on a procedure that stressed partisan and personal considerations rather than a formal and impersonal review process in which the bar assumed responsibility for determining the technical expertise of candidates. The competence of nominees concerned every administration, but the process of discerning professional qualities was more informal and diffuse than it has been under the mid-twentieth-century aegis of the American Bar Association's Committee on Federal Judiciary.

Party was the most significant modernizing force in the selection process. It linked the president, the Congress, and the states and territories in a web of commitment. In an era of limited bureaucratic differentiation in government, party imposed adminstrative as well as political coherence on the selection process. The Democratic and Whig parties became administrative agencies through which the authority of the federal courts was planted, nurtured, and sustained in distant states and territories.

These loosely knit, state-centered, and factionalized parties had a limited capacity to fill judgeships in the established states and to extend judicial authority to newly organized territories. In emphasizing the crucial role of party during the era, there is a danger in flattening into a deceptive symmetry the rich transitional character of the second party system. A traditional mode of selection persisted during an era frequently characterized as a period of unrelenting political modernization. Kinship and instrumental friendship connections were most prominent at the inception and the demise of the party system. In the midst of party realignment these informal and personal ties afforded greater assurance of a candidate's political suitability than did a formal shared party affiliation. During periods of party equilibrium, the patron-client mode of selection diminished, although it never disappeared entirely.

The diverse pressures that shaped the lower federal judiciary defy the neat compartmentalizations of the "electoral machine" and ideological interest descriptions usually assigned to parties of the era. Judicial nominations were important to the party in power, but presidents and principal mediators usually realized that appointees to the constitutional courts were likely to outlast them in public office. In the territories, chief executives also wanted judges who would sustain administrative policy and whose appointments might also enhance the party at the ballot box. There were not, however, meaningful differences in the ideological commitments of Whig and Democratic presidents; both wanted judges who would maintain federal authority, respect state rights, further the development of the state or territorial economy, and sustain major administrative policies. Whig and Democratic presidents selected nominees with similar backgrounds.

The selection process increasingly reflected the underlying ideological imperatives that eventually destroyed the artificial second party system. Before the Mexican War, chief executives sometimes sought guarantees that judicial nominees would uphold the Fugitive Slave Law of 1793, but after the war slavery dramatically insinuated itself into the fabric of federal justice. The party system was conditioned to ignore the moral imperative raised by slavery; the lower federal courts became a principal means of sustaining that myopia. By thrusting political responsibility for settlement of the sectional controversy on the federal courts, the Compromise of 1850 and later the Kansas-Nebraska Act compelled presidents and sectional spokesmen in the legislative wings of the two parties to examine the political and constitutional views of judicial nominees. In the territories, judges became the representatives of conflicting sectional interests. In the states, presidents after 1848 were anxious for district court judges to sustain political tranquillity by encouraging effective enforcement of the Fugitive Slave Act of 1850 and the neutrality and slave trade laws. The Civil War quickly obliterated the moral and legal contradictions that the leaders of the second party system had attempted to maintain through the selection process.

Of course, no president ever entirely succeeded in molding the federal judiciary to his will. The openness of the process, the constitutionally mandated separation of powers, and administrative exigencies frustrated the boldest and most imaginative appointment strategies. This was especially the case with territorial nominations. The limited tenure, enforced family separations, meager pay, harsh working conditions, and skepticism of residents that accompanied a territorial judgeship restricted the pool of candidates from which a chief executive might choose. The result was a youthful, ambitious, and inexperienced territorial judiciary that frequently compounded rather than eased the political and administrative turmoil that beset every territory.

The politics of federal justice derived from the contradictory and contentious qualities of a transitional two-party system. At least in the selection of lower federal court judges, the political culture of the era moved gradually, incrementally, unevenly, and incompletely toward political modernity.

Appendix A

SOCIAL ORIGINS AND
SOCIAL-CLASS POSITIONS

Social status is an elusive historical phenomenon. A host of conditions, including scholarly disagreement over what socio-economic and other conditions contribute to an individual's status, how best to measure status, and how most effectively to relate specific findings to society as a whole, contributes to the ambiguity. The customary separation of men into the "better, middling, and inferior" sorts undoubtedly holds for the late colonial and antebellum eras, but fitting individuals into class levels remains problematic. The historical investigation of status has relied heavily upon occupation. Social origin has been viewed as the consequence of a father's occupational pursuits; social-class position has been deemed the product of a son's particular calling. Social mobility has been the consequence of occupational differences between father and son. Ralph Dahrendorf and Edward Pessen, among others, have rejected occupation as a guide to status, finding it useful but uncertain. Both social origin and social-class position are multidimensional; they involve other attributes such as wealth, tradition of family importance, level of education, public service, and spouse's status.[1] This study attempts to reconstruct the social origins and social-class positions (tables 12 and 13) of the pre–Civil War lower federal judiciary by systematically combining a variety of variables.

SOCIAL ORIGINS

Estimates of social origins were based on eight indicators. These were drawn from the works of Sidney Aronson, Edward Pessen, and (jointly) Charles Westoff, Marvin Bressler, and Philip C. Sagi.[2] The specific weights assigned to each indicator reflect the rank order developed by Westoff, Bressler, and Sagi. However, this study includes variables (political activism, occupational prominence) they did not stipulate and gives more emphasis to paternal occupation and wealth than they believe is justified.

The occupation and wealth of a father were important but not definitive indicators of a judge's social origins. The order of occupations (table 14) closely follows the scheme developed by Aronson.[3] When fathers held multiple occupations, the highest ranking occupation was used. Estate records, tax lists, state censuses, and the federal censuses of 1850 and 1860 provided wealth data. These valuable sources suffer serious shortcomings. Estate inventories are the most accurate, but they treat only the end of a man's life and often deal only with personal instead of real property holdings. Tax lists invariably understate the actual value of property; often it is impossible to determine the degree of underestimation.[4] The federal manuscript census is a comprehensive source of wealth data, but it is concentrated at the end of the antebellum period. The data taken from these sources were used at face value in all but two cases. In the first,

TABLE 12
INDICATORS OF NOMINEES' SOCIAL ORIGINS

Indicator	Rank	Value
Father's Occupation	High Ranking	10
	Middle Ranking	5
	Low Ranking	1
Father's Wealth	Great—$25,000 plus	10
	Impressive—$5,000–$25,000	8
	Modest—$1,000–$5,000	6
	Little—Less than $1,000	4
Father's Political Activity	National Office	8
	State Office	6
	Local Office	4
Father's Highest Level of Education	College Graduate	8
	Attended College	6
	Secondary	4
Prominence of Father in Occupation	National	6
	State	3
	Local	1
Family's Generational Level in North America	5 or More Generations	3
	3–4	2
	1–2	1
Tradition of Family Importance	National	3
	State	2
	Local	1
Father's Military Service	Field Officer	3
	Junior Officer	2
	Enlisted	1

TABLE 13
INDICATORS OF NOMINEES' SOCIAL-CLASS POSITIONS

Indicator	Rank	Value
Prominence in Legal Profession	National	10
	State	8
	Local	4
Judge's Wealth	Great—$25,000 plus	10
	Impressive—$5,000–$25,000	8
	Modest—$1,000–$5,000	6
	Little—Less than $1,000	4
Political Activity	National Office	8
	State Office	6
	Local Office	4
Education	College Graduate	8
	Attended College	6
	Secondary	4
Secondary Occupation	High	6
	Middle	3
	Low	1

TABLE 14
RANKING OF OCCUPATIONAL CATEGORIES

High Ranking

Landed Gentry	Living on estate but holding no slaves, so described in secondary source.
Planter	Living in agricultural setting with 20 or more slaves.
Merchant	Conducting business beyond limits of a single store.
Professional	Doctor, lawyer, minister, military or naval officer, professor, surveyor.

Middle Ranking

Artisan	Skilled tradesman.
Proprietor	Owner of manufacturing or mining enterprise.
Large Farmer	Owner of 100 acres or more or indicated in secondary literature as a "prosperous" farmer.
Teacher	
Sea Captain	
Shopkeeper	Seller of goods, not engaged in manufacture.
Tavern/Innkeeper	

Low Ranking

Small Farmer	Farming less than 100 acres or described as lacking signs of prosperity.
Laborer—Seaman	Working for wage doing manual labor on land or sea.

estimates of the real property holding in the 1850 census were assumed to constitute 80 percent of total wealth; an additional 20 percent was added to arrive at an estimate of total wealth. In the second, when fathers held slaves not included in the specific wealth record, an additional $500 for each slave was added to their holdings.[5] The highest found value was used to determine the father's wealth.

Lee Soltow and Robert Gallman provide the most explicit statements of wealth distribution. Alice Hansen Jones is helpful on the late eighteenth century. Thus, their estimates, while undoubtedly high for satisfactory use in the early national period, are the best available.[6]

Estimates of occupational prominence and family importance were based on four sources: genealogies, obituaries, county histories, and the voluminous letters of application and recommendation in the National Archives. Although often uneven in quantity and accuracy, these sources offered invaluable clues to a father's occupational prominence and the importance of a judge's family. If a source or sources identified a father's occupation but failed to suggest his prominence, the father was deemed locally important. If a father's calling were known to a county historian, genealogist, obituary writer, or supporter of an applicant, then he must have been at least locally prominent.

These indicators of social origins are ranked on a scale from one to ten, with one the lowest. The ranking attempts to account not only for internal differences within a variable, but also the relative importance of variables in relation to one another. This technique has the value of making implicit assumptions explicit, but the numbers are, and should be treated as, approximations. A total score was achieved by summing a father's values. Elite fathers had between thirty-five and fifty-one points, prominent fathers between eighteen and thirty-four, and modest fathers between four and seventeen. The breaking points in these divisions represented the sums of the high, middle, and low values of each indicator. An arbitrary rule specified that two conditions had to be met to estimate social origins. First, at least four of the eight indicators had to be known. Second, of these four indicators one had to be either father's wealth or occupation. When all indicators were not established, a score was obtained by dividing the number of known variables into total points. The quotient was then compared with the quotient obtained by dividing the total number of indicators (eight) into the sums of the highest and lowest values for each indicator.

Elite, prominent, and modest social origins do not equate with high, middle, and low status. Modest probably corresponded to the bulk of the population in the late colonial and early national eras. Certainly, the evidence leaves no doubt that the sons of the lowest elements of the social order—slaves, free blacks, Indians, and white laborers—did not contribute to the antebellum lower federal courts. Elite and prominent origins suggest that a judge's background offered exceptional advantages, although significant differences existed between the two categories. The lowest elements of society provided no judges; the top of the social order provided few. Until more is known about the contours of early American society, historians will have to accept clarity rather than precision; the social origins of the judiciary remain open to further refinement.[7]

SOCIAL-CLASS POSITIONS

Social origins and adult social status may vary. In order to understand the social bases of the recruitment process, the relative positions of appointees within society must be established. The five indicators of social-class position (table 13) were derived primarily from Aronson and Pessen. The most critical indicators of social-class position were wealth and occupation; secondary occupation, political activity, and education were given less emphasis. Insufficient data negated an attempt to analyze the impact of marriage on social position. Wealth records, however, often did reveal a wife's contribution to her husband's financial position.

The federal manuscript censuses of 1850, 1860, and 1870, tax rolls, and estate records provided wealth data. Slaveholding was treated in the same fashion as described under social origins. While useable wealth data were obtained on 70 percent of the judges, they were concentrated in the period after appointment; evidence of preappointment wealth holding could be found for only 33 percent of the judges. Three reasons explain the paucity of preappointment wealth data. First, the federal manuscript censuses cover the end of the second party system, but about 49 percent of the judges were appointed before 1850. Second, not all of the judges had values recorded in the 1850 or 1860 censuses. Failure to list wealth was often as much a manifestation of the census taker's inefficiency as a judge's impoverishment. When wealth information was not listed, it was considered missing datum. Third, state and local tax lists and censuses, while invaluable supplements to the federal census, do not provide comprehensive coverage for the pre-1850 period. When multiple wealth values were obtained, the judge was assigned the highest value.

Other indicators of preappointment social-class position were more accessible than wealth data. Two of particular importance were a nominee's prominence in legal practice and his secondary, nonlegal occupation. Without undertaking the laborious, time-consuming, and probably impossible task of preparing detailed analyses of each judge's legal practice, estimates of professional prominence are tentative and subject to error. Histories of the bench and bar, county histories, genealogies, obituaries, and, perhaps most importantly, letters of application and recommendation in the National Archives offer some insight into a nominee's prominence. These last, whether favorable or antagonistic to a candidate, usually addressed an applicant's standing in the legal profession, the scope of his legal practice, and whether he was uniformly respected by the local or state bars. Often vague, excessively adulatory, and frustratingly contradictory, the letters nevertheless provide the readiest means of assessing an appointee's professional standing. When used in conjunction with other sources, they provide a crude measure of a complex and changing phenomenon.

The judges' preappointment secondary occupations (table 14) were also used to determine social-class position. Holding a secondary occupation equal to or lesser than the status of a lawyer influenced the appointee's social-class position. All secondary occupations held from adulthood (age eighteen) to appointment were considered, but only the highest ranking nonlegal occupation was used to compute social-class position.

The five indicators of social-class position were weighted and totaled to provide a composite score. Judges with elite positions scored between thirty and forty-two, prominent between eighteen and twenty-nine, and modest between four and seventeen. At least three of the five indicators had to be present to establish social-class position; one of these had to be either wealth or prominence in legal profession. Missing data were treated in the same fashion as under social origins.

The social-class position did not mirror basic divisions in the social order from low to high. Modest position did not equate with the lowest elements of the antebellum social order. Modest social position indicated that a jurist probably occupied a place, despite his occupation, in the middle of the social order. Of course, the nominees' legal occupations differentiated them from the essentially nonprofessional and agricultural work force. Men of modest position had no special claim to either wealth or professional prominence. Men of prominent status were a distinct minority. The elite were truly unique.

Appendix B

KINSHIP AND PARTISANSHIP IN THE SELECTION PROCESS

KINSHIP RELATIONS BETWEEN LOWER FEDERAL COURT NOMINEES AND PRINCIPAL MEDIATORS OF THE SELECTION PROCESS

Andrew Jackson's Administration

Philip P. Barbour, Eastern District of Virginia, was the cousin of John Strode Barbour, a Democratic congressman from Culpepper County, Virginia. *Biographical Directory of American Congress* (Washington, D.C.: Government Printing Office, 1971), p. 550.

Charles Scott Bibb, associate justice of Arkansas territory, was the son of Sen. George M. Bibb of Kentucky. L. F. Johnson, *The History of Franklin County, Kentucky* (Frankfort, Ky.: Roberts Printing Co., 1912), p. 84.

Charles Biddle, rejected nominee for associate justice of Florida territory, was the brother of Nicholas Biddle, president of the Second Bank of the United States. *Biddle Family* (Philadelphia: Historical Society of Pennsylvania, 1932), pp. 22–23.

Morgan W. Brown, district of Tennessee, was the brother of William L. Brown, a prominent Jackson party leader in Nashville, and the brother-in-law of Supreme Court Justice John Catron. Biographical Sketch No. 33, TSLA.

John A. Cameron, associate justice of Florida territory, was the brother of Duncan Cameron, judge of North Carolina Supreme Court, and Thomas Nash Cameron, a North Carolina state legislator. John H. Wheeler, *Historical Sketches of North Carolina*, 2 vols. (Philadelphia: Lippincott, Grambo & Co., 1851), 2:130.

Edward Cross, associate justice of Arkansas territory, was the brother-in-law of Chester A. Ashley, a Jackson party organizer in Arkansas, and the cousin of Gov. John Pope. John Hallum, *Biographical and Pictorial History of Arkansas*, 2 vols. (Albany, N.Y.: Weed, Parsons and Company, 1887), 1:120.

Samuel H. Harper, district of Louisiana, was the brother-in-law of Dr. William Lattimore, a former delegate from Mississippi territory and a Jackson organizer in Louisiana, and cousin of Pryor Lea, congressman from Tennessee. Mrs. Sam A. McPherson, "Lea Genealogy," *Louisiana Genealogical Register* 17 (June 1971): 166–69.

Matthew Harvey, district of New Hampshire, was the brother of Congressman Jonathan Harvey. *BDAC*, p. 1082.

Upton Scott Heath, district of Maryland, was the brother of Congressman James P. Heath and a distant kinsman of Roger B. Taney, Jackson's secretary of the treasury and later chief justice of the Supreme Court. "Heath Family of Maryland," Genealogical Section, HSP.

David Irvin, associate justice of Michigan territory, was the brother of Congressman and Ohio Supreme Court Justice William W. Irvin. Edgar Woods, *Albemarle County Virginia* (Charlottesville, Va.: The Michie Company, 1901), pp. 232–34.

Benjamin Johnson, chief justice of Arkansas territory and district judge of Arkansas, was the brother of Representative and Senator Richard M. Johnson of Kentucky. Leland Meyer, *The Life and Times of Col. Richard Mentor Johnson of Kentucky* (New York: Columbia University Press, 1932), pp. 13–47.

Thomas Lacy, associate justice of Arkansas territory, was the nephew of John Overton of Nashville, Tennessee, a friend of Jackson and Democratic organizer. Hallum, *Biographical and Pictorial History of Arkansas*, 1:97.

Thomas Bell Monroe, district of Kentucky, was the son-in-law of John Adair, a Jackson leader in Kentucky. Lewis Collins and Richard H. Collins, *History of Kentucky*, 2 vols., (Louisville, Ky.: By the authors, 1877), 2:32.

Benjamin Tappan, rejected district judge for Ohio, was the brother-in-law of former Congressman John M. Goodnow and former Congressman and Ohio Supreme Court Justice John C. Wright. Genealogical File, Benjamin Tappan Papers, LC.

Thomas Randall, associate justice of Florida territory, was the nephew of Peter Hagner, the third auditor of the treasury, and the son-in-law of William Wirt, a former attorney general of the United States. Genealogical File, Randall Family Papers, MHS.

Ross Wilkins, associate justice of Michigan territory and district judge of Michigan, was the nephew of Sen. William Wilkins of Pennsylvania. "John Wilkins, A Merchant of Carlisle in 1763—His Ancestry and Autobiography," *Collections of the Kittochtinny Historical Society* 2 (1904): 209–20; Wilkins Family Folder, WPHS.

Martin Van Buren's Administration

Isaac H. Bronson, associate justice of Florida territory, was the brother-in-law of Micah Sterling, a former congressman and member of the New York State Senate. Albert Mack Sterling, *The Sterling Genealogy*, 2 vols. (New York: The Grafton Press, 1909), 1:403.

Mahlon Dickerson, district of New Jersey, was the brother of Congressman Philemon Dickerson. *History of Morris County New Jersey* (New York: W. W. Munsell & Co., 1882), pp. 25, 63.

Philemon Dickerson, district of New Jersey, was the brother of Mahlon Dickerson, Van Buren's secretary of the navy.

Isaac Pennybacker, district of Western Virginia, was the cousin of Democratic Congressman Green B. Samuels. Pennypacker Genealogical Materials, Manuscript Division, UWV.

John Tyler's Administration

William Henry Brockenbrough, who declined to serve as associate justice of Florida territory, was a nephew of Thomas Ritchie and a distant kinsman of Sen. William H. Roane of Virginia. He was also the cousin of John White Brockenbrough, whom Polk appointed to the Western District of Virginia. "Brockenbrough Family," *The Virginia Magazine of History and Biography*, 5 (April 1898): 447–49; 6 (July 1898): 82–85.

John B. Christian, rejected as judge for the Eastern District of Virginia, was the brother-in-law of President John Tyler. Robert Seager II, *And Tyler Too: A Biography of John and Julia Gardiner Tyler* (New York: McGraw Hill, 1963), p. 131.

Theodore Howard McCaleb, district of Louisiana, was the brother-in-law of Mississippi Democratic Congressman William H. Hammett. *Biographical and Historical Memoirs of Louisiana* (Chicago: Goodspeed Publishing Co., 1892), pp. 212–13.

Samuel Prentiss, district of Vermont, was the brother of Congressman John H. Prentiss of Vermont. *BDAC*, p. 1566.

Thomas S. Wilson, associate justice of Iowa territory, was a second cousin of Congressman Samuel Stokely of Ohio and a distant kinsman of Congressman Green B. Samuels of Virginia. Joseph B. Doyle, *Twentieth Century History of Steubenville and Jefferson County, Ohio* (Chicago: Lewis Historical Publishing Co., 1910), p. 423. Thomas S. Wilson to Stephen A. Douglas, June 17, 1859, Douglas Papers, UC.

James K. Polk's Administration

John W. Brockenbrough, Western District of Virginia, was the
nephew of Thomas Ritchie. *The Virginia Magazine of History and
Biography,* 5 (April 1898): 447–49; 6 (July 1898): 82–85.
John J. Dyer, district of Iowa, was the brother-in-law of Sen. Isaac S.
Pennybacker of Virginia. *Pennypacker Genealogical Materials,*
UWV.
William A. Hall, who declined to serve as associate justice of Oregon
territory, was the brother of Congressman Willard P. Hall of Mis-
souri. John F. Philips, "Governor Willard Preble Hall," *Missouri
Historical Review* 5 (January 1911): 70–71.
James Turney, who declined to be associate justice of Oregon terri-
tory, was a cousin of Sen. Hopkins L. Turney of Tennessee. Turney
Genealogical File, TSLA.

Zachary Taylor's Administration

David Cooper, associate justice of Minnesota territory, was the
brother of Sen. James Cooper of Pennyslvania. John Livingston,
*Portraits of Eminent Americans now Living: Biographical and Historical
Memoir of Their Lives and Actions* (New York: R. Graighead, Printer,
1854), 4:15–19.
Bradley Burr Meeker, associate justice of Minnesota territory, was the
nephew of Sen. Truman Smith of Connecticut. *Commemorative and
Biographical Record of Fairfield County Connecticut,* 2 vols. (Chicago: J.
H. Beers & Co., 1899), 2:683, 1118–19. John M. Clayton to John J.
Crittenden, April 18, 1849, John J. Crittenden Papers, LC.
Daniel Ringo, district of Arkansas, was the brother-in-law of influen-
tial Whig leader Frederick Trapnall. Daniel Ringo Biographical
Folder, AHC.

Millard Fillmore's Administration

Thomas Nelson, chief justice of Oregon territory, was the son of Whig
Congressman William Nelson of New York. Sidney Teiser, "The
Second Chief Justice of Oregon Territory: Thomas Nelson," *Oregon
Historical Quarterly* 48 (September 1947): 214–15.
Ogden Hoffman, Jr., Northern District of California, was the son of
Ogden Hoffman, an influential Whig leader in New York City.
Eugene A. Hoffman, *Genealogy of the Hoffman Family* (New York:
Dodd, Mead & Co., 1899), pp. 279–81, 383–88.
Rush Elmore, associate justice of Kansas territory, was the brother-

in-law of Sen. Benjamin Fitzpatrick of Alabama. Elmore Family
Collection, ADHA.

John James Gilchrist, chief justice of the Court of Claims, was the
son-in-law of former New Hampshire governor and prominent
Democratic leader Henry Hubbard. Henry Saunderson, *History of
Charleston, New Hampshire* (Claremont, N. H.: The Claremont Manufacturing Co., n.d.), pp. 361–62.

Edward Randolph Harden, associate justice of Nebraska territory,
was the brother-in-law of Supreme Court Justice James Moore
Wayne. Genealogical Folder, Edward Harden Papers, DU.

Franklin Pierce's Administration

Perry E. Brocchus, associate justice of New Mexico, was a distant
kinsman of Senators Clement C. Clay, Jr., and Jeremiah Clemens of
Alabama. Clement C. Clay, Jr., to Franklin Pierce, December 17,
1853, RRAFJ, New Mexico, RG 60, NA. Jeremiah Clemens to Caleb
Cushing, March 18, 1853, Caleb Cushing Papers, LC. John M.
Bernhisel to Brigham Young, February 5, 1853, Brigham Young
Papers, CALDS.

Sterling G. Cato, associate justice of Kansas territory, was the brother
of Lewis Cato, a prominent Democratic party organizer in southern
Alabama. Cato Family File, ADHA.

West Hughes Humphreys, district of Tennessee, was the brother-in-
law of prominent Tennessee Democratic leaders Aaron V. Brown
and Gideon Pillow. Allan Sparrow Humphreys, *Humphreys Genealogy* (Fayetteville, Ark.: n.p., n.d.), p. 64–65.

Charles Anthony Ingersoll, district of Connecticut, was the uncle of
Congressman Colin M. Ingersoll. Charles S. Ripley, *The Ingersolls of
Hampshire* (Boston: A. Mudge & Son, Printers, 1893), pp. 142–43,
158–59.

John Fitch Kinney, chief justice of Utah territory, was the brother-
in-law of prominent Iowa Democrat Augustus Hall. John Fitch
Kinney File, Biography Division, NHS.

Joseph Henry Lumpkin, who declined to serve as associate justice of
the Court of Claims, was the nephew of Democratic Congressman
John H. Lumpkin of Georgia. Florrie Carter Smith, *The History of
Oglethorpe County, Georgia* (Washington, Ga.: Wilkes Publishing Co.,
1972), pp. 110–14.

William Matthews Merrick, circuit court of the District of Columbia,
was the son of former senator William D. Merrick, the son-in-law of
prominent Kentucky politician Charles A. Wickliff, and a

brother-in-law of Joseph Holt, another prominent Kentucky politician. *Washington Evening Star,* February 4, 1889, p. 5; Daniel D. Huyett, *Huyett, Merrick and Kindred Families of Maryland* (Baltimore: For the Author, 1963), pp. 7–37.

Victor Monroe, associate justice of Washington territory, was the son of District Judge Thomas Bell Monroe of Kentucky and the brother-in-law of the daughter of Supreme Court Justice Robert Grier. James Barnett Adair, *Adair History and Genealogy* (Los Angeles: Boylan and Boylan, 1924), pp. 88–90.

John William Henderson Underwood, who declined to serve as associate justice of Utah territory, was the son of Judge William Henderson Underwood, a prominent judicial figure and Democratic organizer in Georgia. *Appleton's Cyclopedia of American Biography,* 6 vols. (New York: D. Appleton and Company, 1889), 6:210.

James Buchanan's Administration

Samuel W. Black, associate justice of Nebraska territory, was the son-in-law of District Judge Thomas Irwin of Pittsburgh. Robert W. Furnas, ed., *Transactions and Reports of the Nebraska State Historical Society* 1 (1885): 94–95.

William G. Blackwood, associate justice of New Mexico territory, was the brother-in-law of New Mexico territorial delegate Miguel A. Otero. Otero to Jeremiah S. Black, January 31, 1859, RRAFJ, New Mexico, RG 60, NA.

Perry E. Brocchus, associate justice of New Mexico territory, was a distant kinsman of Senator Clement C. Clay, Jr., of Alabama. John M. Bernhisel to Brigham Young, February 5, 1853, Young Papers, CALDS.

John Cadwalader, Eastern District of Pennsylvania, was the son-in-law of Horace Binney. *Philadelphia North American,* June 16, 1907, pp. 27–29.

William Davidson, associate justice of New Mexico territory, was the son of Democratic Congressman Thomas Green Davidson of Louisiana. Miguel A. Otero to Jeremiah S. Black, January 15, 1860, RRAFJ, New Mexico, RG 60, NA.

Rush Elmore, associate justice of Kansas territory, was the brother-in-law of Sen. Benjamin Fitzpatrick of Alabama. Elmore Family Collection, ADHA.

Charles Eugene Flandrau, associate justice of Minnesota territory, was a distant kinsman of Judge Wilson McCandless of Pittsburgh. Theodore Agnew, *Address Before the Allegheny County Bar Association*

(Pittsburgh: Pittsburgh Gazette Press, 1882), pp. 17–18.

Robert Patterson Flenniken, associate justice of Utah territory, was the brother-in-law of former district judge Thomas Irwin of Pittsburgh and uncle of Gov. Samuel W. Black of Nebraska territory. Franklin Ellis, *History of Fayette County, Pennsylvania* (Philadelphia: L. H. Everts & Co., 1882), p. 145.

Augustus Hall, associate justice of Nebraska territory, was the brother-in-law of Chief Justice John F. Kinney of Utah and a prominent Nebraska Democratic leader. Augustus Hall File, Biography Division, NHS.

Edward Randolph Harden, who declined to serve as associate justice of Utah, was the brother-in-law of Supreme Court Justice James Moore Wayne. Genealogical Folder, Edward Harden Papers, DU.

John F. Kinney, chief justice of Utah territory, was the brother-in-law of Augustus Hall, associate justice of Nebraska territory and a prominent Democratic party figure in Iowa and Nebraska. John F. Kinney File, NHS.

Rensselaer Russell Nelson, associate justice of Minnesota territory and district judge of Minnesota, was the son of Supreme Court Justice Samuel Nelson. *Progressive Men of Minnesota* (Chicago: W. H. Beers Co., 1897), pp. 370–71.

William E. Niblack, who was not confirmed as associate justice of Nebraska territory, was a cousin of Congressman Silas Leslie Niblack of Florida. *BDAC*, p. 1470.

TABLE 15
FEDERAL LOWER COURT NOMINEES WITH KNOW KINSHIP TIES TO PRINCIPAL MEDIATORS AT NOMINATION, 1829–61[1]

PRESIDENTAL ADMINISTRATIONS

Type of Relationship[2]	Jackson No.	%	Van Buren No.	%	Tyler No.	%	Polk No.	%	Taylor No.	%	Fillmore No.	%	Pierce No.	%	Buchanan No.	%
Primary																
Father-son	1	3	—	—	—	—	—	—	—	—	2	9	2	4	3	7
Brothers	7	18	2	12	1	4	1	6	1	10	—	—	1	2	—	—
Secondary																
Uncle-nephew	4	10	—	—	1	4	2	13	1	10	1	4	2	4	—	—
Father-in-law-son-in-law	1	3	—	—	—	—	—	—	—	—	—	—	—	—	2	5
Brother-in-law	4	10	1	6	2	9	1	6	1	10	—	—	3	5	6	14
Tertiary																
Cousins	1	—	1	6	—	—	—	—	—	—	—	—	—	—	1	2
Great-uncle-great-nephew	—	—	—	—	—	—	—	—	—	—	—	—	—	—	—	—
Distant kinsman	1	3	—	—	1	4	—	—	—	—	—	—	1	2	2	5
Percent of all nominess in category	47		23		23		25		30		13		17		33	
Total number	(19)		(4)		(5)		(4)		(3)		(3)		(9)		(14)	

1. Principle mediators were defined as presidents, senators, representatives, delegates, Supreme Court justices, cabinet or high civil service officers serving at the time of nomination and state and territorial party leaders.

2. While multiple kinship connections may have existed between one candidate and several mediators, only the closest was used.

TABLE 16
NOMINATING PRESIDENT BY NOMINEES' PARTISAN AFFILIATIONS
AT NOMINATION

| President | Number in Category[1] | POLITICAL AFFILIATION | | | Total % |
		Jacksonian Democrat	Whig	Unknown	
Jackson	40	100.0	—	—	100.0
Van Buren	17	100.0	—	—	100.0
Tyler	22	50.0	45.0	5.0	100.0
Polk	16	100.0	—	—	100.0
Taylor	10	—	100.0	—	100.0
Fillmore	23	9.0	91.0	—	100.0
Pierce	54	100.0	—	—	100.0
Buchanan	42	100.0	—	—	100.0
Percent in Category		81.0	18.0	1.0	100.0
Total Number	(224)	(182)	(41)	(1)	

1. Includes renominations of territorial judges from the same or previous administrations.

ABBREVIATIONS USED IN NOTES

AAE, RG 60, NA	Abstracts of Applications and Endorsements for Judicial Office, Record Group 60, National Archives.
ADHA	Alabama Department of History and Archives
AG, LR, RG 60, NA	Attorney General's Papers, Letters Received, RG 60, NA
AG, LS, RG 60, NA	Attorney General's Papers, Letters Sent, RG 60, NA
AOC, RG 59, NA	Acceptances and Orders for Commissions, RG 59, NA
AHC	Arkansas History Commission
BECHS	Buffalo and Erie County Historical Society
BHC, DPL	Burton Historical Collection, Detroit Public Library
CALDS	Church Archives, Church of Jesus Christ of Latter-Day-Saints
CHS	Chicago Historical Society
CR, RG 59, NA	Correspondence Registers, Secretary of State, RG 59, NA
DU	Duke University
GSLDS	Genealogical Society Library, Church of Jesus Christ of Latter-Day-Saints
HSP	Historical Society of Pennsylvania
HU	Huntington Library
JH	*Journal History*
IP, RG 233, NA	Impeachment Papers, RG 233, NA
LAR, M-639, RG 59, NA	Letters of Application and Recommendation During the Administration of Andrew Jackson, Microfilm Publication 639, RG 59, NA
LAR, M-687, RG 59, NA	Letters of Application and Recommendation During the Administrations of Martin Van Buren, William Henry Harrison, and John Tyler, Microfilm Publication 687, RG, 59, NA

LAR, M-873, RG 59, NA	Letters of Application and Recommendation During the Administrations of James K. Polk, Zachary Taylor, and Millard Fillmore, Microfilm Publication 873, RG 59, NA
LC	Library of Congress
LRD, RG 59, NA	Letters of Resignation and Declination, RG 59, NA
LSU	Louisiana State University
MHS	Maryland Historical Society
MINNHS	Minnesota Historical Society
MISDHA	Mississippi Department of History and Archives
MOHS	Missouri Historical Society
MPTC, RG 59, NA	Miscellaneous Permanent and Temporary Commissions of Federal Judges, RG 59, NA
NHS	Nebraska Historical Society
NJHS	New Jersey Historical Society
OHS	Oregon Historical Society
RAEJ, RG 60, NA	Register of Applicants and Endorsements for Appointment as Judges, U.S. Attorneys and Marshals, RG 60, NA
RRAFJ, RG 60, NA	Records Relating to the Appointment of Federal Judges, District Attorneys and Marshals, RG 60, NA
SCJ, RG 46, NA	Senate Committee on the Judiciary Files, RG 46, NA
SEJ	*Journal of the Executive Proceedings of the Senate of the United States*
SHC, UNC	Southern Historical Collection, University of North Carolina
SNF, RG 46, NA	Senate Nominations File, RG 46, NA
TSLA	Tennessee State Library and Archives
UC	University of Chicago
UCB	University of California—Berkeley
UHS	Utah Historical Society
UR	University of Rochester
UTX	University of Texas
UWV	University of West Virginia
WPHS	Western Pennsylvania Historical Society

NOTES

INTRODUCTION

1. For a discussion of the literature on political parties, patronage, and judicial selection, see the bibliographical essay.

2. James K. Polk, *The Diary of James K. Polk During His Presidency, 1845–1849*, ed. Milo C. Quaife, 3:419.

3. Samuel P. Huntington, *Political Order in Changing Societies*, pp. 8–24, 93–139.

4. See Appendix B.

5. See Appendix B.

CHAPTER 1

1. Andrew W. McDonald to William Armstrong, February 19, 1832, James G. Bryce Folder, SNF, RG 46, NA.

2. The quotes are from Robert Remini, *The Revolutionary Age of Andrew Jackson* (New York: Harper & Row, 1976), p. 3; and Lynn L. Marshall, "The Strange Stillbirth of the Whig Party," *American Historical Review* 72 (January 1967): 445–68.

3. James Sterling Young, *The Washington Community, 1800–1828*, pp. 227–54. Young reaches the dubious conclusion that Jackson succeeded in transcending the confines of Washington.

4. Andrew Jackson to Martin Van Buren, November 11, 1832, Andrew Jackson Papers, LC.

5. As quoted in John S. Bassett, *The Life of Andrew Jackson*, 2:447.

6. John S. Bassett and J. Franklin Jameson, eds., *The Correspondence of Andrew Jackson*, 4:11–12.

7. *Pittsburgh Gazette*, January 17, 1832; Erik M. Erikson, "The Federal Civil Service Under President Jackson," *Mississippi Valley Historical Review* 13 (March 1927): 517–38.

8. Carl Russell Fish, "Removals of Officials by the Presidents of the United States," in *Annual Report of the American Historical Association* 1 (1893): 73.

9. Richard P. Longaker, "Andrew Jackson and the Judiciary," *Political Science Quarterly* 71 (September 1956): 341–64; Homer Cummings and Carl McFarland, *Federal Justice*, pp. 507–8; Curtis P. Nettles, "The Mississippi Valley and the Federal Judiciary, 1807–1837," *Mississippi Valley Historical Review* 12 (September 1925): 202–26.

10. Erwin C. Surrency, "A History of Federal Courts," *Missouri Law Review* 28 (1963): 214–44; R. Kent Newmyer, "Justice Story on Circuit and a Neglected Phase of American Legal History," *American Journal of Legal History* 14 (April 1970): 112–35.

11. William W. Blume and Elizabeth G. Brown, "Territorial Courts and Law: Unifying Factors in the Development of American Legal Institutions," *Michigan Law Review* 61 (November 1962, January 1963): 39–106, 467–538.

12. U. S., *Constitution*, Art. II, sec. 2. Harold W. Chase, *Federal Judges: The Appointing Power* (Minneapolis: University of Minnesota Press, 1972), pp. 4–6, argues that lower constitutional court judges can be viewed as inferior in a relational sense and, therefore, susceptible to appointment without the advice and consent of the Senate. Such an argument seems dubious in view of the debates at Philadelphia in 1787 over the appointing power. The framers consciously determined to avoid vesting the power exclusively in the executive. See John Ferling, "The Senate and Federal Judges: The Intent of the Founding Fathers," *Capitol Studies* 2 (Winter 1974): 57–70.

13. U. S., *Statutes at Large*, vol. 1, p. 73.

14. *American Insurance Company* v. *Canter*, 1 Peters 11 (1828).

15. Andrew Jackson to Martin Van Buren, October 27, 1834, in Samuel G. Heiskell, *Andrew Jackson and Early Tennessee History*, 3:507; John A. Bryan to Benjamin Tappan, October 19, 1833, Benjamin Tappan Papers, LC.

16. Caleb Atwater to Andrew Jackson, March 13, 1829, Andrew Jackson Papers, LC.

17. Carl Wittke, ed., *The History of the State of Ohio*, vol. 3, *The Passing of the Frontier: 1825–1850*, Francis P. Weisenburger, pp. 213, 233, 236–37; William Burke to Andrew Jackson, February 9, 1829; Thomas Gillespie to Elijah Hayward, February 18, 1829; James Ross to William B. Lewis, February 25, 1829; LAR, M-639, RG 59, NA.

18. Joseph G.Tregle, "Louisiana in the Age of Jackson: A Study in Ego Politics" (Ph.D. diss., University of Pennsylvania, 1954), pp. 210–13, 360–71.

19. Alexander Porter to Josiah S. Johnston, January 23, 1830, Josiah S. Johnston Papers, HSP; Andrew Davidson to Andrew Jackson, January 28, 1829; Sebastian Hiriart to Jackson, February 12, 1829, LAR, M-639, RG 59, NA; Tregle, "Louisiana in the Age of Jackson," pp. 204–5, 371–74.

20. Alexander Porter to Josiah S. Johnston, December 4, 1828, Johnston Papers, HSP; Alfred Hannan et al. to John Quincy Adams, November 28, 1828; Thomas H. Williams to Martin Gordon, February 26, 1829, LAR, M-639, RG 59, NA.

21. Samuel H. Harper to Andrew Jackson, February 26, 1829, LAR, M-639, RG 59, NA; Alexander Porter to Josiah S. Johnston, January 23, 1830, Johnston Papers, HSP.

22. *Portsmouth Journal*, August 7, 1830.

23. Andrew Dunlap to Andrew Jackson, August 4, 1830, Jackson Papers, LC; Leonard D. White, *The Jacksonians: A Study in Administrative History* (New York: Macmillan Co., 1954), p. 107; Richard P. McCormick, *The Second American Party System: Party Formation in the Jacksonian Era* (Chapel Hill: University of North Carolina Press, 1966), pp. 54–62.

24. Felix Grundy to Andrew Jackson, September 1, 1830; Levi Woodbury to John MacPherson Berrien, September 18, 1830, LAR, M-639, RG 59, NA.

25. John Anderson to Martin Van Buren, August 6, 1830, LAR, M-639, RG 59, NA; Martin Van Buren to Mattew Harvey, September 28, 1830, Martin Van Buren Papers, LC; MPTC, RG 59, NA. The Senate confirmed Harvey without incident. See *SEJ*, 4:127, 130.

26. Jackson in June, 1836, nominated Benjamin Johnson, brother of Kentucky Senator Richard M. Johnson, judge of the federal district court for Arkansas. There is no evidence, as there is for the Tennessee and Maryland nominations, that this kinship connection figured directly in the selection. Johnson had the overwhelming support of influential Arkansas Democrats. See William Fulton to Andrew Jackson, February 9, 1836, Jackson Papers, LC.

27. George C. Childress to Andrew Jackson, August 21, 1833; John Catron to Jackson, August 22, 1833; William L. Brown to Jackson, August 24, 1833, LAR, M-639, RG 59, NA; John H. Dew to James K. Polk, January 21, 1834, James K. Polk Papers, LC.

28. Roger B. Taney to Andrew Jackson, March 15, 1836, LAR, M-687, RG 59, NA; Taney to Martin Van Buren, March 15, 1836, Van Buren Papers, LC.

29. John P. Frank, *Justice Daniel Dissenting*, pp. 63–76, 140–49; Joseph H. Harrison, "Martin Van Buren and His Southern Supporters," *Journal of Southern History* 22 (November 1956): 438–58.

30. Weisenburger, *The Passing of the Frontier*, pp. 272–96.

31. Humphrey H. Leavitt, *Autobiography of Humphrey Howe Leavitt*, pp. 4–17; John Thomson et al. to Andrew Jackson, September 30, 1833; Humphrey H. Leavitt to Martin Van Buren, September 28, 1833; Van Buren to Jackson, October 4, 1833, LAR, M-639, RG 59, NA.

32. Joseph Benham to John McLean, January 20, 1829, John McLean Papers, LC; Robert Lucas to Benjamin Tappan, October 10, 1833; John A. Bryan to Tappan, October 19, 1833, Tappan Papers, LC.

33. Elijah Hayward to Benjamin Tappan, November 4, 1833, Tappan Papers, LC; MPTC, RG 59, NA.

34. Adam A. Leonard, "Personal Politics in Indiana," *Indiana Magazine of History* 14 (March, June, September 1923): 1–56, 132–68, 241–81; William Hendricks to John Forsyth, July 24, 1835; Amos Lane to Jesse Lynch Holman, September 7, 1835, LAR, M-639, RG 59, NA; Amos Lane to Holman,

August 24, 1835; Ethan A. Brown to Holman, September 16, 1835, in "Seeking a Federal Judgeship," *Indiana Magazine of History* 35 (March 1939): 311–12.

35. Landon F. Sharp to Andrew Jackson, August 1, 1835, LAR, M-639, RG 59, NA. Sen. Richard M. Johnson discounted this plea by his fellow Kentuckians and urged Jackson to appoint Holman.

36. Jesse Lynch Holman to Amos Lane, September 7, 1835; Stephen C. Stevens to John Forsyth, September 23, 1835, LAR, M-639, RG 59, NA. Holman's response convinced Jackson; Stevens's letter was dated one week after the president appointed Holman. See MPTC, RG 59, NA.

37. V. P. Van Antwerp to Martin Van Buren, November 20, 1835, Van Buren Papers, LC; *Indiana Democrat*, October 21, 1835.

38. Ratliff Boon to Andrew Jackson, December 21, 1835; Amos Lane to Jackson, December 21, 1835; Boon et al. to Jackson, December 12, 1835; John Tipton to Jesse Lynch Holman, January 20, 1836, in "Seeking a Federal Judgeship," p. 318.

39. Jesse Lynch Holman to Allen Hamilton, February 10, 1836; John Tipton to Holman, February 1, 1836, in "Seeking a Federal Judgeship," p. 321; Ratliff Boon to Andrew Jackson, March 7, 1836, Jackson Papers, LC; *SEJ*, 4:524.

40. John Quincy Adams, *Memoirs of John Quincy Adams* ed. Charles Francis Adams, 5:442; Robert P. Fogerty, "An Institutional Study of the Courts of the Old Northwest, 1788–1848" (Ph.D. diss., University of Minnesota, 1942), pp. 55–70.

41. *American Insurance Company* v. *Canter*, 1 Peters 511 (1828); John W. Smurr, *Territorial Jurisprudence*, 1:223–33.

42. In 1836 Arkansas and Michigan achieved statehood, but at the same time Congress organized Wisconsin territory.

43. Frank B. Woodford, *Lewis Cass: Last Jacksonian*, pp. 150–51; Floyd B. Streeter, *Political Parties in Michigan, 1837–1860*, pp. 8, 24–29.

44. *Detroit Gazette*, May 16, 1828, September 20, December 11, 1827, February 28, 1828.

45. *Detroit Gazette*, October 22, November 19, December 17, 1824, May 3, 17, 31, September 18, 25, November 8, 1825; *Detroit Free Press*, May 12, 1831; Lewis Cass to William Woodbridge, February 1, 1826; William Woodbridge Papers; Solomon Sibley to Cass, November 28, 1828, Solomon Sibley Papers, BHC, DPL.

46. *U.S.* v. *John P. Sheldon, U.S.* v. *Henry L. Ball, U.S.* v. *John Reed*, in William W. Blume, ed., *Transactions of the Supreme Court of the Territory of Michigan, 1825–1836*, 5:104–6, 337–40; *Detroit Gazette*, January 22, 29, February 13, 19, 22, 26, 1829.

47. *Detroit Gazette*, December 3, 1829; Letter of Ebenezer Reed, December 27, 1829, in Friend Palmer, *Early Days in Detroit: Papers Writen by General Friend Palmer*, pp. 325–27.

48. John Biddle to Solomon Sibley, February 16, 1830; Lewis Cass to

Sibley, February 17, 1830, Sibley Papers; Jacob Burnett to William Woodbridge, February 24, 1830; John McKinney to Woodbridge, March 14, 1830;
Austin Wing to Woodbridge, January 4, 13, 18, 26, 1832; Cass to Woodbridge, January 25, 1832, Woodbridge Papers, BHC, DPL; George B. Porter
to David R. Porter, August 31, 1831, W. W., Porter Collection; George B.
Porter to Henry D. Gilpin, January 25, 1832, Henry D. Gilpin Papers, HSP.

49. *Detroit Journal and Michigan Advertiser*, February 20, 1832; *New York
Daily Advertiser*, January 30, February 15, 1832; William Wilkins to Andrew
Jackson, December 14, 1831, William Woodbridge Folder; William W. Irvin
to Jackson, December 17, 1831, David Irvin Folder, SNF, RG 46, NA; William
W. Irvin to William Woodbridge, January 12, 1832, Woodbridge Papers,
BHC, DPL; George Morell to William L. Marcy, January 22, 1832, Simeon
Gratz Collection, HSP.

50. *Detroit Free Press*, May 19, 1831, February 2, 16, March 16, April 12,
May 17, 1832; William Woodbridge to Lewis Cass, January 13, 1839, Woodbridge Papers, BHC, DPL.

51. Herbert Doherty, Jr. *Richard Keith Call*, pp. 41–42, 46–51, 70–83, 110,
119.

52. Thomas Randall Daybook, Randall Family Genealogical Records,
MHS; *Florida Herald*, May 17, 1832; Peter Hagner to John Forsyth, December
14, 1831, LAR, M-639, RG 59, NA.

53. Doherty, *Richard Keith Call*, pp. 36, 80; SEJ, 4:206.

54. Rowland W. Rerick, *Memoirs of Florida*, 2:63–65, 75; Joseph L. Smith
to Andrew Jackson, November 18, 1829; Charles Downing et al. to Jackson,
January 11, 1830; Report of the Senate Committee on the Judiciary, April 30,
1822; Memorial of the Grand Juries of DuVal, Nassau, Alachua, St. Johns,
and Musquite Counties to Andrew Jackson, n.d.; John M. Niles et al. to
Jackson, January, 1832; Democratic Members of the City Council of New
York to Jackson, January, 1832, Joseph L. Smith Folder, SNF, RG 46, NA.
The president consistently refused throughout his term to remove any
Florida judge. See the endorsement by Jackson on Thomas Baltzell to John
Forsyth, September 11, 1835, Thomas Randall Folder, SNF, RG 46, NA.

55. William Pope DuVal to Andrew Jackson, April 23, 1832, in (Washington, D.C.) *Globe*, May 11, 1832. See also *Globe*, May 15, 1832; *United States
Telegraph*, April 17, 1832.

56. Peter V. Daniel to Andrew Jackson, January 17, 1832; Daniel to William Barry, January 17, 1832; Richard M. Johnson to Carter L. Stevenson,
February 1, 1832, James G. Bryce Folder, SNF, RG 46, NA.

57. Charles Biddle, *Autobiography of Charles Biddle, Vice-President of the Su-
preme Executive Council of Pennsylvania*, p. 371; James K. Polk et al. to Andrew
Jackson, n.d.; George G. Pieper et al. to Charles Biddle, February 27, 1830,
Charles Biddle Folder, SNF, FG 46, NA.

58. Lonnie J. White, *Politics on the Southwestern Frontier*, pp. 88–98,
115–25.

59. Ambrose H. Sevier to Martin Van Buren, March 31, 1830; Sevier to

Andrew Jackson, December 7, 1829, William Trimble Folder, SNF, RG 46, NA.

60. U.S., *Statutes at Large*, vol. 3, p. 495; *Arkansas Advocate*, May 19, June 2, 15, July 14, 1830; *Arkansas Gazette*, August 4, 1830.

61. *Arkansas Gazette*, June 15, 1830; Ambrose H. Sevier to Martin Van Buren, March 31, 1830; Felix Grundy to Andrew Jackson, April 3, 1830, William Trimble Folder, SNF, RG 46, NA.

62. *Arkansas Gazette*, April 25, June 27, July 18, August 15, September 26, 1832; John S. Goff, "The Last Leaf: George Mortimer Bibb," *Register of the Kentucky Historical Society* 59 (Fall 1961): 337–39.

63. William Fulton to Andrew Jackson, February 9, 1836, Thomas J. Lacy to Jackson, June 4, 1834, Jackson Papers, LC; Cave Johnson to Jackson, October 30, 1832; Benjamin Johnson et al. to Jackson, October 29, 1834, LAR, M-639, RG 59, NA. The quote is from Archibald Yell to James K. Polk, October 18, 1834, Polk Papers, LC.

64. Martin Van Buren, *The Autobiography of Martin Van Buren*, ed. John C. Fitzpatrick, 2:253.

65. Andrew Jackson to John Coffee, December 28, 1830, Jackson Papers, LC.

66. Joseph Kent, *Speech in Support of an Amendment to the Constitution*, pp. 10–11.

67. Elijah Hayward to Benjamin Tappan, November 4, 1833, Tappan Papers, LC.

68. *Historical Statistics of the United States, Colonial Times to 1957*, p. 691; Claude G. Bowers, *Party Battles of the Jackson Period*, pp. 64–87.

69. William L. Marcy to W. J. McNeven, October 14, 1833, Marcy Papers, LC; Ronald P. Formisano, "Political Character, Antipartyism and the Second Party System," *American Quarterly* 21 (Winter 1969): 683–709.

70. Philip S. Klein, *Pennsylvania Politics, 1817–1832: A Game Without Rules*, pp. 297–323; Isaac D. Barnard to Andrew Jackson, February 24, 1831, Thomas Irwin Folder, SNF, RG 46, NA.

71. Walter Forward et al. to Andrew Jackson, March 10, 1832; Stephen Colwell to John C. Calhoun, March 10, 1832, Thomas Irwin Folder, SNF, RG 46, NA; George M. Dallas to Bedford Brown, n.d., Bedford Brown Papers, DU; *Niles Register*, April 9, 1831, April 21, 1832; *Pittsburgh Gazette*, January 6, 1832; *Allegheny Democrat*, January 6, 1832.

72. See "Recommendations in Favor of Thomas Irwin," Thomas Irwin Folder, SNF, RG 46, NA; *SEJ*, 4:225, 232. The Supreme Court subsequently sustained Marcy's position in *United States* v. *Hartwell*, 6 Wallace 385 (1865).

73. *SEJ*, 4:218, 230; James Duane Doty to Secretary of State, July 12, 1824, in Clarence E. Carter and John Porter Bloom, eds. and comps., *Territorial Papers of the United States*, 11:567. Doty protested his "removal"; he refused to allow Irvin to hold court, although he subsequently relented. See Alice Smith, *James Duane Doty, Frontier Promoter*, pp. 241–42.

74. *SEJ*, 4:244.

75. Ibid. Ross Wilkins and Irvin were confirmed unanimously, but George Morell, perhaps because of his association with Marcy, was confirmed on a roll-call vote of twenty-seven to ten.

76. William Cummins to Andrew Jackson, December 3, 1832; Endorsement by Andrew Jackson on Cummins to Jackson, December 3, 1832, Benjamin Johnson Folder, SNF, RG 46, NA; *SEJ*, 4:280, 286, 287, 301; White, *Politics on the Southwestern Frontier*, p. 145n.

77. Carter and Bloom, *Territorial Papers of the United States* 21:669–71.

78. Endorsement by Andrew Jackson on Thomas Baltzell to John Forsyth, September 11, 1835, Thomas Randall Folder, SNF, RG 46, NA.

79. The quote is from A. W. McDonald to William Armstrong, March 1, 1832; see also Joseph M. White to President of the Senate, March 4, 1832; James G. Bryce to John Tyler, March 4, 1832, James G. Bryce Folder, SNF, RG 46, NA.

80. Extract of a Letter from a Gentleman in Nashville, n.d.; John Overton to Andrew Jackson, May 9, 1832, Charles Biddle Folder, SNF, RG 46, NA; *Globe*, February 16, 1832.

81. Joseph M. White to President of the Senate, February 21, 1832, James G. Bryce Folder, SNF, RG 46, NA.

82. *SEJ*, 4:248–49, 250–1.

83. Andrew Jackson to William B. Lewis, February 28, 1842, in Bassett and Jameson, *The Correspondence of Andrew Jackson*, 6:142.

84. *SEJ*, 4:248–49; Doherty, *Richard K. Call*, pp. 80–83.

85. Elijah Hayward to Benjamin Tappan, November 4, 1833, Tappan Papers, LC.

86. John C. Wright to Benjamin Tappan, December 24, 1833; Benjamin Tappan to Benjamin Tappan, Jr., January 22, 1834; Charles Anthony to Thomas Ewing, January 18, 1834; James Wilson to Ewing, March 19, 1834; Benjamin Tappan to Ewing, March 19, 1834, Ewing Family Papers, LC; *Western Herald and Steubenville Gazette*, March 26, 1834.

87. P. Hitchcock to Thomas Ewing, January 9, 1834, Ewing Family Papers, LC.

88. The quote is from William Miner to Thomas Ewing, June 24, 1834, Ewing Family Papers, LC; see, also Thomas Morris to Benjamin Tappan, July 10, 1834, Tappan Papers, LC.

89. Benton of Missouri, Forsyth of Georgia, and Grundy and White of Tennessee voted for Tappan. See *SEJ*, 4:412; Lewis Tappan to Benjamin Tappan, June 19, 1834; Thomas Morris to Tappan, July 10, 1834, Tappan Papers, LC.

90. The quote is from the *Ohio Sun*. See, also, James Wilson to Thomas Ewing, June 17, 1834; Nathan Dike to Ewing, June 18, 1834, Ewing Family Papers, LC; *Western Herald and Steubenville Gazette*, July 16, 1834. The Senate on June 28 quickly confirmed Leavitt. See *SEJ*, 4:435–36.

91. *United States Telegraph*, March 31, 1832.

CHAPTER 2

1. From the masthead of the *Albany Argus*, August 5, 1836.

2. Henry R. Warfield to Henry Clay, May 30, 1822 in James F. Hopkins, ed., *The Papers of Henry Clay*, 3:211; Robert Remini, *Martin Van Buren and the Making of the Democratic Party*, pp. 1–11, 186–98.

3. Richard Hofstadter, *The Idea of a Party System: The Rise of Legitimate Opposition in the United States, 1780–1840* (Berkeley: University of California Press, 1970), pp. 214–31, 236–53; James C. Curtis, *The Fox at Bay: Martin Van Buren and the Presidency, 1837–1841*, pp. 51, 206.

4. Curtis, *The Fox at Bay*, pp. 52–63, 138–51.

5. Ibid., pp. 52–53, 63.

6. Martin Van Buren, *The Autobiography of Martin Van Buren*, ed. John C. Fitzpatrick, p. 107; Charles Warren, *The Supreme Court in United States History*, 2:116n., 124, 130, 136–37, 139, 143, 209, 480.

7. Martin Van Buren to Andrew Jackson, March 12, 1841, Andrew Jackson Papers, LC. Van Buren was referring to the selection of Peter V. Daniel to the Supreme Court. But see also Van Buren, *Autobiography*, pp. 183, 185, 229, 290–93; and John W. Kenney to William Woodbridge, February 9, 1830, William Woodbridge Papers, BHC, DPL. Van Buren left no evidence to suggest he had more specific selection criteria.

8. Cooperation typified Van Buren's relationship with the Senate in dispensing the patronage; the upper chamber rejected only thirty-two of the president's nominees, and none of these were to major posts. See Curtis, *The Fox at Bay*, p. 63.

9. Richard P. McCormick, *The Second American Party System: Party Formation in the Jacksonian Era*, p. 341.

10. George Adams to John Forsyth, September 30, 1838, LRD, RG 59, NA.

11. Joseph G. Tregle, Jr., "Louisiana in the Age of Jackson: A Study in Ego Politics" (Ph.D. diss., University of Pennsylvania, 1954), pp. 460–64; McCormick, *The Second American Party System*, pp. 316–17.

12. John Slidell to John Forsyth, August 4, 1837; William Christy to Martin Van Buren, July 21, 1837; Alexander Mouton to Van Buren, July 24, 1837, LAR, M-687, RG 59, NA.

13. Samuel H. Laughlin to James K. Polk, April 12, 1836, James K. Polk Papers, LC; Philip K. Lawrence to John Forsyth, September 28, 1837, AOC, RG 59, NA; Philip K. Lawrence to William S. Hamilton, April 17, 1830, William S. Hamilton Papers, LSU; Albert E. Fossier, *New Orleans: The Glamour Period, 1800–1840*, p. 189.

14. As quoted in Edwin Miles, *Jacksonian Democracy in Mississippi*. p. 170.

15. J. Willie Cooper, "A History of Federal Judges in Mississippi," typescript in Federal Records Center, East Point, Georgia.

16. George N. Terrill to James K. Polk, October 15, 1838, Polk Papers, LC; Robert J. Walker to Thomas H. Williams, February, 1839; Stephen Cocke to Thomas H. Williams, February 7, 1839, LAR, M-687, RG 59, NA.

17. James M. Banner, Jr., "The Problem of South Carolina," in Stanley Elkins and Eric McKitrick, eds., *The Hofstadter Aegis: A Memorial,* pp. 60–93; William W. Freehling, "Spoilsmen and Interests in the Thought and Career of John C. Calhoun," *Journal of American History* 52 (June 1965): 25–42.

18. William W. Freehling, *Prelude to Civil War: The Nullification Controversy in South Carolina, 1816–1836,* pp. 118–19, 140–44, 152–54, 157–58, 186–91, 243–44; Curtis, *The Fox at Bay,* pp. 98–99; Gerald M. Capers, *John C. Calhoun—Opportunist: A Reappraisal,* p. 189.

19. Robert B. Rhett to Joel R. Poinsett, November 4, 1839, Joel R. Poinsett Papers, HSP. Van Buren was also aware that Finley suffered from a chronic heart condition.

20. Edward McCrady to Joel R. Poinsett, October 25, 1839; Robert B. Gilchrist to Poinsett, October 25, 1839, LAR, M-687, RG 59, NA.

21. Joseph Johnson to Joel R. Poinsett, October 25, 1839, LAR, M-687, RG 59, NA.

22. Thomas Condy to Joel R. Poinsett, October 26, 1839, Poinsett Papers, HSP; James R. Pringle to Joel R. Poinsett, October 25, 1839; Alfred Huger to James M. Wayne, October 26, 1839, LAR, M-687, RG 59, NA.

23. James Moore Wayne to John Forsyth, October 26, 1839, LAR, M-687, RG 59, NA.

24. Joel R. Poinsett to Joseph Johnson, October 30, 1839, Gilpin Family Papers, HSP. Van Buren did conciliate the supporters of McCrady by appointing him to Gilchrist's post.

25. *SEJ,* 4:252, 258.

26. Green B. Samuels to John Forsyth, April 11, 1839, LAR, M-687, RG 59, NA; Pennypacker Family Folder, Manuscripts Division, UWV. Van Buren, in May, 1839, appointed John C. Nicoll to the federal bench in Georgia. Nicoll, like Gilchrist and Pennybacker, was a Union Democrat. See N. B. [Fannier] to Forsyth, May 8, 1839; Matthew Hall McAllister to Forsyth, May 7, 1839, LAR, M-687, RG 59; MPTC, RG 59, NA.

27. Richard P. McCormick, "Party Formation in New Jersey in the Jacksonian Era," *Proceedings of the New Jersey Historical Society* 83 (July 1965): 161–73.

28. U.S. Congress, *House Report 541,* 26th Cong., 1st sess.

29. John R. Thomason to John Forsyth, June 25, 1840; James Nelson et al. to Daniel B. Ryall, June 22, 1840, LAR, M-687, RG 59, NA.

30. Stacy G. Potts to Martin Van Buren, July 7, 1840, Van Buren Papers, LC.

31. Silas Wright to Martin Van Buren, June 26, 1840, Van Buren Papers, LC.

32. Mahlon Dickerson to Martin Van Buren, July 28, 1840, Van Buren Papers, LC; *SEJ,* 5:302, 308–9.

33. *Morristown* (N.J.) *True Democratic Banner,* October 12, 1853; Mahlon Dickerson Diary, July 21–28, 1840, Mahlon Dickerson Papers, NJHS; Robert R. Beckwith, "Mahlon Dickerson of New Jersey, 1770–1853" (Ph.D. diss., Columbia University, 1964), pp. 453–55.

34. *SEJ*, 5:342, 345.

35. Louis Pelzer, "The History and Principles of the Democratic Party of the Territory of Iowa," *Iowa Journal of History and Politics* 6 (January 1908): 3–54; Alice E. Smith, *James Duane Doty, Frontier Promoter*, pp. 224, 240–41.

36. George W. Jones to Martin Van Buren, June 11, 1838, LAR, M-687, RG 59, NA; Jacob A. Swisher, "The Judiciary of the Territory of Iowa," *Iowa Journal of History and Politics* 4 (April 1922): 244–45, 248–49.

37. Charles McCool Snyder, *The Jacksonian Heritage: Pennsylvania Politics, 1833–1848*, pp. 50–67, 122–23; Curtis, *The Fox at Bay*, pp. 58, 62.

38. Henry Muhlenberg to Martin Van Buren, March 24, 1838; Joseph Williams to Van Buren, March 30, 1838; Endorsement by Henry Baldwin on John Kennedy to Henry Baldwin, April 2, 1838; Edward B. Aubley et al. to John Forsyth, April 3, 1838, LAR, M-687, RG 59, NA; T. S. Parvin, "Hon. Joseph Williams," *Iowa Historical Record* 12 (January 1896): 387–92, notes the influence of Jeremiah S. Black in the selection of Williams.

39. George Espy to Martin Van Buren, May 30, 1838, LAR, M-687, NA.

40. *SEJ*, 5:134, 140. Van Buren in January, 1839, appointed another Muhlenberg supporter, Andrew G. Miller, to be chief justice of Wisconsin territory. See *SEJ*, 5:186, 197.

41. Arthur W. Thompson, *Jacksonian Democracy on the Florida Frontier*, pp. 17–41; Herbert J. Doherty, Jr., "Political Factions in Territorial Florida," *Florida Historical Quarterly* 28 (October 1949): 131–42.

42. Herbert J. Doherty, Jr., *The Whigs of Florida, 1845–1854*, pp. 1–11; Doherty, *Richard Keith Call: Southern Unionist*, pp. 70–83.

43. Charles Downing to Martin Van Buren, July 7, 1838; Robert R. Reid to John Forsyth, February 12, 1838, LAR, M-687, RG 59, NA; *SEJ*, 5:152–53.

44. Robert Strange and Robert Brown to Martin Van Buren, February 15, 1838; Dixon H. Lewis to John Forsyth, July 11, 1838, LAR, M-687, RG 59, NA; *SEJ*, 5:145, 153.

45. Thompson, *Jacksonian Democracy on the Florida Frontier*, pp. 49–52.

46. Robert R. Reid to Joel R. Poinsett, April 15, 1840, Gilpin Family Collection, HSP.

47. David Levy, "Brief Remarks Concerning the Democratic Cause in Florida, with a Suggestion, Respectfully Submitted to the President," n.d., Van Buren Papers, LC.

48. Doherty, *Richard Keith Call*, pp. 70–83.

49. James Webb to John Forsyth, January 1, 1839; Webb to Forsyth, January 7, 1839, LAR, M-687, RG 59, NA; Charles D. Farris, "The Courts of Territorial Florida," *Florida Historical Quarterly* 19 (April 1941): 346–66.

50. David Lord, Jr., to Charles Walker, November 28, 1838; William Kent to William P. Hallett, November 28, 1838, LAR, M-687, RG 59, NA.

51. James Webb to Charles Downing, January 29, 1839, LAR, M-687, RG 59, NA.

52. Robert R. Reid to John Forsyth, January 20, 1839; O[liver] O'Hara et al. to Charles Downing, December 8, 1838, LAR, M-687, RG 59, NA; Dwight

H. Bruce, *Onondaga's Centennial Gleanings of a Century*, 2 vols. (Boston: The Boston History Publishers, 1896), 2:48.

53. The secretary of state on February 4, 1839, received Webb's letter of resignation. Reid's letter reached the Department of State on March 8. Marvin's letters were also before the administration well before the adjournment of Congress. See clerk's endorsements on James Webb to John Forsyth, January 1, 1839, LRD, RG 59, NA; Robert R. Reid to Forsyth, January 20, 1839, LAR, M-687, RG 59, NA. Although Marvin was from New York, he was not acquainted with the president. See William Marvin to Martin Van Buren, October 17, 1839, AOC, RG 59, NA. For Marvin's commission see MPTC, RG 59, NA.

54. Stephen Mallory et al. to John Forsyth, February 8, 1840; Robert R. Reid to Forsyth, February 26, 1840; William Marvin to Reid, February 28, 1840, LAR, M-687, RG 59, NA; Forsyth to Reid, January 17, 1840, in Clarence E. Carter and John Porter Bloom, comps. and eds., *Territorial Papers of the United States: The Territory of Florida, 1823–1844*, 26:50–51.

55. William Marvin to John Forsyth, February 28, 1840, LAR, M-687, RG 59, NA.

56. *SEJ*, 5:268, 280.

57. Thomas Baltzell to John Forsyth, September 11, 1835, Thomas Randall Folder, SNF, RG 46, NA; Benjamin F. Hall, comp., *Official Opinions of the Attorney General of the United States*, 3:409–11; Alfred Balch to Martin Van Buren, April 3, 1840, Van Buren Papers, LC.

58. John Quincy Adams, *Memoirs of John Quincy Adams*, ed. Charles Francis Adams, 9:87; Micah Sterling to Joel R. Poinsett, Gilpin Family Papers, HSP; Robert R. Reid to Poinsett, January 16, 1840, Poinsett Papers, HSP; Charles Downing to John Forsyth, December 10, 1839, LAR, M-687, RG 59, NA.

59. As quoted in Glyndon G. Van Deusen, *The Jacksonian Era, 1828–1848*, p. 114.

CHAPTER 3

1. As quoted in Arthur W. Thompson, *Jacksonian Democracy on the Florida Frontier*, p. 49.

2. Roy F. Nichols, *The Invention of American Political Parties* (New York: Macmillan Co., 1967), pp. 359–77.

3. "Memoirs of a Senator and Representative from Pennsylvania, Jonathan Roberts, 1771–1854," *Pennsylvania Magazine of History and Biography* 62 (October 1938): 525.

4. Henry Clay to E. M. Letcher, June 11, 1841, in Mrs. Chapman Coleman, ed., *The Life of John J. Crittenden with Selections from his Correspondence and Speeches*, 2:156–57.

5. Lyon G. Tyler, *Parties and Patronage in the United States*, pp. 66–77;

Robert J. Morgan, *A Whig Embattled: The Presidency under John Tyler*, pp. 4–5, 69–70, 80–89, 163.

6. James D. Richardson, comp., *Compilation of the Messages and Papers of the Presidents, 1789–1897*, 4:12, 51, 105; Leonard D. White, *The Jacksonians: A Study in Administrative History, 1829–1861*, pp. 564–66.

7. William B. Campbell to David Campbell, February 27, 1841, Campbell Family Papers, DU; Carl Russell Fish, *The Civil Service and the Patronage* (New York: Longmans and Co., 1905), p. 149–54.

8. William B. Campbell to David Campbell, July 16, 1841, Campbell Papers, DU; Fish, *The Civil Service and the Patronage*, p. 153.

9. *Pennsylvanian*, (Philadelphia) February 17, 1842.

10. *Harrisburg Telegraph*, May 31, 1843.

11. Fish, *The Civil Service and the Patronage*, p. 153.

12. John C. Calhoun to T. G. Clemson, April 3, 1842, in J. Franklin Jameson, ed., *The Correspondence of John C. Calhoun*, 2:507–9.

13. Claude M. Fuess, *Daniel Webster*, 2:97–99.

14. Charles Warren, *The Supreme Court in United States History*, 2:124, 129, 136–37, 143, 284; Felix Frankfurter and James M. Landis, *The Business of the Supreme Court: A Study in the Federal Judicial System*, pp. 38, 40.

15. The quote is from Claude H. Hall, *Abel Parker Upshur, Conservative Virginian, 1790–1844*, p. 117. John C. Calhoun also observed that in making nominations Tyler was secretive and independent. See Calhoun to Robert M. T. Hunter, July 30, 1844, in Jamison, *The Correspondence of John C. Calhoun*, 2:602.

16. *Crescent City* (New Orleans), May 20, 1841. At the time of his death, Lawrence was under investigation for incompetence and malfeasance in office. See U.S. Congress, *House Report 272*, 25th Cong., 3rd sess., pp. 1–38. There are no existing letters that suggest who mediated Ogden's nomination. See, however, John Smith Kendall, "The Chronicles of a Southern Family," *Louisiana Historical Quarterly* 29 (April 1946): 280, 286, 290; Abner Nash Ogden to Daniel Webster, August 4, 1841, LRD, RG 59, NA. The latter suggests that Ogden was unaware of his selection until the commission arrived. As with other district court nominations, Webster may have been instrumental in mediating the Ogden selection.

17. Theodore H. McCaleb to Henry Clay, November 27, 1840; S. S. Prentiss to John Henderson, January 13, 1841; McCaleb to Henderson, January 18, 1841; William Christy to William H. Harrison, February 9, 1841; LAR, M-687, RG 59, NA; *Louisiana Sunday Review* (New Orleans), December 23, 1894; *SEJ*, 5:404–5, 425, 431. Shortly after appointing McCaleb, the administration received erroneous information that the new judge had died. The president promptly granted a recess commission to Bennett A. Crawford, who refused the post, informing Webster that McCaleb was still alive. See Rice Garland to Webster, October 1, 1841; McCaleb to Webster, November 6, 1841, AOC, RG 59, NA.

18. Pierre Duponceau to William H. Harrison, January 20, 1841; Members of the Bar of Boston to Daniel Webster, February 15, 1841; Peleg Sprague to Daniel Webster, April 5, 1841; John Homans to John Gray, July 9, 1841, LAR, M-687, RG 59, NA; Peleg Sprague to Daniel Webster, July 15, 1841, in Charles M. Wiltse, ed., *The Papers of Daniel Webster*, microfilm ed.

19. Herbert J. Doherty, Jr., *The Whigs of Florida, 1845–1854*, pp. 9–13; Doherty, *Richard Keith Call: Southern Unionist;* William Wyatt to Phillip Fendall, August 10, 1841, LAR, M-687, RG 59, NA.

20. Biographical sketch of Carmack in Joseph Greer Papers, TSLA.

21. William Wyatt to Phillip Fendall, August 10, 1841, LAR, M-687, RG 59, NA; William H. Brockenbrough to John Tyler, September 27, 1841, LRD, RG 59, NA; *SEJ,* 5:424, 439–40; 6:12, 30; MPTC, RG 59, NA.

22. Henry R. Mueller, *The Whig Party in Pennsylvania,* pp. 60–67, 83–84, 237, 240.

23. Nicholas B. Wainwright, ed., *A Philadelphia Perspective: The Diary of Sidney George Fisher* (Philadelphia: Historical Society of Pennsylvania, 1964), p. 132; "Memoirs of a Senator and Representative from Pennsylvania," p. 514.

24. "Memoirs of a Senator and Representative from Pennsylvania," pp. 516, 520.

25. Carl B. Swisher, *The Taney Period 1836–64,* pp. 133–49.

26. *North American* (Philadelphia), January 11, 21, 1842; *Public Ledger* (Philadelphia), January 20, 1842. The Senate confirmed Binney one week after his nomination. See *SEJ,* 6:12, 24.

27. Horace Binney to Daniel Webster, February 1, 1842, in Wiltse, *Papers of Daniel Webster;* Horace Binney, "Manuscript Autobiography of Horace Binney," Horace Binney Papers, HSP.

28. Horace Binney to Joseph R. Ingersoll, January 18, 1842; Binney to John Sergeant, January 18, 1842; Thomas J. Wharton to Richard S. Coxe, February 3, 1842, LAR, M-687, RG 59, NA; Joel Jones to Thomas Bradford, January 18, 1842; John B. Gibson et al. to [Daniel Webster], February 19, 1842, Thomas Bradford Folder, SNF, RG 46, NA; William Rawle to Abel P. Upshur, January 15, 1842; James M. Porter to James Buchanan, February 18, 1842, James Buchanan Papers, HSP.

29. Nicholas Biddle to Daniel Webster, January 18, 1842; Webster to Biddle, February 19, 1842, in Wiltse, *Papers of Daniel Webster; Pennsylvanian,* January 25, 1842; *SEJ,* 6:24.

30. *Pennsylvanian,* February 25, 1842; *North American,* February 19, 23, 1842; *SEJ,* 6:24, 32.

31. Nicholas Biddle to Daniel Webster, February 24, March 2, 1842, in Wiltse, *Papers of Daniel Webster; United States Gazette,* February 23, 1842.

32. Daniel Webster to Nicholas Biddle, March [4], 1842, in Wiltse, *Papers of Daniel Webster;* Job R. Tyson to James F. Maculey, February 27, 1842, LAR, M-687, RG 59, NA.

33. Nicholas Biddle to Daniel Webster, March 10, 1842, in Wiltse, *Papers*

of Daniel Webster. The quote is from *Public Ledger,* March 4, 1842. See also *North American,* March 4, 1842. He was confirmed on March 9, 1842, without opposition. See *SEJ,* 6:34, 36.

34. Prentiss replaced retiring Judge Elijah Paine. The latter had intended to retire the previous year but the "great rush" of officeseekers raised his ire sufficiently that he postponed his resignation until "the furor" abated. The Senate followed its tradition of approving one of its members without question; Prentiss was confirmed the same day as his nomination. Politically, Prentiss was identified with Webster. See Elijah Paine to Daniel Webster, March 9, 1842, in Wiltse, *Papers of Daniel Webster;* William Upham to Samuel Phillips, March 12, 1842, LAR, M-687, RG 59, NA; *SEJ,* 6:50.

35. Adam A. Leonard, "Personal Politics in Indiana," *Indiana Magazine of History* 19 (June, September 1923): 167, 241–81; Roger H. Van Bolt, "The Hoosier Politician of the 1840s," *Indiana Magazine of History* 48 (1952): 26–31; Logan Esarey, *A History of Indiana,* 1:531.

36. John McLean to Daniel Webster, April 1, 1842, in Wiltse, *Papers of Daniel Webster.*

37. Albert S. White to Daniel Webster, April 18, 1842, ibid.; *SEJ,* 6:57.

38. Charles Dewey to Daniel Webster, April 16, 1842, LRD, RG 59, NA; William Wesley Woollen, *Biographical and Historical Sketches of Early Indiana,* pp. 360–65.

39. Stephen C. Stevens to Joseph L. White, April 1, 1842; William Hendricks to White, April 8, 1842; Miles C. Eggleston to White, March 3, 1842, LAR, M-687, RG 59, NA; William Hendricks to Daniel Webster, April 7, 1842, in Wiltse, *Papers of Daniel Webster.*

40. Johnathan McCarty to Daniel Webster, April 18, 1842, in Wiltse, *Papers of Daniel Webster.*

41. Daniel Webster to Thomas Clayton, April 29, 1842, Elisha M. Huntington Folder, SNF, RG 46, NA; Leander J. Monks, *Courts and Lawyers of Indiana,* 1:76; 2:411–12.

42. Joseph L. White and James H. Cravens to Oliver H. Smith and Albert S. White, April 28, 1842, Huntington Folder, SNF, RG 46, NA. The remainder of the Whig delegation refused to sustain the protest and, thereby, isolated White and Cravens. See James H. Cravens to David Wallace and Henry S. Lane, April 29, 1842, Huntington Folder, SNF, RG 46, NA.

43. Albert S. White to James H. Cravens, April 28, 1842; White to Thomas Clayton, April 24, 1842, Huntington Folder, SNF, RG 46, NA: Thomas Clayton to Daniel Webster, April 28, 1842, LAR, M-687, RG 59, NA; *SEJ,* 6:57, 62.

44. Tyler reappointed three Democratic judges in Florida: in June, 1842, Dillon Jordan, Jr., to the Western District and in March, 1844, Isaac H. Bronson to the Eastern District and William Marvin to the Southern District. Administratively, the appointments retained experienced judges on the bench. Politically, the selections enraged the leadership of the nascent Florida Whig party. See William Pope DuVal to Abel P. Upshur, January 28, 1844, LAR, M-687, RG 59, NA.

45. Louis Pelzer, "The History and Principles of the Whigs of the Territory of Iowa," *Iowa Journal of History and Politics* 5 (January 1907): 46–90; Pelzer, "The History and Principles of the Democratic Party of the Territory of Iowa," *Iowa Journal of History and Politics* 6 (January 1908): 3–54.

46. Pelzer, "The Whigs of Iowa," p. 63.

47. Francis Springer to William Pitt Fessenden, January 17, 19, 1842, LAR, M-687, RG 59, NA.

48. John McLean to Samuel Stokely, March 22, 1842, LAR, M-687, RG 59, NA; J. H. Clay Mudd to Daniel Webster, April 25, 1842, in Wiltse, *Papers of Daniel Webster;* Bruce E. Mahan, "Judge Joseph Williams," *The Palimpsest* 5 (March 1924): 90–92.

49. Isaac Leffler to Abel P. Upshur, March 8, 1842; Francis Springer to William Pitt Fessenden, January 17, 1842; Alfred Hebard to [Abel P. Upshur], January 18, 1842; David Clark to Albert S. White, February 10, 1842, LAR, M-687, RG 59, NA.

50. Daniel Webster to John Tyler, June 22, 1842, in Wiltse, *Papers of Daniel Webster.*

51. Williams also benefited from a bit of good fortune. He shared part of his journey to Washington with Tyler's wife, who purportedly intervened with her husband on behalf of the embattled judge. See Mahan, "Joseph Williams," pp. 90–93; *SEJ,* 6:112, 116.

52. *Iowa City Standard,* September 28, 1842; *Iowa Capital Reporter,* July 16, August 20, October 8, 1842; *Davenport Gazette,* April 20, 1843.

53. Glyndon G. Van Deusen, *The Jacksonian Era, 1828–1848,* pp. 177–81.

54. Henry H. Simms, *The Rise of the Whigs in Virginia, 1824–1840,* p. 40; Howard Braverman, "The Economic and Political Background of the Conservative Revolt in Virginia," *Virginia Magazine of History and Biography* 60 (April 1972): 283–89.

55. *Richmond Whig,* May 17, 1844; Roy M. Curry, "James A. Seddon, A Southern Prototype," *Virginia Magazine of History and Biography* 63 (April 1955): 126–50.

56. Robert Seager, *And Tyler Too: A Biography of John and Julia Gardiner Tyler,* p. 131. Christian's sister was Tyler's first wife.

57. Beverly Tucker to Robert Saunders, March 25, 1844; George W. Southall to John Tyler, March 25, 1844; C. G. Griswold to Tyler, March 25, 1844; John B. Christian to Tyler, March 29, 1841, Christian Folder, SNF, RG 46, NA.

58. P[hilip] Mayo to William C. Rives, May 16, 1844, William C. Rives Papers, LC; *SEJ,* 6:252.

59. Louis C. Bouldin to George C. Dromgoole, April 6, 1844, Edward Dromgoole Papers, SHC, UNC.

60. *Richmond Whig,* April 12, May 14, 24, 1844.

61. John B. Christian to William C. Rives, March 29, April 1, 1844, Rives Papers, LC.

62. *SEJ,* 6:252, 341–42; P[hilip] Mayo to William C. Rives, May 16, 1844, Rives Papers, LC.

63. *Petersburg Index*, March 4, 1870; Robert C. Collier to William C. Rives, June 19, July 26, 1844, Rives Papers, LC; *SEJ*, 6:348–49.
64. *Richmond Whig*, June 18, 1844. See also ibid., April 30, May 3, 17, June 21, 1844; *SEJ*, 6:348, 350.
65. Curry, "James A. Seddon, A Southern Prototype," p. 126; Charles G. Sellers, Jr., *James K. Polk, Jacksonian: 1795–1843*, pp. 135–37.
66. As quoted in Oscar D. Lambert, *Presidential Politics in the United States, 1841–1844* (Durham: Duke University Press, 1936), p. 87.

CHAPTER 4

1. James K. Polk, *The Diary of James K. Polk During His Presidency, 1845–1849*, ed. Milo C. Quaife, 2:314–15.
2. James MacGregor Burns, *The Deadlock of Democracy: Four-Party Politics in America*, pp. 10–21.
3. Charles G. Sellers, Jr., *James K. Polk, Continentalist: 1843–1846* (Princeton: Princeton University Press, 1966), pp. 212–13, 350–53; Joel H. Sibley, *The Shrine of Party: Congressional Voting Behavior, 1841–1852* (Pittsburgh: Univ. of Pittsburgh Press, 1967), pp. 35–82, 142–46. For an excellent firsthand summary of the problems confronting Polk, see James Hamilton to John C. Calhoun, October 12, 1846, James Hamilton Papers, SHC, UNC.
4. Polk, *The Diary of James K. Polk*, 2:20.
5. Francis P. Blair to Martin Van Buren, November 16, 30, 1848, Martin Van Buren Papers, LC. See also Charles A. McCoy, *Polk and the Presidency*, p. 203; and Norman Grabener, "James K. Polk: A Study in Federal Patronage," *Mississippi Valley Historical Review* 38 (March 1952): 613–32.
6. Sellers, *Polk, Continentalist*, pp. 267–68, 301–3, 324, 352–53, 447–48.
7. Polk, *The Diary of James K. Polk*, 4:360, 2:315, 1:483.
8. Carl Russell Fish, *The Civil Service and the Patronage*, pp. 160–61; Eugene I. McCormac, *James K. Polk: A Political Biography*, pp. 342–43.
9. Polk, *The Diary of James K. Polk*, 1:51–52, 138.
10. McCormac, *James K. Polk*, pp. 329, 341; Philip Shriver Klein, *President James Buchanan: A Biography*, p. 165.
11. Job Barnard, "Early Days of the Supreme Court of the District of Columbia," *Records of the Columbia Historical Society* 22 (1919): 1–22; Members of the Bar of Fairfax County to James K. Polk, August 30, 1845; Christopher Neale to Polk, August 30, 1845, LAR, M-873, RG 59, NA; Francis Thomas to Polk, September 6, 1845, James K. Polk Papers, LC.
12. W[illiam] W. Payne to James K. Polk, October 28, 1845; H. G. Williams to Polk, September 2, 1845, LAR, M-873, RG 59, NA.
13. Sellers, *Polk, Continentalist*, pp. 13, 49, 149–50.
14. Alfred Balch to James K. Polk, September 13, 1845, Polk Papers, LC.
15. Proceedings of the Bar of the District of Columbia, September 4,

1845; Elizabeth M. Fendall to James K. Polk, September 1, 1845; Ransom H. Gillett to Polk, September 3, 1845; C. P. Singstack to James Buchanan, September 2, 1845; "A True Democrat" to Polk, October [18], 1845, LAR, M-873, RG 59, NA.

16. Henry M. Morfit to James K. Polk, October 9, 1845, Polk Papers, LC; *SEJ*, 7:10, 41; MPTC, RG 59, NA.

17. Charles Ambler, *Thomas Ritchie: A Study in Virginia Politics*, pp. 227–29; Joseph H. Harrison, Jr., "Oligarchs and Democrats—The Richmond Junto," *Virginia Magazine of History and Biography* 78 (April 1970): 184–98.

18. Henry H. Simms, *Life of Robert M. T. Hunter: A Study in Sectionalism and Secession*, pp. 50–52; Roy W. Curry, "James A. Seddon, A Southern Prototype," *Virginia Magazine of History and Biography* 63 (April 1955): 128–29; Sellers, *Polk, Continentalist*, p. 319.

19. The senators from Virginia had little impact on the selection process; William S. Archer was a Whig and Pennybacker promoted his uncle, Joseph Samuels. Isaac Pennybacker to James K. Polk, December 11, 1845, LAR, M-873, RG 59, NA. Pennybacker in October, 1846, played a more influential part in the selection of his brother-in-law, John J. Dyer, as district judge of Iowa. The Iowa Democratic congressional delegation also endorsed Dyer. See Isaac S. Pennybacker to James K. Polk, October 12, 1846; Serranus C. Hastings to Polk, January 12, 1848, Polk Papers, LC; Pennybacker to Polk, December 19, 1846; Hastings to Polk, January 20, 1847, LAR, M-873, RG 59, NA.

20. Augustus A. Chapman to James K. Polk, December 17, 1845; Virginia Members of the House of Representatives to Polk, December 15, 1845; Archibald Atkinson to Polk, December 8, 1845, LAR, M-873, RG 59, NA; Polk, *The Diary of James K. Polk*, 1:466–67.

21. John Brockenbrough to James K. Polk, December 10, 1845; George W. Hopkins to Polk, December 15, 22, 1845, LAR, M-873, RG 59, NA.

22. Democratic Members of the House of Representatives from Western Virginia to James K. Polk, December 22, 1845, LAR, M-873, RG 59, NA; *SEJ*, 7:10, 34.

23. Polk, *The Diary of James K. Polk*, 1:382; Arthur W. Thompson, *Jacksonian Democracy on the Florida Frontier*, pp. 45–47.

24. U.S., *Statutes at Large*, vol. 5, p. 788; William H. Brockenbrough to James K. Polk, March 5, 1846, Polk Papers, LC.

25. Thompson, *Jacksonian Democracy*, p. 51.

26. Benjamin F. Hall, comp., *Official Opinions of the Attorney General of the United States*, 4:362–63; David L. Yulee to James K. Polk, April 19, 1846, Polk Papers, LC.

27. Polk, *The Diary of James K. Polk*, 1:382; William D. Moseley to James K. Polk, November 25, 1845, Polk Papers, LC; Isaac Bronson to Polk, January 3, 1846; Stephen Mallory and James B. Brome to David L. Yulee, James D. Westcott, and William H. Brockenbrough, January 6, 1846, LAR, M-873, RG 59, NA.

28. James D. Westcott to James K. Polk, August 6, 1846, Polk Papers, LC.

210   *Notes*

29. Polk, *The Diary of James K. Polk,* 1:383–84; U.S., *Statutes at Large,* vol. 9, 131–32; *SEJ,* 7:70, 148, 227, 236.

30. Ernest W. Winkler, ed., *Platforms of Political Parties in Texas,* pp. 11–41; Louis F. Blount, "A Brief Study of Thomas J. Rusk Based on his Letters to his Brother, David, 1835–1856," *Southwestern Historical Quarterly* 34 (January, April 1931): 181–202, 271–92.

31. James Webb to Mirabeau B. Lamar, September 30, 1845; Lamar to James K. Polk, October 17, 1845; Thomas H. DuVal to Lamar, June 27, 1846, in Charles A. Gulick and Winnie Allen, eds., *The Papers of Mirabeau Buonaparte Lamar,* 4:104–8, 128–29, 135; Lamar to John C. Calhoun, February 25, 1846; Calhoun to Polk, January 8, 1846, LAR, M-873, RG 59, NA; Sam Houston to James Buchanan, November 19, 1845, in Amelia A. Williams and Eugene C. Barker, eds., *The Writings of Sam Houston, 1813–1863,* 4:430.

32. James K. Polk to Sam Houston, January 13, 1846, Polk Papers, LC.

33. James Webb to Mirabeau B. Lamar, March 23, 1846 in Gulick and Allen, *Papers of Mirabeau Buonaparte Lamar,* 4:128–29; Thomas J. Rusk to David Rusk, March 27, 1846, in Blount, "A Brief Study of Thomas J. Rusk," p. 285.

34. Mirabeau B. Lamar to James K. Polk, January 31, 1846, LAR, M-873, RG 59, NA.

35. Dixon H. Lewis to James K. Polk, February 26, 1846, LAR, M-873, RG 59, NA; Wallace Hawkins, *The Case of John C. Watrous, United States Judge for Texas: A Political History of High Crimes and Misdemeanors,* pp. 9–16.

36. Thomas J. Rusk to Sam Houston, May 25, 1846; Houston to James K. Polk, May 26, 1846, LAR, M-873, RG 59, NA; John C. Watrous to James Webb, April 3, 1846, Thomas Rusk Papers, UTX; *SEJ,* 7:79, 82.

37. Charles McCool Snyder, *The Jacksonian Heritage: Pennsylvania Politics, 1833–1848,* pp. 187–99; Sellers, *Polk, Continentalist,* pp. 54, 78–81, 116–21, 151–55, 193–95, 292–95, 351–55.

38. Snyder, *The Jacksonian Heritage,* pp. 169, 189–91, 211.

39. James Buchanan to James K. Polk, [December, 1845], James Buchanan Papers, HSP. Buchanan drafted but apparently never sent this letter; Klein, *President James Buchanan,* 170–71.

40. As quoted in Lee F. Crippen, *Simon Cameron, Antebellum Years,* p. 82.

41. Henry Horn to James K. Polk, June 8, 1846; Edward King to Polk, June 8, 1846; George M. Dallas to Polk, June 9, 1846; Joel B. Sutherland to Polk, June 9, 10, 1846, Polk Papers, LC; John W. Forney to James Buchanan, June 7, 8, 1846, Buchanan Papers, HSP; Presidents of the Insurance Companies of Philadelphia to Polk, June 10, 1846; Henry M. Maine to Polk, June 11, 1846, LAR, M-873, RG 59, NA.

42. Francis Shunk to James K. Polk, June 9, 1846; George M. Dallas to Polk, June 9, 1846; Daniel Sturgeon to Polk, June 9, 1846; William J. Leiper to Polk, June 9, 10, 1846, Polk Papers, LC.

43. Sellers, *Polk, Continentalist,* pp. 119–27, 327–28.

44. George M. Krim to James K. Polk, June 11, 1846; William J. Leiper to Polk, June 10, 1846, Polk Papers, LC.

45. Polk, *The Diary of James K. Polk,* 1:463. Buchanan in June, 1848, helped his old political friend Andrew G. Miller secure the post of district judge for the new state of Wisconsin. Miller, however, was also endorsed by the Democratic congressional delegation from Wisconsin. See Andrew G. Miller to James Buchanan, December 21, 1846, December 4, 1847, Buchanan Papers, HSP; Mason C. Darling and William P. Lynde to James K. Polk, June 21, 1848, AOC, RG 59, NA.

46. James K. Polk to Jesse Miller, June 11, 1846, Polk Papers, LC; *SEJ,* 7:86.

47. *SEJ,* 7:86, 91–92. Only Whigs Alexander Barrow of Louisiana and Thomas Corwin of Ohio voted in the negative.

48. Augustus C. Dodge to James K. Polk, May 4, 1845, Polk Papers, LC; Dodge to James Buchanan, May 20, 1845, LAR, M-873, RG 59, NA; *SEJ,* 7:104, 115, 152.

49. W. C. Woodward, "The Rise and Early History of Political Parties in Oregon," *Quarterly of the Oregon Historical Society* 2 (December 1910): 35, 325–54.

50. Ibid., p. 35.

51. Polk, *The Diary of James K. Polk,* 4:21; William A. Hansen, "Thomas Hart Benton and the Oregon Question," *Missouri Historical Review* 63 (July 1969): 489–97; Robert W. Johannsen, *Stephen A. Douglas,* pp. 223–25.

52. George Abernathey to James K. Polk, February 12, 1847, Polk Papers, LC.

53. David Atchison and John M. Johnson to James K. Polk, June 9, 1848; Stephen A. Douglas to Polk, July 22, 1848; [B.] Jennings et al. to Iowa Congressional Delegation, December 23, 1847, LAR, M-873, RG 59, NA.

54. Frances F. Victor, *The River of the West,* p. 454; Missouri Congressional Delegation to James K. Polk, February 12, 1847, LAR, M-873, RG 59, NA; *SEJ,* 7:484.

55. Kintzing Pritchette of Pennsylvania, Henry C. Whitman of Ohio, and Cyrus Olney of Iowa were recommended for the post. See William Bigler to James K. Polk, January 7, 1847; Benjamin Tappan to Polk, December 28, 1846; Augustus C. Dodge to Polk, June 23, 1848, LAR, M-873, RG 59, NA.

56. Edward A. Hannegan et al. to James K. Polk, n.d.; Thomas J. Turner to Polk, September 2, 1848, LAR, M-873, RG 59, NA; Turney Family Genealogical File, TSLA; Sidney Teiser, "The First Chief Justice of Oregon Territory: William P. Bryant," *Oregon Historical Quarterly* 48 (June 1947): 45–53.

57. James Turney to James Buchanan, August 17, 1848, LRD, RG 59, NA; Senators and Representatives from the State of Missouri to James K. Polk, n.d.; William A. Hall to Buchanan, October 4, 1848, LAR, M-873, RG 59, NA; MPTC, RG 59, NA.

58. John A. McLernand to Joseph Lane, January 13, 1854, Joseph Lane Papers, OHS; "Synopsis of the Life of Honorable O. C. Pratt," Orville C. Pratt Folder, Oregon Manuscripts, UCB; Augustus C. French to James K. Polk, December 27, 1847, LAR, M-873, RG 59, NA; MPTC, RG 59, NA; *SEJ,* 8:6, 8–9.

59. Peter H. Burnett, *Recollections and Opinions of an Old Pioneer,* p. 194. Burnett was also involved in California politics; he in 1850 became the first governor. There is no letter of declination in the records of the secretary of state. In January and February of 1849, several applicants sought the post; Burnett may have been mistaken about the precise timing of his declination.

60. J. Pringle Jones to Simon Cameron, March 19, 1846, Lewis Coryell Papers, HSP.

CHAPTER 5

1. As quoted in Holman Hamilton, *Zachary Taylor: Soldier in the White House,* 2:237.

2. Robert J. Rayback, *Millard Fillmore: Biography of a President,* pp. 137–59, 192–206.

3. Richard P. McCormick, "Political Development and the Second Party System," in William Nisbet Chambers and Walter Dean Burnham, eds., *The American Party System: Stages of Poltical Development,* pp. 90–116; David M. Potter, *The Impending Crisis, 1848–1861* (New York: Harper and Row, 1976), pp. 225–33.

4. James D. Richardson, comp., *A Compilation of the Messages and Papers of the Presidents, 1789–1897,* 5:6.

5. Nicholas Dean to Thomas Ewing, April 4, 1849, Ewing Family Papers, LC; Zachary Taylor to John J. Crittenden, November 1, 1849, John J. Crittenden Papers, LC.

6. Brainerd Dyer, *Zachary Taylor,* pp. 321–23.

7. Isaac Crary to James Buchanan, January 27, 1849, LAR, M-873, RG 59, NA; Carl Russell Fish, *The Civil Service and the Patronage,* pp. 162–63; Richardson, *Messages and Papers of the Presidents,* 5:6.

8. *Historical Statistics of the United States, Colonial Times to 1957,* p. 691. Democrats controlled 35 Senate seats in both the Thirty-first and Thirty-second Congresses while Whigs occupied 25 and 24 seats respectively. In the House, Whigs in the Thirty-first Congress claimed 109 members and Democrats 112, but in the next Congress this changed to 80 Whigs and 140 Democrats.

9. As quoted in Hamilton, *Zachary Taylor,* 2:162–63.

10. David Outlaw to Emily Outlaw, December 9, 1849, David Outlaw Papers, SHC, UNC.

11. Hamilton, *Zachary Taylor,* 2:205.

12. Jeremiah Clemens to C. C. Clay, January 19, 1840, SCJ, RG 46, NA;

C. C. Clay to James K. Polk, November 27, 1845, Polk Papers, LC; U.S., *Statutes at Large*, vol. 5, p. 210.

13. William R. King et al. to Zachary Taylor, March 3, 1849; Franklin W. Bowdon to Taylor, March 5, 1849; A. C. Beard to Taylor, March 23, 1849, LAR, M-873, RG 59, NA. Silas Parsons of Huntsville and Chancellor David G. Ligon of Moulton were the leading contenders from north Alabama. See Thomas M. Peter et al. to Taylor, March 12, 1849; Samuel F. Rice to Taylor, March 21, 1849, LAR, M-873, RG 59, NA.

14. Henry W. Hilliard to Zachary Taylor, March 5, 1849, LAR, M-873, RG 59, NA. Hilliard also grudgingly endorsed Gayle.

15. John Gayle to Zachary Taylor, March 5, 1849, LAR, M-873, RG 59, NA; John Gayle Biographical File, ADHA; *Montgomery Daily Advertiser*, July 22, 1859; *SEJ*, 8:73, 78.

16. As quoted in Theodore C. Blegen, *Minnesota: A History of the State*, p. 162.

17. Robert M. Brown, "A Territorial Delegate in Action," *Minnesota History* 31 (September 1950): 172–78.

18. Seward recommended Moses B. Butterfield, Albert Smith, and Levi Beardsley, all residents of Wisconsin who had formerly resided in New York. Fillmore supported Daniel Garnsey of Gowanda, New York, and Nathan K. Hall of Buffalo. See Seward to John M. Clayton, March 10, 1849; Seward to Zachary Taylor, March 29, 1849, LAR, M-873, RG 59 NA; Garnsey to Fillmore, March 10, 1849, Millard Fillmore Papers, BECHS; Holman Hamilton, "Zachary Taylor and Minnesota," *Minnesota History* 30 (June 1949): 104–5.

19. John M. Clayton to John J. Crittenden, April 18, 1849, Crittenden Papers, LC; Hamilton, *Zachary Taylor*, 2:63–64, 108, 110, 205, 206; Joseph H. Parks, *John Bell of Tennessee*, pp. 229–32.

20. John M. Clayton to John J. Crittenden, April 18, 1849, Crittenden Papers, LC; James Cooper to Millard Fillmore, March 13, 1851, Fillmore Papers, BECHS; Truman Smith to Thomas Ewing, April 6, 1849, Ewing Papers, LC; Andrew J. Ogle to Zachary Taylor, March 10, 1849, LAR, M-873, RG 59, NA; Gideon Tomlinson to Smith, January 10, 1850, Bradley B. Meeker Folder, SNF, RG 46, NA; Henry R. Mueller, *The Whig Party in Pennsylvania*, pp. 149–57; *SEJ*, 8:84, 89.

21. John J. Crittenden to John M. Clayton, April 10, 1849, Clayton Papers, LC; Albert D. Kirwan, *John J. Crittenden: The Struggle for the Union*, pp. 247–64.

22. Leslie Combs to John M. Clayton, April 29, 1849, Clayton Papers, LC.

23. John M. Clayton to John J. Crittenden, April 18, 1849, Crittenden Papers, LC.

24. John M. Clayton to John J. Crittenden, May 7, 12, 1849; B. Rowan Hardin to Crittenden, May 8, 1849; Leslie Combs to Crittenden, May 25, 1849, Crittenden Papers, LC.

25. Meeker's first name was spelled Benjamin instead of Bradley on his

original commission. On April 3, 1849, a recess commission was granted before Kentucky Whigs communicated their displeasure to the administration. When Taylor submitted a regular nomination, the Senate Committee on the Judiciary undertook its investigation. The most serious charge against Meeker was that he had failed repeatedly to pay rent due his landlady. On the entire affair see Meeker's extensive folder in SNF, RG 46, NA; *SEJ*, 8:84, 89.

26. Daniel G. Garnsey to John M. Clayton, March 26, 1849, LAR, M-873, RG 59, NA.

27. Parks, *John Bell*, pp. 266–67.

28. Alonzo M. A[zeno] to Alpheus Felch, January 9, 1849; John Bell to John M. Clayton, March 15, 1849, LAR, M-873, RG 59, NA; Robert C. Voight, "Defender of the Common Law: Aaron Goodrich, Chief Justice of Minnesota Territory" (Ph.D. diss., University of Minnesota, 1962), pp. 13–34; *SEJ*, 8:84, 89.

29. Samuel H. Harper to Josiah S. Johnston, February 3, 1830, Josiah S. Johnston Papers, HSP; U.S., Congress, Senate, *Congressional Globe*, 30th Cong., 2nd sess., 1848, pp. 474, 483, 697; U.S., *Statutes at Large*, vol. 9, pp. 401–2.

30. Benjamin Winchester to Zachary Taylor, March 13, 1849; James G. Campbell to Taylor, April 9, 1849, LAR, M-873, RG 59, NA; Campbell to John M. Clayton, April 9, 1849, LRD, RG 59, NA.

31. James G. Campbell to John M. Clayton, April 12, 1849; Henry Boyce to Zachary Taylor, March 19, 1849, LAR, M-873, RG 59, NA; John Kingsbury Elgee to Taylor, May 15, 1849, LRD, RG 59, NA; MPTC, RG 59, NA.

32. Henry Ba[lrieu] to Millard Fillmore, August 4, 1849, LAR, M-873, RG 59, NA; Henry Boyce to John Byrne, July 6, 1849, Mullanphy Family Papers, MOHS; Boyce to John M. Clayton, June 18, 1849, AOC; MPTC, RG 59, NA; William Hyde and Howard L. Conrad, eds., *Encyclopedia of the History of St. Louis*, 1:206–7.

33. Brian G. Walton, "The Second Party System in Arkansas," *Arkansas Historical Quarterly* 28 (Summer 1969): 120–55; Lonnie J. White, *Politics on the Southwestern Frontier: Arkansas Territory, 1819–1836*, pp. 142–48.

34. Albert Rho to Zachary Taylor, October 18, 1849; John Drennen and Phi[llip] Pennywit to Taylor, October 18, 1849, LAR, M-873, RG 59, NA; D[aniel] J. Baldwin to Thomas Ewing, October 19, 1844, Ewing Family Papers, LC; U.S., *Statutes at Large*, vol. 5, p. 51, vol. 9, pp. 594–95.

35. W. H. Sutton to Zachary Taylor, October 29, 1849, LAR, M-873, RG 59, NA. Westerns urged the president to select either William Byers of Batesville or Jesse Turner of Van Buren.

36. Fredrick Trapnall to John Bell, June 22, 1849; John Bell to Thomas Ewing, November 3, 1849; Trapnall to Ewing, October 14, 1849, Ewing Family Papers, LC; [Daniel] Butler to Zachary Taylor, October 16, 1849, LAR, M-873, RG 59, NA; Daniel Ringo Folder, AHC; MPTC, RG 59, NA.

37. Thomas Ewing to John M. Clayton, September 15, 1849; Seabury Ford to Ewing, September 12, 1849, LAR, M-873, RG 59, NA; Samuel F.

Vinton to Ewing, September 10, 1849, Ewing Family Papers, LC; MPTC, RG 59, NA.

38. Daniel Webster to Charles Augustus Stetson, February 15, 1850, in Charles M. Wiltse, ed., *The Papers of Daniel Webster*, microfilm ed.; Hamilton, *Zachary Taylor*, 2:203–9.

39. William D. Fenton, "Edward Dickinson Baker," *Quarterly of the Oregon Historical Society*, 2 (March 1908): 1–23.

40. Nathaniel Coffin to Daniel Webster, January 31, 1850, in Wiltse, *Papers of Daniel Webster*; Abraham Lincoln to Zachary Taylor, January 25, 1850; David Davis et al. to Taylor, January 28, 1850; Endorsement by Joseph R. Underwood on Moses Bledsoe to Joseph R. Underwood, January 27, 1850; Endorsement by John McLean on William Thomas to John McLean, January 22, 1850, LAR, M-873, RG 59, NA.

41. Edward D. Baker to Thomas Ewing, February 2, 1850, Ewing Family Papers, LC.

42. William Thomas to Joseph R. Underwood, February 7, 11, 1850, LAR, M-873, RG 59, NA; *SEJ*, 8:135.

43. Daniel Webster to Franklin Haven, January 18, 1850, in Wiltse, *Papers of Daniel Webster*.

44. Zachary Taylor to John J. Crittenden, November 1, 1847, Crittenden Papers, LC.

CHAPTER 6

1. U. S. Congress, *House Executive Documents*, 32nd Cong., 1st sess., p. 509.

2. As quoted in David M. Potter, *The Impending Crisis, 1848–1861*, p. 114.

3. Homan Hamilton, *Prologue to Conflict: The Crisis and Compromise of 1850*.

4. Wallace Mendelson, "Dred Scott's Case—Reconsidered," *Minnesota Law Review* 38 (December 1953): 16–28.

5. Millard Fillmore to Washington Hunt, February 23, 1851, Millard Fillmore Papers, BECHS; Robert J. Rayback, *Millard Fillmore: Biography of a President*, pp. 238–92.

6. James D. Richardson, comp., *Compilation of the Messages and Papers of the Presidents, 1789–1897*, 6:2616; Millard Fillmore to Daniel Webster, September 10, 1851, in Charles M. Wiltse, ed., *The Papers of Daniel Webster*, microfilm ed.

7. Rayback, *Millard Fillmore*, p. 335.

8. U. S. Congress, *House Executive Documents*, 32nd Cong., 1st sess., p. 509.

9. Ibid. Fillmore wanted to nationalize the lower federal courts by centralizing their administration under a more powerful attorney general. See Kermit L. Hall, "The Taney Court in the Second Party System: The Congres-

sional Response to Federal Judicial Reform" (Ph.D. diss., University of Minnesota, 1972), pp. 128–83.

10. See the various synopses in LAR, M-873, RG 59, NA.

11. William Henry Ellison, *A Self-Governing Domain: California, 1849–1860*, pp. 167–91; U. S., *Statutes at Large*, vol. 9, pp. 521–22.

12. As quoted in Earl Pomeroy, "California, 1846–1860: Politics in a Representative Frontier State," *California Historical Society Quarterly* 32 (December 1953): 297.

13. Robert V. P. Steele, *Between Two Empires: The Life Story of California's First Senator, William McKendree Gwin*, p. 77.

14. James M. Carne to Millard Fillmore, August 31, 1850, March 9, 1852, Fillmore Papers, BECHS.

15. J. H. Clay Mudd to Thomas Corwin, February 16, 26, 1852; John Wilson to Corwin, June 25, 1850, Thomas Corwin Papers, LC; Truman Smith to Wilson, November 29, 1850, December 6, 1851, John Wilson Papers, UCB.

16. Synopsis of Applicants for the California Judgeships, LAR, M-873, RG 59, NA.

17. Daniel Webster to Millard Fillmore, October 19, 1850, Fillmore Papers, BECHS; Louis Gruss, "Judah Philip Benjamin," *Louisiana Historical Quarterly* 19 (October 1936): 970–80; *SEJ*, 8:266–67.

18. John Wilson to Thomas Ewing, March 30, 1850, Ewing Family Papers, LC; Daniel Webster to Millard Fillmore, October 29, 1850, Fillmore Papers, BECHS; Judah P. Benjamin to Webster, October 18, 1850, LRD, RG 59, NA; John P. Healy to Webster, October 2, 1850, in Wiltse, *Papers of Daniel Webster*. On Fillmore's chagrin, see Fillmore to Webster, October 23, 1850, Fillmore Papers, BECHS.

19. Daniel Webster to Millard Fillmore, October 19, 1850; Fillmore to Leslie Combs, April 13, 1852, Fillmore Papers, BECHS; Truman Smith to John Wilson, November 29, 1850, Wilson Papers, UCB.

20. King endorsed two San Francisco lawyers: Kimball H. Dimmick and John Satterlee. Carne supported John Wilson. T. Butler King to Daniel Webster, November 11, 1850, LAR, M-873, RG 59, NA; Satterlee to Millard Fillmore, September 15, 1850, January 23, 1851; James Carne to Fillmore, August 31, 1850, Fillmore Papers, BECHS.

21. William Nelson to Millard Fillmore, December 21, 26, 1850, LAR, M-873, RG 59, NA; *SEJ*, 8:280; Fillmore to Daniel Webster, October 23, 1850, Fillmore Papers, BECHS. The president also appointed Nelson's son, Thomas, chief justice of Oregon.

22. Memorandum of Recommendation for Peabody Morse, December 12, [1850], LAR, M-873, RG 59, NA; George Cosgrave, "James McHall Jones," *California Historical Society Quarterly* 20 (January 1941): 111.

23. William Nelson to Millard Fillmore, January 24, 1851, LAR, M-873, RG 59, NA; Nelson to Andrew Pickens Butler, January 12, 1851; Nelson to Daniel Dickinson, January 1, 1851; Samuel F. Reynolds to Dickinson, January 13, 1850, John Currey Folder, SNF, RG 46, NA; *SEJ*, 8:286.

24. Marshall O. Roberts to Millard Fillmore, December 14, 1850; William H. Aspinwall to Fillmore, December 20, 1850, Fillmore Papers, BECHS; [James A.] Dorr to Aspinwall, January 25, 1851; Benjamin D. Silliman to Aspinwall, January 25, 1851; Dorr to John V. Plume, January 25, 1851, LAR, M-873, RG 59, NA.

25. William M. Gwin, George W. Wright, and Edward Gilbert to Millard Fillmore, February 1, 1851, LAR, M-873, RG 59, NA; *SEJ*, 8:287, 289.

26. J. H. Clay Mudd to Alexander H. H. Stuart, December 22, 1851, LAR, M-873, RG 59, NA; Daniel Webster to Millard Fillmore, February 15, 1852, Fillmore Papers, BECHS.

27. Andrew Pickens Butler to Millard Fillmore, February 2, 1852, LAR, M-873, RG 59, NA; J. H. Clay Mudd to John Wilson, May 9, 1852, Wilson Papers, UCB; *SEJ*, 8:370; U. S., *Statutes at Large*, vol. 10, pp. 84, 264–65.

28. John W. Crisfield to Mary Crisfield, January 13, 1851, John W. Crisfield Papers, MHS; Charles E. P. Smith to Millard Fillmore, November 12, 1850, Fillmore Papers, BECHS; Jean H. Baker, *The Politics of Continuity: Maryland Political Parties from 1858 to 1870*, pp. 1–6.

29. James A. Pearce to Thomas Corwin, March 8, 1852, Corwin Papers, LC; Pearce to Millard Fillmore, March 8, 1852, LAR, M-873, RG 59, NA.

30. Thomas Yates Walsh to Millard Fillmore, February 27, 1852; Reverdy Johnson to Fillmore, February 21, 1852; Roger B. Taney to Thomas G. Pratt, March 3, 1852, LAR, M-873, RG 59, NA.

31. John M. S. Causin to Millard Fillmore, March 11, 1857, LAR, M-873, RG 59, NA; Charles W. March to Daniel Webster, February 24, 1852, in Wiltse, *Papers of Daniel Webster;* John Barney to Fillmore, February 26, 1852, Fillmore Papers, BECHS.

32. Wallace Burr to Millard Fillmore, March 7, 1852; George E. Langston to Fillmore, March 17, 1852, LAR, M-873, RG 59, NA.

33. James A. Pearce to Thomas Corwin, March 1, 1852, Corwin Papers, LC; Jonathan Meredith to Daniel Webster, March 9, 1852, in Wiltse, *Papers of Daniel Webster,* Reverdy Johnson to David M. Perine, February 26, 1852, David M. Perine Correspondence, MHS.

34. Reverdy Johnson to Alexander H. H. Stuart, February 27, 1852, LAR, M-873, RG 59, NA; George E. Badger to Millard Fillmore, February 27, 1852, Fillmore Papers, BECHS; James A. Pearce to Thomas Corwin, March 5, 1852, Corwin Papers, LC.

35. James A. Pearce to Millard Fillmore, March 18, 1852, Fillmore Papers, BECHS.

36. Alfred Conkling to Millard Fillmore, August 17, 1852, Fillmore Papers, BECHS; Hamilton Fish to Thurlow Weed, September 1, 1852, Thurlow Weed Papers, UR; *SEJ*, 8:433, 436, 449.

37. Mendelson, "Dred Scott's Case," pp. 18–19.

38. Brigham Young to James K. Polk, August 19, 1849, James K. Polk Papers, LC.

39. Norman F. Furniss, *The Mormon Conflict, 1850–1859*, p. 13.

40. George Morey to Millard Fillmore, December 17, 1850, Fillmore Papers, BECHS; William R. King to Fillmore, September 14, 1850, RRAFJ, New Mexico, RG 60, NA.

41. Furniss, *The Mormon Conflict,* p. 7.

42. John M. Bernhisel to Millard Fillmore, September 16, 1850; Bernhisel to Brigham Young, August 9, 1850, John M. Bernhisel Papers, CALDS. The Mormons considered Fillmore a distinct improvement over Zachary Taylor, who condemned them as a "pack of outlaws . . . not fit for self-government." See Almon W. Babbitt to Young, July 7, 1850, John M. Bernhisel Papers, UHS.

43. William D. Gallagher to Millard Fillmore, February 25, 1851; John M. Bernhisel to Fillmore, September 16, 1850, Fillmore Papers, BECHS; John MacPherson Berrien and William G. Dawson to Fillmore, September 24, 1850, LAR, M-873, RG 59, NA.

44. John M. Bernhisel to Millard Fillmore, September 16, 1850, Fillmore Papers, BECHS; Thomas Leiper Kane to Brigham Young, September 24, 1850, Young Papers, CALDS; Almon W. Babbitt to Daniel Webster, September 21, 1850; Zerubbabel Snow to David K. Cartter, September 17, 1850; Joseph Casey and Thaddeus Stevens to Fillmore, n.d., LAR, M-873, RG 59, NA; William R. King to Fillmore, September 14, 1850, RRAFJ, New Mexico, RG 60, NA.

45. Alexander H. H. Stuart to Millard Fillmore, n.d.; John W. Allen to Fillmore, September 18, 1850, LAR, M-873, RG 59, NA; Daniel Webster to Fillmore, September 28, 1850, Fillmore Papers, BECHS; *SEJ,* 8:252, 253, 266.

46. Joseph Buffington to Millard Fillmore, January 23, 1851, LRD, RG 59, NA; Thaddeus Stevens to Fillmore, n.d.; Joseph Casey to Thomas Ewing, March 9, 1849; Lemuel G. Brandebury to Fillmore, February 17, 25, 1851, LAR, M-873, RG 59, NA.

47. Loomis Morton Ganaway, *New Mexico and the Sectional Controversy, 1846–1861,* pp. 120–44; Arrie W. Poldervaart, *Black-Robed Justice: A History of the Administration of Justice in New Mexico from the American Occupation in 1846 until Statehood in 1912,* pp. 28–37.

48. John W. Folger to Daniel Webster, n.d., LAR, M-873, RG 59, NA; *Republican* (St. Louis), December 28, 1850.

49. J. H. Peters to Thomas Corwin, January 15, 1851, Corwin Papers, LC; Corwin to Millard Fillmore, January 10, 1851, LAR, M-873, RG 59, NA.

50. George S. Yerger to Henry Clay, December 25, 1850, LAR, M-873, RG 59, NA; W. D. Gallagher to Millard Fillmore, February 25, 1851, Fillmore Papers, BECHS; Endorsement by William Gwin on Henry Foote to Fillmore, January 12, 1851, LAR, M-873, RG 59, NA; *SEJ,* 8:288, 291.

51. Edward McGaughey to Millard Fillmore, February 4, 1851; Jesse D. Bright to Fillmore, December 27, 1850, January 30, 1851; Indiana Congressional Delegation to Fillmore, n.d., LAR, M-873, RG 59, NA.

52. William D. Sprague to Daniel Webster, December 9, 1850; George S.

Bates to Webster, February 1, 1851; John McLean to Webster, December 14, 1850, LAR, M-873, RG 59, NA.

53. *SEJ,* 8:288, 291, 298, 305, 313.

54. Alexander Wilkin to Millard Fillmore, November 30, 1850; A. M. Mitchell to Fillmore, January 6, 1851, LAR, M-873, RG 59, NA; Robert C. Voight, "Defender of the Common Law: Aaron Goodrich, Chief Justice of Minnesota Territory" (Ph.D. diss., University of Minnesota, 1962), pp. 52–73.

55. Endorsement by Millard Fillmore on A. M. Mitchell to Fillmore, January 6, 1851, LAR, M-873, RG 59, NA; Daniel Webster to Fillmore, January 7, 1851, Fillmore Papers, BECHS; Henry H. Sibley to Alexander Ramsey, February 20, 1851, Alexander Ramsey Papers, MINNHS.

56. Henry H. Sibley to Alexander Ramsey, December 26, 1851, Ramsey Papers, MINNHS.

57. Benjamin F. Hall, comp., *Official Opinions of the Attorney General of the United States,* 5:288; Daniel Webster to Millard Fillmore, January 7, 1851, Fillmore Papers, BECHS.

58. CR, vol. 39, p. 310, RG 59, NA. Goodrich attributed his removal to an earlier dispute with Fillmore that had taken place when both men lived in Buffalo, New York. See Voight, "Defender of the Common Law," pp. 71–73. On the reaction in Minnesota, see Alexander Ramsey Diary, November 1, 1851, Ramsey Papers, MINNHS; Henry H. Sibley to Fillmore, July 13, 1852, Fillmore Papers, BECHS.

59. Sidney Teiser, "First Associate Justice of Oregon Territory: O. C. Pratt," *Oregon Historical Quarterly* 49 (September 1948): 180–84; William Nelson to Millard Fillmore, February 4, 1852, Fillmore Papers, BECHS; Memorandum of Charges against Grafton Baker, n.d., LAR, M-873, RG 59, NA.

60. John M. Bernhisel to Brigham Young, March 10, 1852, Young Papers, CALDS.

61. U. S., Congress, House, *Congressional Globe,* 32nd Cong., 1st sess., 1851, pp. 1235–38, 1377, 1409–13, 1531–33; U. S., *Statutes at Large,* vol. 10, pp. 98, 188.

62. Millard Fillmore to Luke Lea, May 8, 1852, LAR, M-873, RG 59, NA; Lemuel G. Brandebury to Daniel Webster, May 5, 1852, LRD, RG 59, NA; Matthew P. Deady to Joseph Lane, July 16, 1852, Joseph Lane Papers, OHS; CR, vol. 39, p. 329, RG 59, NA.

63. John Bernhisel to Brigham Young, February 13, 1852, Young Papers, CALDS.

64. John M. Bernhisel to Brigham Young, May 8, June 8, 1852, Young Papers, CALDS; Daniel Webster to Fillmore, December 31, 1851; Edwin C. Wilson to Thomas Corwin, April 30, 1852; Samuel Stokely to Fillmore, July 15, 1852, Fillmore Papers, BECHS; Bernhisel to Fillmore, April 30, 1852, LAR, M-873, RG 59, NA; Louis B. Schmidt, "The Miller-Thompson Election Contest," *Iowa Journal of History and Politics* 12 (January 1914): 43–53, 58–61.

65. Fred S. Martin to Millard Fillmore, February 11, 1852, LAR, M-873,

RG 59, NA; Reuben Robie et al. to John Bernhisel, August 4, 1852, Bernhisel Papers, CALDS.

66. Endorsement by David R. Atchison on Leonidas Shaver to Atchison, February 6, 1852, LAR, M-873, RG 59, NA; John Bernhisel to Brigham Young, August 13, 1852, Young Papers, CALDS.

67. Daniel Webster to Millard Fillmore, August 26, July 3, 1852; Fillmore to Webster, August 27, 1852, Fillmore Papers, BECHS; Arthur Train, *Puritan's Progress*, pp. 171–74.

68. Hamilton Fish to Thurlow Weed, September 1, 1852, Weed Papers, UR. Fillmore nominated and the Senate confirmed Henry Z. Hayner of Troy, New York. He was removed by Franklin Pierce before he ever reached Minnesota. See W. W. David to Millard Fillmore, September 20, 1852, Fillmore Papers, BECHS; *SEJ*, 8:477, 452.

69. Daniel Webster to Franklin Haven, April 28, 1851, in Wiltse, *Papers of Daniel Webster*.

CHAPTER 7

1. Samuel Treat to Caleb Cushing, August 26, 1853, Caleb Cushing Papers, LC.

2. Roy F. Nichols, *Franklin Pierce: Young Hickory of the Granite Hills*, pp. 285–93.

3. Roy F. Nichols, *The Democratic Machine, 1850–1854*, p. 189; Edmund Burke to Stephen A. Douglas, January 9, 1854, Stephen A. Douglas Papers, UC.

4. William L. Marcy to Caleb Cushing, March 31, 1853, Cushing Papers, LC; RAEJ, RG 60, NA.

5. Kermit L. Hall, "The Taney Court in the Second Party System: The Congressional Response to Federal Judicial Reform" (Ph.D. diss., University of Minnesota, 1972), pp. 184–285.

6. Caleb Cushing to Daniel Sickles, March 24, 1853, Cushing Papers, LC.

7. Memorandum on Appointment Policies, n.d., Cushing Papers, LC.

8. *Tribune Almanac and Political Register for 1854*, pp. 7–9.

9. Truman Powers to Joseph Lane, July 23, 1852, Joseph Lane Papers, OHS; J[ames] L. Collins to Millard Fillmore, March 22, 1852, LAR, M-873, RG 59, NA; Henry H. Sibley to Franklin Pierce, March 30, 1853, RRAFJ, Minnesota, RG 60, NA.

10. Norman F. Furniss, *The Mormon Conflict, 1850–1859*, p. 38.

11. *SEJ*, 9:74, 143.

12. W. C. Woodward, "The Rise and Early History of Political Parties in Oregon," *Quarterly of the Oregon Historical Society* 11 (December 1910): 43–55; Sidney Teiser, "The Second Chief Justice of Oregon Territory: Thomas Nelson," *Oregon Historical Quarterly* 48 (September 1947): 214–24.

13. Joseph Lane to William L. Marcy, March 9, 1853, RRAFJ, Oregon,

RG 60, NA; Lane to James Nesmith, December 13, 1853, Lane Papers, OHS.

14. Joseph Lane to Franklin Pierce, June 20, 1853, RRAFJ, Oregon, RG 60, NA. Apparently, Douglas believed Pratt had speculated in the English-owned Hudson's Bay Company. Pratt claimed he was innocent. See Pratt to Matthew P. Deady, November 30, 1853; Joseph Lane to Deady, June 18, 1854, Matthew P. Deady Papers, OHS; Pratt to Douglas, June [19], 1853, Douglas Papers, UC; *SEJ*, 9:155, 160.

15. Amory Holbrook to Caleb Cushing, May 30, 1853, Cushing Papers, LC; Matthew P. Deady to William L. Marcy, June 11, 1853, RRAFJ, Oregon, RG 60, NA.

16. Joseph Lane to Matthew P. Deady, June 18, 1854, Deady Papers, OHS; Cyrus Olney to Lane, November 1, 1853, RRAFJ, Oregon; Endorsement by Franklin Pierce on James Buchanan to Pierce, March, 1853, RRAFJ, Minnesota, RG 60, NA; Sidney Teiser, "Obadiah B. McFadden, Oregon and Washington Territorial Judge," *Oregon Historical Quarterly* 66 (March 1965): 25–37.

17. James Nesmith to Matthew P. Deady, January 9, 1854; Joseph Lane to Deady, June 18, 1854, Deady Papers; Orville C. Pratt to Lane, December 1, 1853, Lane Papers, OHS; *SEJ*, 9:225, 229.

18. *St. Anthony Express* (Minn.), May 6, 1854; *Minnesota Democrat*, May 8, 1854.

19. Henry H. Sibley to William L. Marcy, March 21, 1853; Sibley to Franklin Pierce, March 30, 1853, RRAFJ, Minnesota, RG 60, NA; Sibley to Stephen A. Douglas, March 16, 1853, Douglas Papers, UC; *SEJ*, 9:147, 149.

20. Alfred O. P. Nicholson to Franklin Pierce, September 19, 1853, RRAFJ, New Mexico, RG 60, NA.

21. Endorsement by Jefferson Davis on James J. Deavenport to Davis, January 30, 1853; Clement C. Clay, Jr., to Franklin Pierce, December 17, 1853; Stephen A. Douglas et al. to Pierce, March 7, 1853; Memorandum on Nominees for the New Mexico Judgeships, n.d., RRAFJ, New Mexico, RG 60, NA; Perry E. Brocchus to Caleb Cushing, September 27, 1854, Cushing Papers, LC.

22. John M. Bernhisel to Brigham Young, February 5, 1853, January 13, 1854, Brigham Young Papers, CALDS; Robert W. Johannsen, *Stephen A. Douglas*, p. 378.

23. Brigham Young to Franklin Pierce, March 30, 1853, Young Papers, CALDS.

24. John M. Bernhisel to Brigham Young, March 11, April 11, 1854, Young Papers, CALDS; Franklin Pierce to Caleb Cushing, June 23, [1854], Cushing Papers, LC; Louis B. Schmidt, "The Miller-Thompson Election Contest," *Iowa Journal of History and Politics* 12 (January 1914): 34–127.

25. Joseph H. Lumpkin to Caleb Cushing, September 10, 1853; Elijah W. Chastain to Cushing, September 11, 1853; Howell Cobb to Cushing, September 12, 1855, RRAFJ, Utah, RG 60, NA; *SEJ*, 9:224, 265.

26. Joseph H. Lumpkin to Caleb Cushing, August 26, 1855, RRAFJ, Kansas; George P. Stiles to Jeremiah S. Black, February 26, 1858, RRAFJ, Utah,

RG 60, NA; John M. Bernhisel to Brigham Young, April 15, 17, 18, October 18, 1854; Young to Bernhisel, June 29, 1854, Young Papers, CALDS; William W. Drummond to Stephen A. Douglas, December 30, 1854, Douglas Papers, UC; Dennis L. Lythgoe, "Negro Slavery In Utah," *Utah Historical Quarterly* 39 (Winter 1971): 48–49.

27. *St. Anthony Express*, May 6, 1854.

28. Pierce's appointees reflected the wish of the administration and the Senate to achieve sectional representation on this court. Chief Justice John J. Gilchrist of New Hampshire represented the East, while Associate Justices Isaac Newton Blackford of Indiana and George Parker Scarburgh of Virginia represented the West and the South respectively. See *RRAFJ*, Court of Claims, RG 60, NA.

29. The quote is attributed to Pierce in O. H. Brown to Caleb Cushing, June 10, 1854, Cushing Papers, LC.

30. On the recommendation of Cushing, Pierce on June 22, 1854, nominated Fenner Ferguson of Michigan chief justice and James Bradley of Laporte, Indiana, and Edward R. Harden of Dalton, Georgia, associate justices of Nebraska. The Democratic congressional delegates of these respective states mediated the selection process. See generally RRAFJ, Nebraska, RG 60, NA; *SEJ*, 9:340, 345; Nichols, *Franklin Pierce*, pp. 407–18.

31. John A. Campbell to Franklin Pierce, May 27, 1854, RRAFJ, Kansas, RG 60, NA.

32. Alfred P. Edgerton to Franklin Pierce, June 8, 1854; Democratic Members of the Ohio Legislature to Pierce, June 12, 1854, RRAFJ, Kansas, RG 60, NA; Stephen A. Douglas to Pierce, March 30, 1853, LAR, M-967, RG 59, NA; Saunders W. Johnston to Douglas, March 24, 1854, Douglas Papers, UC; *SEJ*, 9:341, 345.

33. James Bridges et al. to Franklin Pierce, February 6, 1854; Sterling Price to Pierce, May 4, 1854; Madison Brown to Caleb Cushing, August 9, 1854, RRAFJ, Kansas, RG 60 NA; Endorsement by Cushing on Brown to Henry May, June 4, 1854, Cushing Papers, LC; *SEJ*, 9:340, 345.

34. Richard H. Jackson to Franklin Pierce, September 20, 1854; Henry May to Caleb Cushing, August 13, 1853, Philip S. Thomas to Pierce, October 2, 1854, RRAFJ, Kansas, RG 60, NA; MPTC, RG 59, NA; *SEJ*, 9:399–400.

35. T. M. Lillard, "Beginnings of the Kansas Judiciary," *Kansas Historical Quarterly* 5 (February 1941): 91–95.

36. Caleb Cushing to Associate Justices of Kansas Territory, June 14, 1855, in *Kansas State Historical Society Collections* 5 (1889–1896): 227–28.

37. Rush Elmore to Caleb Cushing, August 23, 1855, AG, LR, RG 60, NA.

38. John A. Campbell to Caleb Cushing, August 31, April 31, 1855; C. C. Clay, Jr., to Franklin Pierce, August 26, 1855; Memorandum of Applicants for the Kansas Associate Judgeship, n.d., RRAFJ, Kansas, RG 60, NA.

39. James Campbell to Caleb Cushing, August 31, 1855; Campbell to Franklin Pierce, September 5, 1855, RRAFJ, Kansas, RG 60, NA; MPTC, RG 59, NA; *SEJ*, 10:3, 36.

40. Elmer L. Craik, "Southern Interest in Territorial Kansas, 1854–1858," *Kansas State Historical Society Collections* 15 (1919–1922): 395–99.

41. Memorandum of Applicants for the Associate Judgeship in Kansas vice J. Burrell, n.d.; Thomas Cunningham to Franklin Pierce, November 6, 1856, RRAFJ, Kansas, RG 60, NA; *SEJ*, 10:164, 169.

42. John W. Geary to Franklin Pierce, September 19, 1856, LAR, M-967, RG 59, NA; Geary to Pierce, December 22, 1856, January 12, 1857, Franklin Pierce Papers, LC; James Guthrie to John C. Breckenridge, November 27, December 4, 1856, John C. Breckenridge Papers, LC; Samuel D. Lecompte to Caleb Cushing, January 9, 1857, AG, LR, RG 60, NA.

43. Paul H. Bergeron, "The Jacksonian Party on Trial: Presidential Politics in Tennessee, 1836–1856" (Ph.D. diss., Vanderbilt University, 1965), pp. 321–32.

44. A. O. P. Nicholson to Franklin Pierce, April 12, 1853, in Joseph H. Parks, ed., "Some Tennessee Letters, 1849–1864," *Tennessee Historical Quarterly* 4 (September 1945): 244.

45. John Catron to Franklin Pierce, March 10, 1853; Catron to Andrew P. Butler, March 10, 1853, RRAFJ, Tennessee, RG 60, NA.

46. Gideon Pillow to Caleb Cushing, March 7, 9, 1853, Cushing Papers, LC; Aaron V. Brown to Franklin Pierce, March 11, 1853, RRAFJ, Tennessee, RG 60, NA.

47. A. O. P. Nicholson to Caleb Cushing, April 19, 1853, Cushing Papers, LC; Memorandum on Candidates for District Judge of East and West Tennessee vice Morgan W. Brown, Deceased, n.d., RRAFJ, Tennessee, RG 60, NA; Andrew Johnson to William L. Marcy, June 26, 1856, Andrew Johnson Papers, LC; *SEJ*, 9:104, 109.

48. Henry B. Payne to Franklin Pierce, February 16, 1854; Members of Congress from the Northern Judicial District of Ohio to Pierce, February 8, 1855, RG 60, NA; Hiram V. Willson to Stephen A. Douglas, November 18, 1852, Douglas Papers, UC.

49. Arthur W. Thompson, *Jacksonian Democracy on the Florida Frontier*, pp. 18–29.

50. William G. Davis to Franklin Pierce, December 15, 1855, RRAFJ, North Florida, RG 60, NA.

51. Stephen R. Mallory to Franklin Pierce, August 29, 1855; Endorsement by Mallory on John K. Samis to Mallory, November 12, 1855, RRAFJ, North Florida, RG 60, NA.

52. Memorandum on Candidates for District Judge of North Florida, n.d.; Stephen R. Mallory to Franklin Pierce, January 14, 1854; Augustus E. Maxwell to Pierce, January 10, 1856, RRAFJ, North Florida, RG 60, NA.

53. David L. Yulee to Franklin Pierce, February 11, 1856, RRAFJ, North Florida, RG 60, NA.

54. On the South Carolina and Texas appointments see Andrew P. Butler to Josiah Evans, May 3, 1856, RRAFJ, South Carolina; Thomas J. Rusk to Franklin Pierce, n.d., RRAFJ, Western District of Texas, RG 60, NA; *SEJ*, 10:58, 64, 90, 91, 206, 208.

55. The president, on the recommendation of Senators Gwin and Weller of California, appointed Matthew H. MacAllister judge of the new circuit court for California. See William H. Ellison, "Memoirs of Honorable William M. Gwin," *California Historical Society Quarterly* 19 (September 1940): 261; Herschel V. Johnson to Franklin Pierce, February 3, 1855, RRAFJ, Southern California, RG 60, NA.

56. George Cosgrave, *Early California Justice: The History of the United States District Court for the Southern District of California*, pp. 33–48.

57. David A. Williams, *David C. Broderick: A Political Portrait*, pp. 50–55, 74–76.

58. Isaac Martineau to Robert McClellan, December 1, 1853; Milton S. Latham to Franklin Pierce, January 15, 1853; James A. McDougall to Pierce, January 13, 1853, RRAFJ, Southern District of California, RG 60, NA.

59. Isaac S. K. Ogier to [John B. Weller], January 22, 1853; Weller and William M. Gwin to Franklin Pierce, January 17, 1854, RRAFJ, Southern District of California, RG 60, NA; Ogier to Abel Stearns, n.d., Abel Stearns Papers, HU.

60. See Isaac Toucey to Franklin Pierce, April 1, 1853, RRAFJ, Connecticut; Stephen A. Douglas to Pierce, February 20, 1855, RRAFJ, Southern Illinois; George W. Jones to Pierce, February 1, 1856, RRAFJ, Iowa, RG 60, NA.

61. U. S., Congress, House, *Congressional Globe*, 32nd Cong., 1st sess., Appendix, p. 678.

62. The single exception was his selection of John J. Gilchrist, chief justice of the New Hampshire Supreme Court, to be chief justice of the Court of Claims. See Nichols, *Franklin Pierce*, p. 378; *SEJ*, 9:438, 443.

CHAPTER 8

1. Jefferson Buford to James Buchanan, September 17, 1856, RRAFJ, Alabama, RG 60, NA.

2. Allan Nevins, *The Emergence of Lincoln*, vol. 1, *Douglas, Buchanan and Party Chaos, 1847–1859*, p. 64.

3. Philip Shriver Klein, *President James Buchanan: A Biography*, pp. 304–5, 428–29.

4. Eric Foner, *Free-Soil, Free Labor, Free Men: The Idelology of the Republican Party before the Civil War* (New York: Oxford University Press, 1970), pp. 292–93; Stanley W. Campbell, *The Slave Catchers: Enforcement of the Fugitive Slave Law, 1850–1860*, pp. 49–96, 148–86.

5. Arthur Bestor, "State Sovereignty and Slavery: A Reinterpretation of Proslavery Constitutional Doctrine, 1846–1860," *Journal of the Illinois State Historical Society* 54 (Summer 1961): 117–80; Norman Furniss, *The Mormon Conflict, 1850–1859*, pp. 21–94.

6. David M. Potter, *The Impending Crisis, 1848–1861*, p. 313; *Tribune Almanac and Political Register for 1860*, pp.7–8.

7. Roy F. Nichols, *The Disruption of American Democracy* (New York: Macmillan Co., 1948), pp. 86–103.

8. Potter, *The Impending Crisis*, pp. 56–62, 71–72, 82, 171–75, 271, 328, 402, 421–22.

9. Joseph Lane to Matthew P. Deady, April 17, 1858, Matthew P. Deady Papers, OHS.

10. James Buchanan to Robert Tyler, June 27, 28, 1859, James Buchanan Papers, HSP.

11. John Bassett Moore, ed., *The Works of James Buchanan*, 5:205, 209; James Buchanan to Robert C. Grier, November 14, 1856; Buchanan to Fernando Wood, December 1, 1856, Buchanan Papers, HSP.

12. The quote is from William Norwood Brigance, *Jeremiah Sullivan Black: A Defender of the Constitution and the Ten Commandments*, p. 56.

13. Moore, *The Works of James Buchanan*, 1:149, 444–45; 5:311.

14. James Buchanan to William M. Gwin, March 30, 1853, William M. Gwin Papers, UCB.

15. James Buchanan to Fernando Wood, December 1, 1856, Buchanan Papers, HSP.

16. David Meerse, "James Buchanan, the Patronage and the Northern Democratic Party, 1857–1858" (Ph.D. diss., University of Illinois, 1969), pp. 566–90.

17. Donald Bruce Johnson and Kirk H. Porter, comps., *National Party Platforms, 1840–1972*, p. 27.

18. *JH*, January 7, 8, April 7, 1857, January 7, 1858, CALDS.

19. George P. Stiles to Jeremiah S. Black, February 26, 1858, AG, LR, RG 60, NA. The judges criticized the Mormon-manned territorial probate courts for circumventing the federal courts. See John F. Kinney to Black, n.d., RRAFJ, Utah, RG 60, NA.

20. Record of Interviews with the President, Fall, 1857, John M. Bernhisel Papers, CALDS.

21. "Notes Regarding Utah," Buchanan Papers, HSP; George P. Stiles to Jeremiah S. Black, February 26, 1858; John F. Kinney to Black, [1857], AG, LR, RG 60, NA.

22. Memorandum for the President of the United States on Utah Affairs, [1858], Thomas L. Kane Papers; John M. Bernhisel to Brigham Young, March 18, 1858, Brigham Young Papers, CALDS.

23. Delana R. Eckles to Lewis Cass, March 26, 1857; Eckles to Jacob S. Thompson, March 25, 1857; Jesse D. Bright to Lewis Cass, April 11, 1857, LAR, M-967, RG 59, NA; AAE, Utah, RG 60, NA; MPTC, RG 59, NA.

24. Emery D. Potter to Lewis Cass, April 1, 1857; Lawrence W. Hall et al. to James Buchanan, March 30, 1857, RRAFJ, Utah; AAE, Utah, RG 60, NA; MPTC, RG 59, NA; *JH*, October 27, 1858.

25. Alfred Cumming to James C. Orr, May 12, 1858, Buchanan Papers,

HSP; John M. Bernhisel to Brigham Young, June 29, 1858, Young Papers, CALDS.

26. Jeremiah S. Black to Alexander Wilson, August [17], 1858, AG, LS, RG 60, NA.

27. William H. Hooper to Brigham Young, February 12, March 12, 1860, William H. Hooper Papers, CALDS; Furniss, *The Mormon Conflict*, pp. 211–27.

28. William H. Hooper to Brigham Young, February 12, 1860, Hooper Papers, CALDS; Jeremiah S. Black to James Buchanan, March 17, 1860, Buchanan Papers, HSP.

29. William H. Hooper to Brigham Young, February 12, 1860, Hooper Papers, CALDS.

30. Jeremiah S. Black to Brigham Young, July 12, 1860, AG, LS, RG 60, NA; Thomas L. Kane to Brigham Young, July 24, 1859, Young Papers, CALDS.

31. Brigham Young to William H. Hooper, January 30, 1860, Hooper Papers, CALDS; AAE, Utah, RG 60, NA.

32. William H. Hooper to Brigham Young, June 24, 1860, Hooper Papers, CALDS; *JH*, September 24, 1860; AAE, Utah, RG 60, NA; *SEJ*, 11:210, 221, 226, 265, 277.

33. A. G. Eye to Jeremiah S. Black, March 12, 1857, Jeremiah S. Black Papers, LC.

34. Meerse, "James Buchanan, the Patronage and the Northern Democratic Party," pp. 262–66.

35. *Kansas State Historical Society Collections,* 16 (1923–1925): 659.

36. Thomas M. Jett to James Buchanan, February 23, 1857; George W. Jones to Lewis Cass, March 17, 1857; James Craig to Buchanan, March 17, 1857, RRAFJ, Kansas; AAE, Kansas, RG 60, NA.

37. Robert J. Walker to James Buchanan, June 28, 1857, Buchanan Papers, HSP.

38. Moore, *The Works of James Buchanan,* 10:192, 235, 341.

39. James W. Denver to James Buchanan, January 16, 1858, Buchanan Papers, HSP; John Martin, "Biographical Sketch of Judge Rush Elmore," *Kansas State Historical Collections* 8 (1903–1904): 435–36.

40. John Pettit to James Buchanan, December 20, August 21, 1858; Jesse D. Bright to Buchanan, August 23, 1858; Judah P. Benjamin to Buchanan, September 6, 1858; Benjamin Fitzpatrick to Buchanan, September 20, 1858, RRAFJ, Kansas, RG 60, NA.

41. *New York Tribune,* March 2, 1859. The vote was thirty-two to sixteen in favor of Elmore and twenty-nine to thirteen in favor of Pettit. The vote followed party lines. *SEJ,* 11:38, 93.

42. Joseph Lane to James Buchanan, August 31, 1857, RRAFJ, Oregon; Henry M. Rice to Jeremiah S. Black, April 1, 1857, RRAFJ, Minnesota; Isaac Stevens to Black, March 16, 1858, RRAFJ, Washington, RG 60, NA; Loomis

Morton Ganaway, *New Mexico and the Sectional Controversy, 1846–1861*, pp. 60–76, 84, 85, 92, 95; Meerse, "James Buchanan, the Patronage and the Northern Democratic Party," pp. 245–51.

43. See Appendix B.

44. James Buchanan to William M. Gwin, March 30, 1853, Gwin Papers, UCB.

45. U. S., Congress, House, *Congressional Globe*, 36th Cong., 1st sess., pp. 667, 759; Moore, *The Works of James Buchanan*, 10:143, 342; 11:11.

46. Richard Vaux to James Buchanan, July 24, 1857; Robert Tyler to Buchanan, December 29, 1857, Buchanan Papers, HSP.

47. Nichols, *The Disruption of American Democracy*, pp. 208–9.

48. Papers Relating to the Case of John K. Kane, IP, RG 233, NA; Meerse, "James Buchanan, the Patronage and the Northern Democratic Party," pp. 394–95.

49. William Bigler to James Buchanan, February 24, 1858, Buchanan Papers; James Campbell to Bigler, February 27, 1858, William L. Bigler Papers, HSP; Memorandum of Endorsements for Judge of the Eastern District of Pennsylvania, 1858, RRAFJ, Eastern District of Pennsylvania, RG 60, NA.

50. James C. Van Dyke to James Buchanan, April 6, 1858; Joseph B. Baker to Buchanan, April 12, 1858, Buchanan Papers, HSP; AAE, Eastern District of Pennsylvania, RG 60, NA; *Philadelphia Evening Journal*, April 10, 1858.

51. Joseph B. Baker to James Buchanan, April 12, 1858, Buchanan Papers; John Cadwalader to J. Buchanan Henry, February 24, 27, 1858, John C. Cadwalader Papers, HSP.

52. James C. Van Dyke to James Buchanan, April 6, 1858; Buchanan to Van Dyke, April 7, 1858; Lewis C. Cassidy to Buchanan, April 14, 1858, Buchanan Papers, HSP.

53. Joseph B. Baker to James Buchanan, April 23, 1858, Buchanan Papers, HSP; *Philadelphia North American and United States Gazette*, February 25, March 2, 3, 18, April 12, 1858.

54. James Buchanan to James C. Van Dyke, April 7, 1858, Buchanan Papers, HSP.

55. *New York Tribune*, April 26, 1858; *Philadelphia North American and United States Gazette*, April 21, 22, 26, 1858. Bigler and Republican Senator Simon Cameron of Pennsylvania were among the thirty votes to confirm; eight Republicans voted to reject. *SEJ*, 10:364, 368.

56. Thomas Irwin to Lewis Cass, January 26, 1859, LRD, RG 59; Papers Relating to the Case of Thomas Irwin, IP, RG 233, NA; *Pittsburgh Morning Post*, January 17, 22, 24, 25, 28, 1859; *Pittsburgh Gazette*, January 22, 27, 28, 29, 1859.

57. Joseph B. Baker to James Buchanan, January 28, 1859, Buchanan Papers, HSP; *Pittsburgh Morning Post*, February 4, 1859; *Pittsburgh Gazette*, February 2, 1859.

58. George R. Barrett to William Bigler, February 1, 1859, Bigler Papers, HSP; AAE, Western District of Pennsylvania, RG 60, NA; *Pittsburgh Gazette*, January 31, 1859; *SEJ*, 11:50, 53.

59. Joseph Lane to Matthew P. Deady, April 17, 1859, Deady Papers, OHS; Samuel Nelson to James Buchanan, January 12, 1858; Henry M. Rice to Jeremiah S. Black, May 1, 1858, RRAFJ, Minnesota, RG 60, NA.

60. Memorandum by Attorney General Jeremiah S. Black, "Court Operations in Alabama," [1858], RRAFJ, Alabama, RG 60, NA.

61. John A. Campbell to Jeremiah S. Black, September 5, 1859, RRAFJ, Alabama, RG 60, NA.

62. Clement C. Clay, Jr., to James Buchanan, July 25, 1859; Clay to Jacob Thompson, August 15, 1859; Reuben Chapman to Thompson, July 26, 1859, RRAFJ, Alabama, RG 60, NA.

63. Jeremiah S. Black to James Buchanan, August 3, 1859, RRAFJ, Alabama, RG 60, NA.

64. Benjamin Fitzpatrick to James Buchanan, July 25, 1859, RRAFJ, Alabama, RG 60, NA.

65. John A. Campbell to Jeremiah S. Black, September 5, August 25, 1859; Black to Buchanan, August 3, 1859, RRAFJ, Alabama, RG 60, NA.

66. Sydenham Moore to Jacob Thompson, August 10, 1859, RRAFJ, Alabama, RG 60, NA.

67. John A. Campbell to Jeremiah S. Black, August 25, 1859; Benjamin Fitzpatrick to James Buchanan, August 6, 1859, RRAFJ, Alabama; AAE, Alabama, RG 60, NA.

68. James Buchanan to Virginia C. Clay, October 15, 1859, Buchanan Papers, HSP; MPTC, RG 59, NA.

69. Virginia C. Clay to James Buchanan, October 5, 1859, Buchanan Papers, HSP; Clement C. Clay, Jr., to Jacob Thompson, August 15, 1859, RRAFJ, Alabama, RG 60, NA.

70. James Buchanan to Virginia C. Clay, October 15, 1859, Buchanan Papers, HSP; *SEJ*, 11:128, 134.

71. The "western" associate justiceship was bestowed, at the urging of Sen. Jesse D. Bright, on James Hughes of Indiana. AAE, Court of Claims, [1860], RG 60, NA; Samuel Shapiro, "The Rendition of Anthony Burns," *Journal of Negro History* 44 (June 1959): 34–51.

72. William M. Gwin et al. to James Buchanan, n.d., RRAFJ, Court of Claims, RG 60, NA; John Clark to Buchanan, March 19, 1858, Buchanan Papers, HSP.

73. *New York Tribune*, May 4, 1858. The vote was twenty-seven to thirteen to confirm. *SEJ*, 11:374, 391.

74. *SEJ*, 11:262.

75. Moore, *The Works of James Buchanan*, 11:10; AAE, Kansas, RG 60, NA; John Pettit to John McLean, April 28, 1860, John McLean Papers, LC.

76. *New York Times*, February 22, 1861. The Senate also refused to act on the nomination of Congressman William E. Niblack to be associate justice of

Nebraska territory. See, for both Pettit and Niblack, *SEJ*, 11:274, 275, 288.

77. As quoted in Klein, *James Buchanan*, p. 305.

CHAPTER 9

1. *United States Monthly Law Magazine* 3 (March 1851): 542.

2. Lawrence Stone, "Prosopography," *Daedalus* 100 (Winter 1971): 46–79; John R. Schmidhauser, "The Justices of the Supreme Court: A Collective Portrait," *Midwest Journal of Political Science* 3 (February 1959): 1–57.

3. Robert E. Scott, "Political Elites and Political Modernization: The Crisis of Transition," in Seymour Martin Lipset and Aldo Solari, eds., *Elites in Latin America*, pp. 117–45; Richard D. Brown, *Modernization: The Transformation of American Life, 1600–1865* (New York: Hill and Wang, 1976), pp. 3–22.

4. Presidents nominated 224 judges, but 24 of these were renominations of sitting territorial judges. For purposes of the collective biography, a judge was attributed only to the first administration that appointed him. However, if a judge terminated his service and was nominated months or years later by a different president, then he was attributed to both administrations.

5. Frances Trollope, *Domesitc Manners of the Americans*, p. 121.

6. Lillian C. Tuthill, *Success in Life. The Lawyer; Yale Literary Magazine* 10 (November 1844): 3; *DeBow's Review* 2 (September 1846): 151, 19 (September 1855): 301–8, (October 1855): 389–405, (November 1855): 507–25, (December 1855): 637–48.

7. Edward Pessen, *Jacksonian America: Society, Personality and Politics*, pp. 251–54, 357–59; Ronald P. Formisano, "Toward a Reorientation of Jacksonian Politics: A Review of the Literature, 1959–1975," *Journal of American History* 63 (June 1976):49–52; J. Willard Hurst, *The Growth of American Law: The Law Makers* (Boston: Little, Brown & Co., 1950), pp. 131–49.

8. Edward Pessen, *Riches, Class and Power Before the Civil War*, p. 304.

9. Ibid., pp. 52–58; Maxwell Bloomfield, *American Lawyers in a Changing Society, 1776–1876*, pp. 136–90; Gary B. Nash, "The Philadelphia Bench and Bar, 1800–1861," *Comparative Studies in Society and History* 7 (January 1965): 203–20.

10. See Appendix A.

11. P. K. Whelpton, "Occupational Groups in the United States, 1820–1920," *Journal of the American Statistical Association* 21 (September 1926): 328–42. These and subsequent findings are elaborated in fuller detail in Kermit L. Hall, "240 Men: The Antebellum Lower Federal Judiciary, 1829–1861," *Vanderbilt Law Review* 29 (October 1976): 1089–1129.

12. John Glenn to Elias Glenn, July 5, 1815, Oliver Papers, MHS.

13. Lee Soltow, *Men and Wealth in the United States, 1850–1870*, p. 65. Census, estate, and tax records containing wealth information were available for 63 percent of the fathers. See Appendix A.

14. Personal Tax Roles, 1841, 1849, Claiborne County, Mississippi, MIS-HDA; Seventh Census of the United States, 1850, Claiborne County, Mississippi, NA; Case 1714, July 1821, Probate Court, Philadelphia County, Pennsylvania, GSLDS; Estate Records, Thomas Cadwalader Papers, HSP.

15. See Appendix A.

16. Twenty-one percent of Whig nominees were from elite social-class positions versus 11 percent of the Democrats. Hall, "240 Men," p. 1117.

17. As quoted in Ralph Lerner, "The Supreme Court as a Republican Schoolmaster," in Phillip B. Kurland, ed., *The Supreme Court Review: 1967*, pp. 128, 155.

18. Lawrence M. Friedman, *A History of American Law* (New York: Simon and Schuster, 1973), p. 326.

19. John D. W. Guice, *The Rocky Mountain Bench: The Territorial Supreme Courts of Colorado, Montana, and Wyoming, 1861–1890* (New Haven: Yale University Press, 1972), pp. 60–80.

20. Data on college education before 1840 are uncertain at best. See *American Almanac and Repository of Useful Knowledge for the Year 1831*, 2:167. Judges who attended or graduated from a law school were not included in the totals for academic education.

21. Friedman, *A History of American Law*, pp. 278–92.

22. "The Prospects of the American Lawyer," *Yale Literary Magazine* 10 (March 1844): 1.

23. Alexis de Tocqueville, *Democracy in America*, trans. Henry Reeve, 1:278; Pessen, *Riches, Class and Power*, pp. 52–58.

24. See Appendix A.

25. "Autobiography of Horace Binney," Horace Binney Papers, HSP; *National Intelligencer*, March 5, 1855; Millard Fillmore to Daniel Webster, October 23, 1850, Millard Fillmore Papers, BECHS.

26. Soltow, *Men and Wealth*, pp. 9–19, 27–32, 69–74, 105–8, 174–83. The judges accumulated significant wealth; the average of the highest known wealth, for the 60 percent of the judges for whom data were available, was $28,870, or more than twelve times the average wealth of an adult white male in 1860. See Hall, "240 Men," p. 1105.

27. Edward R. Harden to [Caroline R.] Harden, June 29, 1854, Edward Harden Family Papers, DU.

28. See, for example, Peleg Sprague to William Henry Harrison, April 5, 1841, LAR, M-687, RG 59, NA; John Cadwalader to James Buchanan Henry, February 27, 1858, John Cadwalader Papers, HSP.

29. James M. Jones to Joseph Hornsby, James M. Jones Papers, UCB.

30. The percentage for successful election understates the actual level of political participation; some nominees ran but lost, while others held only appointive offices. See Hall, "240 Men," p. 1108.

31. Alexander Porter to John J. Crittenden, July 2, 1837, John J. Crittenden Papers, LC.

32. Bloomfield, *Lawyers in a Changing Society*, pp. 136–90; *Philadelphia North American and United States Gazette*, February 27, 1858.

33. Robert P. Fogerty, "An Institutional Study of the Territorial Courts of the Old Northwest, 1788–1848" (Ph.D. diss., University of Minnesota, 1942), pp. 141–46.

34. Timothy Walker, "The Administration of Justice," *Western Law Journal* 3 (October 1850): 10.

35. *Western Law Journal* 2 (December 1849): 110.

CHAPTER 10

1. *Western Law Journal* 3 (January 1846): 150.

2. Leonard D. White, *The Jacksonians: A Study in Administrative History, 1829–1861*, p. 124.

APPENDIX A

1. Ralph Dahrendorf, *Class Conflict in Industrial Society*, pp. 118–222; Edward Pessen, *Riches, Class and Power Before the Civil War*, pp. 47, 49–52, 74–75.

2. Sidney H. Aronson, *Status and Kinship in the Higher Civil Service* (Cambridge, Mass.:Harvard University Press, 1964), pp. 56–83; Pessen, *Riches, Class and Power*, p. 74; Charles F. Westoff, Marvin Bressler, and Philip C. Sagi, "The Concept of Social Mobility: An Empirical Inquiry," *American Sociological Review* 25 (June 1960): 375–85.

3. Aronson, *Status and Kinship in the Higher Civil Service*, pp. 56–66; Solomon Fabricant, "The Changing Industrial Distribution of Gainful Workers: Comments on the Decennial Censuses, 1820–1840," *Studies in Income and Wealth* 11 (1949): 31–32; P. K. Whelpton, "Occupational Groups in the United States, 1820–1920," *Journal of the American Statistical Association* 21 (September 1926): 348–52.

4. Wealth and family data were collected in the Genealogical Library of the Church of Jesus Christ of Latter-Day-Saints. See Larry Wimmer and Clane L. Pope, "The Genealogical Society Library of Salt Lake City: A Source of Data for Economic and Social Historians," *Historical Methods Newsletter* 8 (April 1975): 51–59.

5. Kenneth Stampp, *The Peculiar Institution: Slavery in the Antebellum South* (New York: Alfred A. Knopf, 1956), pp. 201–2, 388, 402, 414–17.

6. Lee Soltow, *Men and Wealth in the United States, 1850–1870;* Robert Gallman, "Trends in the Size Distribution of Wealth in the Nineteenth Century: Some Speculations," in Lee Soltow, ed., *Six Papers on the Size Distribution of Wealth and Income*, pp. 1–32; Alice Hansen Jones, "Wealth Estimates for the American Middle Colonies, 1774," *Economic Development and Cultural Change* 18 (1970): 1–172.

7. Note the contradictory assessments of the antebellum social order in Rowland Berthoff, *An Unsettled People: Social Order and Disorder in American History*, pp. 125–275; Stephen Thernstorm, *Poverty and Progress: Social Mobility in a Nineteenth-Century City.*

SELECTED BIBLIOGRAPHY

I

Since the end of the Civil War, historians have probed for the roots of the antebellum political culture. The early literature, with its emphasis on the causes of the war, is ably dissected in Thomas J. Pressly, *Americans Interpret Their Civil War*, 2nd ed. rev. (New York: Free Press, 1962) and William H. Cartright and Richard L. Watson, Jr., eds., *The Reinterpretation of American History and Culture* (Washington, D.C.: National Council for the Social Sciences, 1973). Beginning in the early 1960s, political historians gradually lost interest in the sectional conflict and the coming of the Civil War; instead, they sought the rudiments—party, legislative behavior, and the social bases of popular voting—of the political culture. Roy F. Nichols in many ways provided the indispensable link between generations of historians. Intrigued by the potential of social science methods and intimately familiar with the political issues and leaders of the antebellum era, Nichols did much to crack the traditional emphasis on sectionalism and slavery. His two major works, *The Disruption of American Democracy* (1948) and *The Invention of American Political Parties* (1967)—both published in New York by Macmillan—were especially influential in demonstrating the potential of a cogent analysis of political parties. The message implicit in the work of Nichols was made explicit by Joel H. Silbey, "The Civil War Synthesis in American Political History," *Civil War History* 10 (June 1964): 130–40. Silbey insisted that the traditional emphasis on sectionalism and slavery had badly distorted understanding of antebellum politics and political institutions and that the damage could best be rectified through an infusion of social science methods, especially quantitative analysis of voting and legislative behavior. Silbey's essay coincided with an outpouring of explicitly revisionist historical writing. The best introduc-

233

tions to this literature remain Allan G. Bogue, "United States: The 'New' Political History," *Journal of Contemporary History* 3 (January 1968): 5–27, and Robert P. Swierenga, "Computers and American History: The Impact of the 'New' Generation," *Journal of American History* 60 (March 1974): 1045–70.

The "new" political history was a product of the behavioralist revolution that swept political science in the 1950s. The work of V. O. Key, Jr., was especially influential. In his seminal essay, "A Theory of Critical Elections," *Journal of Politics* 17 (February 1955): 3–18, Key set historians and political scientists to thinking about the common problem of explaining the evolution of the American two-party system in the context of changing patterns of voting behavior. From the historical study of popular voting behavior emerged a sense of developmental unity. Charles G. Sellers, Jr., "The Equilibrium Cycle in Two-Party Politics," *Public Opinion Quarterly* 29 (Spring 1965): 16–37, and William Nisbet Chambers, "Party Development and the American Mainstream," in William Nisbet Chambers and Walter Dean Burnham, eds., *The American Party System: Stages of Political Development* (New York: Oxford University Press, 1967) persuasively argued that significant changes in the social bases and levels of voter participation and the character of party organization occurred during various eras of the two-party system.

The second party system has been the subject of intense inquiry and equally intense dispute. Richard P. McCormick, *The Second American Party System: Party Formation in the Jacksonian Era* (Chapel Hill: University of North Carolina Press, 1966), concluded the new party system of Whigs and Democrats was predicated on consensus and that it was inherently artificial; that is, it persisted only as long as it was able to ignore the reality of slavery. Parties were "electoral machines" that substituted hoopla and organization for ideological content. Attracting and holding voters was more important than settling the critical issues of the day. Herbert Ershkowitz and William G. Shade, "Consensus or Conflict? Political Behavior in the State Legislatures during the Jacksonian Era," *Journal of American History* 58 (December 1971): 591–621, concluded that on the state level a good deal of difference did separate Whigs and Democrats and that they took firm positions on a host of issues. The centrality of party to the new political culture was reinforced by Richard Hofstadter, *The Idea of a Party System: The Rise of Legitimate Opposition in the United States, 1780–1840* (Berkeley: University of California Press, 1970). Hofstadter joined with Nichols to demonstrate that the second party system was rooted in an acceptance of parties as legitimate institutions. Joel H.

Silbey, *The Shrine of Party: Congressional Voting Behavior, 1841–1852* (Pittsburgh: University of Pittsburgh Press, 1967), showed the tenacity of Democratic and Whig allegiances even in the midst of the sectional crisis over the Mexican War. However, David Potter, *The Impending Crisis, 1848–1861* (New York: Harper & Row, 1976), and Eric Foner, *Free Soil, Free Labor, Free Men: The Ideology of the Republican Party before the Civil War* (New York: Oxford University Press, 1970), argued that the powerful sectional and ideological pressures within the Whig and Democratic parties hastened the demise of the second party system. Potter convincingly demonstrates that slavery insinuated itself into the political debate and that the federal judiciary helped to sustain that process. While quantitative analysis of voting and legislative behavior have sharpened understanding of the ethnocultural and social bases of the second party system, Walter Dean Burnham, "Parties and the Ethno-Cultural Variable," *Historical Methods Newsletter* 3 (November 1971): 120–30, has suggested that more must be done to relate local and national political developments. Slavery and sectionalism are far from dead issues in the analysis of antebellum politics.

In two provocative essays, Ronald P. Formisano has questioned the periodization of the second party system and the inability of historians to explore new areas of research. In "Deferential-Participant Politics: The Early Republic's Political Culture, 1789–1840," *American Political Science Review* 68 (June 1974): 473–87, he argued that traditional forms of political behavior persisted well into Andrew Jackson's administration; the rise of the first mass two-party system can be better dated from 1840 than 1828. Formisano correctly questioned the attempt by many historians to dichotomize the antebellum political culture between traditional and modern. While subscribing to the utility of developmental themes for heuristic purposes, he has urged restraint in using modernization theory, exemplified in Richard D. Brown, *Modernization: The Transformation of American Life, 1600–1865* (New York: Hill and Wang, 1976), to explain rather than to illuminate historical change. In "Toward a Reorientation of Jacksonian Politics: A Review of the Literature, 1959–1975," *Journal of American History* 63 (June 1976): 42–65, Formisano insisted that scholars must deal more thoughtfully and systematically with a variety of political practices, including the distribution of patronage.

Historians of the era have devoted slight attention to distribution of the federal patronage. Carl Russell Fish, *The Civil Service and the Patronage* (New York: Longmans and Company, 1905), and Leonard D. White, *The Jacksonians: A Study in Administrative History, 1829–1861*

(New York: Macmillan Co., 1954) remain the classics. White viewed the patronage as an important political function, but, like Fish, he adopted a moralizing tone toward political officials who dispensed it. In the future, patronage studies must cast off the humbug of the "spoils system." Political scientist Frank J. Sorauf, in *Political Parties in the American System* (Boston: Little, Brown & Company, 1964), reminded scholars that the kind of rewards and incentives used and the way in which they are distributed offers insight into the fundamental character of a political culture. Further, Sorauf, "Patronage and Party," *Midwest Journal of Political Science* 3 (May 1959): 115–26, suggested that far from being static, simple, and inherently degrading, allocation of public offices involves the convergence of partisan, personal, and public interests in a rich and complex process.

Anthropologists have done the most provocative work on the social and political significance of patronage, most of it placed in the perspective of political and social development and modernization theory. The changing nature of patronage distribution in a developing nation was analyzed in Sydel Silverman, "Patronage and Community-Nation Relationships in Central Italy," *Ethnology* 4 (April 1965): 183–84. Eric R. Wolf, "Kinship, Friendship and Patron-Client Relations in Complex Societies," in Michael P. Banton, ed., *The Social Anthropology of Complex Societies* (New York: Frederick A. Praeger, 1966), emphasized the importance of informal personal connections in even highly differentiated institutions. Alex Weingrod, "Patrons, Patronage, and Political Parties," *Comparative Studies in Society and History* 10 (July 1968): 377–400, demonstrated that in a modernizing political order the impersonal ties of party replace informal, personal connections. The impact of family ties in ordering political life in a small Italian village is provocatively discussed in John K. Campbell, *Honour, Family and Patronage* (Oxford: Clarendon Press, 1964). The only notable attempt to examine the impact of kinship realtions on federal patronage decisions during even a part of the second party system is Sidney H. Aronson, *Status and Kinship in the Higher Civil Service: Standards of Selection in the Administrations of John Adams, Thomas Jefferson and Andrew Jackson* (Cambridge, Mass.: Harvard University Press, 1964). Leonard Tabachnik, "Political Patronage and Ethnic Groups: Foreign-born in the United States Customhouse Service, 1821–1861," in Robert P. Swierenga, ed., *Beyond the Civil War Synthesis: Political Essays of the Civil War Era* (Westport, Conn.: Greenwood Press, 1975), revealed the impact of ethnicity on the federal patronage.

While distribution of the federal patronage has received slight attention, the selection of lower federal court judges during the second party system has been totally ignored. Both David J. Rothman, "The Promise of American Legal History," *Reviews in American History* 2 (March 1974): 16–21, and J. Willard Hurst, *The Growth of American Law: The Law Makers* (Boston: Little, Brown & Co., 1950) have noted the relevance of the judicial selection process to an understanding of the social bases of American judging. However, Lawrence Friedman, *A History of American Law* (New York: Simon and Schuster, 1973), accepted the stereotypical view that appointment of judges involved little more than an exercise in crass political expediency.

While political, constitutional, and legal historians have neglected judicial selection, political scientists have fashioned a subdiscipline devoted to analyzing the backgrounds, selection, and behavior of judges. Jack W. Peltason, *Federal Courts in the Political Process* (New York: Random House, 1955), was among the first to emphasize the interconnectedness of the federal judiciary and the political culture and legal-constitutional order. This view has been reinforced by Sheldon Goldman and Thomas P. Jahnige, *The Federal Courts as a Political System* (New York: Harper and Row, 1971), and Richard J. Richardson and Kenneth N. Vines, *The Politics of Federal Courts* (Boston: Little, Brown & Company, 1970). Joel Grossman, *Lawyers and Judges: The ABA and the Politics of Judicial Selection* (New York: John Wiley and Sons, 1965), demonstrated that the constitutionally open selection process enabled the bar of the mid–twentieth century to influence the selection of federal district and appeals court judges. Harold Chase, *Federal Judges: The Appointing Process* (Minneapolis: University of Minnesota Press, 1972), illuminated the internal mechanics of the selection process from the Eisenhower through the Johnson administrations, but his discussion of the historical evolution of the selection process was predicated on little research in primary materials. Chase and other political scientists cited above have too willingly accepted the incorrect view propagated by Joseph P. Harris, *The Advice and Consent of the Senate* (Berkeley: University of California Press, 1953), that the practice of senatorial courtesy developed "about 1840." Indeed, while political scientists have shown that analysis of the twentieth-century judicial selection process can illuminate the contemporary political culture, they have all but ignored the nineteenth century. The best available treatment of the intention of the framers, which contradicts the generalizations made by Chase and others about senatorial courtesy, is John Ferling, "The Senate and Federal Judges: The Intent of the Founding Fathers," *Capitol Studies* 2 (Winter 1974): 57–70.

Both political scientist and historians have all but ignored the territorial judiciary. William W. Blume and Elizabeth G. Brown, "Territorial Courts and Law: Unifying Factors in the Development of American Legal Institutions," *Michigan Law Review* 61 (November 1962, January 1963): 39–106, 467–538, cogently analyzed the changing legal and constitutional bases of the territorial judiciary, but they did not address the issue of why or how judges were selected. John D. W. Guice, *The Rocky Mountain Bench: The Territorial Supreme Courts of Colorado, Montana, and Wyoming, 1861–1890* (New Haven: Yale University Press, 1972), argued that in the last half of the nineteenth century, crass political considerations alone did not dictate the composition of the territorial bench, although he did not specify what did. Robert Paul Fogerty, "An Institutional Study of the Courts of the Old Northwest, 1788–1848" (Ph.D. diss., University of Minnesota, 1942), provided the only analysis of the impact of the second party system on the selection of territorial judges.

II

1. MANUSCRIPT SOURCES

Government Manuscripts

National Archives, Washington, D.C.
    Record Group 46: Records of the United States Senate.
        Senate Nominations File.
    Record Group 59: Records of the Department of State.
        Acceptances and Orders for Commissions.
        Correspondence Registers, 1819–1839, 1840–1859, 1860–1862.
        Letters of Application and Recommendation During the Administration of Andrew Jackson. Microfilm Publication M-639.
        Letters of Application and Recommendation During the Administrations of Martin Van Buren, William Henry Harrison and John Tyler, 1837–1845. Microfilm Publication M-687.
        Letters of Application and Recommendation During the Administrations of James K. Polk, Zachary Taylor and Millard Fillmore, 1845–1853. Microfilm Publication M-873.
        Letters of Application and Recommendation During the Administrations of Franklin Pierce and James Buchanan, 1853–1861. Microfilm Publication M-967.
        Letters of Resignation and Declination.
        Miscellaneous Permanent and Temporary Commissions of Federal Judges.

Record Group 60: Records of the Department of Justice.
  Abstracts of Applicants and Endorsements for Judicial Office.
  Attorney General's Correspondence, Letters Received, 1816–1870.
  Attorney General's Correspondence, Letters Sent, 1816–1870.
  Records Relating to the Appointment of Federal Judges, District Attorneys and Marshals.
  Register of Applicants and Endorsements for Appointment as Judges, U. S. Attorneys and Marshals.
Record Group 233: Records of the United States House of Representatives.
  Impeachment Papers, House Committee on the Judiciary.

Personal Manuscripts

Alabama Department of History and Archives, Montgomery, Alabama
  Elmore Family Papers
Arkansas State History Commission, Little Rock, Arkansas
  Biographical Collection
Buffalo and Erie County Historical Society, Buffalo, New York
  Millard Fillmore Papers
Chicago Historical Society, Chicago, Illinois
  Edward D. Baker Papers
  David Davis Papers
Church of Jesus Christ of Latter-Day-Saints, Salt Lake City, Utah
  John M. Bernhisel Papers
  William H. Hooper Papers
  Journal History, 1849–1861
  Thomas L. Kane Papers
  Brigham Young Papers
Detroit Public Library, Burton Historical Collection, Detroit, Michigan
  John Allen Papers
  John P. Sheldon Papers
  Solomon Sibley Papers
  William Woodbridge Papers
Duke University, Perkins Library, Durham, North Carolina
  Bedford Brown Papers
  Campbell Family Papers
  Alfred Cumming Papers
  Edward Harden Papers
Historical Society of Pennsylvania, Philadelphia, Pennsylvania
  William Bigler Papers
  Horace Binney Papers
  James Buchanan Papers
  John C. Cadwalader Papers
  Lewis Coryell Papers
  Gilpin Family Papers
  Henry D. Gilpin Papers
  Simeon Gratz Collection

Josiah S. Johnston Papers
Thomas H. Montgomery Family Notes
Joel R. Poinsett Papers
W. W. Porter Collection
Huntington Library, San Marino, California
Abel Stearns Papers
Illinois State Library, Springfield, Illinois
Turney Family Papers
Indiana Historical Society Library, Indianapolis, Indiana
William H. English Collection
Library of Congress, Washington, D.C.
Jeremiah Sullivan Black Papers
John C. Breckenridge Papers
John M. Clayton Papers
Thomas Corwin Papers
John Jordan Crittenden Papers
Caleb Cushing Papers
Ewing Family Papers
Andrew Jackson Papers
Andrew Johnson Papers
John McLean Papers
William L. Marcy Papers
Franklin Pierce Papers
James K. Polk Papers
William C. Rives Papers
Benjamin Tappan Papers
Martin Van Buren Papers
Louisiana State University Library, Baton Rouge, Louisiana
William S. Hamilton Papers
Maryland Historical Society, Baltimore, Maryland
John W. Crisfield Papers
Oliver Papers
David M. Perine Correspondence
Randall Family Papers
Minnesota Historical Society, St. Paul, Minnesota
Alexander Ramsey Papers
Missouri Historical Society, St. Louis, Missouri
Mullanphy Family Papers
New Jersey Historical Society, Newark, New Jersey
Mahlon Dickerson Papers
Oregon Historical Society, Portland, Oregon
Matthew P. Deady Papers
Joseph Lane Papers
Tennessee State Library and Archives, Nashville, Tennessee
Joseph Greer Papers

Utah Historical Society, Salt Lake City, Utah
    John Bernhisel Papers
University of California, Berkeley, Bancroft Library, Berkeley, California
    William McKendree Gwin Papers
    James McHall Jones Papers
    Oregon Manuscripts
    John Wilson Papers
University of Chicago, Reginstein Library, Chicago, Illinois
    Stephen A. Douglas Papers
University of North Carolina, Southern Historical Collection, Chapel Hill,
    North Carolina
    Edward Dromgoole Papers
    James Hamilton Papers
    David Outlaw Papers
University of Rochester, Rush Rhees Library, Rochester, New York
    Thurlow Weed Papers
University of Texas Library, Austin, Texas
    Thomas J. Rusk Papers
University of West Virginia Library, Morgantown, West Virginia
    Pennypacker Family Papers
Yale University, Sterling Memorial Library, New Haven, Connecticut
    William H. Hooper Papers

2. Newspapers

Albany Argus. 1836.
Allegheny Democrat (Pittsburgh). 1832–33.
Arkansas Advocate (Little Rock). 1830–37.
Arkansas Gazette (Little Rock). 1830–37.
Bee (New Orleans). 1841.
Crescent City (New Orleans). 1841.
Davenport Gazette (Iowa). 1842–43.
Deseret News (Salt Lake City). 1851–60.
Detroit Free Press. 1829–32.
Detroit Gazette. 1828–32.
Detroit Journal and Michigan Advertiser. 1832.
Florida Herald (Tallahassee). 1832.
Globe (Washington, D.C.). 1829–33.
Harrisburgh Telegraph (Pennsylvania). 1843.
Indiana Democrat (Indianapolis). 1835.
Iowa Capital Reporter (Iowa City). 1842–43.
Iowa City Standard. 1842–43.
Journal (Portsmouth, N. H.). 1830.
Louisiana Sunday Review (New Orleans). 1894.
Minnesota Democrat (St. Paul). 1854.
Montgomery Daily Advertiser. 1859.

Morning Oregonian (Portland). 1853–58.
National Intelligencer (Washington, D.C.). 1855.
Nebraska News (Omaha). 1856.
New York Daily Advertiser. 1832.
New York Times. 1858–61.
Niles Register (Washington, D.C.). 1831–49.
North American (Philadelphia). 1842–58.
Ohio Sun (Columbus). 1834.
Pennsylvanian (Philadelphia). 1842.
Petersburgh Index (Virginia). 1844.
Philadelphia Evening Journal. 1858.
Pittsburgh Gazette. 1832–33, 1858.
Pittsburgh Morning Post. 1858.
Public Ledger (Philadelphia). 1842–58.
Republican (St. Louis). 1850–51.
Richmond Whig. 1844.
St. Anthony Express (Minneapolis). 1854.
True Democratic Banner (Morristown, N.J.). 1853.
United States' Telegraph (Washington, D.C.). 1829–32.
Western Herald and Steubenville Gazette (Ohio). 1833–34.

3. PERIODICALS

American Jurist and Law Magazine. Vols. 5–19. (1831–38).
DeBow's Review. Vols. 2–19. (1846–1855).
United States Monthly Law Magazine. Vol. 3 (1851).
Western Law Journal. Vols. 2–3. (1846–50).
Yale Literary Magazine. Vol. 10. (1844).

4. GOVERNMENT PUBLICATIONS

Carter, Clarence E., and Bloom, John Porter, comps. and eds. *The Territorial Papers of the United States.* 27 vols. to date. Washington, D.C.: Government Printing Office, 1949–[77].

Hall, Benjamin F., comp. *Official Opinions of the Attorney General of the United States.* 8 vols. Washington, D.C.: Robert Farnham, 1852–58.

Historical Statistics of the United States, Colonial Times to 1957. Washington, D.C.: Government Printing Office, 1961.

Ohio House of Representatives. *Reports.* 26th Gen. Assm., 1st sess.

Richardson, James D., comp. *A Compliation of the Messages and Papers of the Presidents, 1789–1897.* 10 vols. Washington, D.C.: Government Printing Office, 1907.

Richardson, William A. *History, Jurisdiction and Practice of the Court of Claims (United States).* Washington, D.C.: Government Printing Office, 1885.

U. S. Congress. *Congressional Globe.* 23rd Cong., 1st sess., to 36th Cong., 2nd sess.

U. S. Congress. House. *Documents.* 21st Cong., 1st sess., to 36th Cong., 2nd sess.

U. S. Congress. House. *Reports.* 21st Cong., 1st sess., to 36th Cong., 2nd sess.
U. S. Congress. Senate. *Documents.* 21st Cong., 1st sess., to 36th Cong., 2nd sess.
U. S. Congress. Senate. *Journal of the Executive Proceedings of the Senate of the United States.* Washington, D.C.: Duff Green & GPO, 1828–1861. Reprint, New York: Johnson Reprint Corporation, 1969.
U. S. *Statutes at Large.* Vols. 1-11.
U. S. Supreme Court. *Report.* Washington, 1828–61.

5. PUBLISHED PRIMARY SOURCE MATERIAL

Adams, John Quincy, *Memoirs of John Quincy Adams.* 12 vols. Edited by Charles Francis Adams. Philadelphia: J. B. Lippincott & Co., 1874–77.
American Almanac and Repository of Useful Knowledge for the Year 1831. 2 vols. Boston: Gray and Bowen, 1840.
Bassett, John S., and Jameson, J. Franklin, eds. *The Correspondence of Andrew Jackson.* 7 vols. Washington, D.C.: Carnegie Institution, 1926–35.
Benton, Thomas Hart. *The Thirty Years View.* 2 vols. New York: Appleton, 1854–56.
Biddle, Charles. *Autobiography of Charles Biddle, Vice-President of the Supreme Executive Council of Pennsylvania.* Philadelphia: E. Claxton and Co., 1883.
[Blake, I. George.] "Seeking a Federal Judgeship under Jackson" (Holman Correspondence). *Indiana Magazine of History* 35 (March 1939): 310–25.
Blount, Louis F. "A Brief Study of Thomas J. Rusk Based on his Letters to his Brother, David, 1835–1856." *Southwestern Historical Quarterly* 34 (January, April 1931): 181–202, 271–92.
Blume, William W., ed. *Transactions of the Supreme Court of the Territory of Michigan, 1825–1836.* 6 vols. Ann Arbor: University of Michigan Press, 1935–40.
Burnett, Peter H. *Recollections and Opinions of an Old Pioneer.* New York: D. Appleton and Co., 1880.
Coleman, Mrs. Chapman, ed. *The Life of John J. Crittenden with Selections from his Correspondence and Speeches.* 2 vols. Philadelphia: Lippincott, 1871.
Gulick, Charles A., and Allen, Winnie, eds. *The Papers of Mirabeau Buonaparte Lamar.* 7 vols. Austin: Library and Historical Commission, 1924.
"Historical Register of Kansas," *Kansas State Historical Scoiety Collections* 16 (1923–1925): 659–65.
Hopkins, James F., ed. *The Papers of Henry Clay.* 3 vols. Lexington: University of Kentucky Press, 1959–[1977].
Jameson, J. Franklin, ed. *The Correspondence of John C. Calhoun.* 2 vols. Washington, D.C.: Government Printing Office, 1900.
Johnson, Donald Bruce, and Porter, Kirk H., comps. *National Party Platforms, 1840–1972.* 5th ed. Urbana: University of Illinois Press, 1973.
Kent, Joseph. *Speech in Support of an Amendment to the Constitution.* Washington, D.C.: Duff Green, 1832.
Klein, Philip S., ed. "Memoirs of a Senator and Representative from Pennsylvania, Johnathan Roberts, 1771–1854." *Pennsylvania Magazine of History and*

Biography 61 (October 1937): 446–74; 62 (January, April, July, October 1938): 64–97, 213–48, 361–409, 502–51.

Leavitt, Humphrey H. *Autobiography of Humphrey Howe Leavitt.* New York: Macmillan Co., 1893.

Moore, John Bassett, ed. *The Works of James Buchanan.* 12 vols. Philadelphia: J. B. Lippincott & Co., 1908–11.

Palmer, Friend. *Early Days in Detroit: Papers Written by General Friend Palmer.* Detroit: Hunt & June, 1906.

Parks, Joseph H., ed. "Some Tennessee Letters, 1849 to 1864." *Tennessee Historical Quarterly* 4 (September 1945): 76–82.

Polk, James Knox *The Diary of James K. Polk.* 4 vols. Edited by Milo M. Quaife. Chicago: A. C. McClurg & Co., 1910.

Rerick, Rowland W. *Memoirs of Florida.* 2 vols. Atlanta: Southern Historical Association, 1902.

Tocqueville, Alexis de. *Democracy in America.* Translated by Henry Reeve. 2 vols. New York: A. S. Barnes & Co., 189[1].

Tribune Almanac and Political Register. New York: Tribune Publishing Co., 1854–61.

Trollope, Frances. *Domestic Manners of the Americans.* London: Whittaker, Treacher & Co., 1832.

Tuthill, Lillian C. *Success in Life. The Lawyer.* Cincinnati: Henry W. Derby, 1854.

Van Buren, Martin. *The Autobiography of Martin Van Buren.* 2 vols. Edited by John C. Fitzpatrick. Washington, D.C.: American Historical Association, 1920.

Williams, Amelia A., and Barker, Eugene C., eds. *The Writings of Sam Houston, 1813–1863.* 8 vols. Austin: University of Texas Press, 1943.

Wiltse, Charles M., ed. *The Papers of Daniel Webster.* Ann Arbor: University Microfilms, 1971.

Winkler, Ernest W., ed. *Platforms of Political Parties in Texas.* Austin: University of Texas Press, 1916.

6. Books

Abraham, Henry J. *Justices and Presidents: A Political History of Appointments to the Supreme Court.* New York: Oxford University Press, 1974.

Ambler, Charles. *Thomas Ritchie: A Study in Virginia Politics.* Richmond: Hastings Press, 1913.

Baker, Jean H. *The Politics of Continuity: Maryland Political Parties from 1858 to 1870.* Baltimore: Johns Hopkins University Press, 1973.

Bashful, Emmet W. *The Florida Supreme Court: A Study in Judicial Selection.* Tallahassee: University of Florida Press, 1958.

Bassett, John S. *The Life of Andrew Jackson.* 2 vols. New York: Macmillan Co., 1911.

Berthoff, Rowland. *An Unsettled People: Social Order and Disorder in American History.* New York: Harper & Row, 1971.

Blegen, Theodore C. *Minnesota: A History of the State.* Minneapolis: University of Minnesota Press, 1963.

Bloomfield, Maxwell. *American Lawyers in a Changing Society, 1776–1876.* Cambridge: Harvard University Press, 1976.

Bowers, Claude G. *Party Battles of the Jackson Period.* New York: Houghton Mifflin Co., 1922.

Brauer, Kinley J. *Cotton versus Conscience: Massachusetts Whig Politics and Southwestern Expansion, 1843–1848.* Lexington: University of Kentucky Press, 1967.

Brigance, William Norwood. *Jeremiah Sullivan Black: A Defender of the Constitution and the Ten Commandments.* Philadelphia: University of Pennsylvania Press, 1934.

Burns, James MacGregor. *The Deadlock of Democracy: Four Party Politics in America.* Englewood Cliffs N.J.: Prentice-Hall, 1963.

Calhoun, Daniel. *Professional Lives in America: Structure and Aspirations, 1750–1850.* Cambridge: Harvard University Press, 1965.

Campbell, Stanley W. *The Slave Catchers: Enforcement of the Fugitive Slave Law, 1850–1860.* New York: W. W. Norton & Co., Inc., 1970.

Capers, Gerald M. *John C. Calhoun—Opportunist: A Reappraisal.* Gainesville: University of Florida Press, 1960.

Chambers, William Nisbet, and Burnham, Walter Dean, eds. *The American Party System: Stages of Political Development.* New York: Oxford University Press, 1967.

Chourst, Anton-Herman. *The Rise of the Legal Profession in America.* 2 vols. Norman: University of Oklahoma Press, 1965.

Cole, Arthur C. *The Whig Party in the South.* Washington, D.C.: American Historical Association, 1913.

Corwin, Edward S. *The Constitution and What It Means Today.* 13th ed. Edited by Harold W. Chase and Craig R. Ducat. Princeton: Princeton University Press, 1973.

Cosgrave, George. *Early California Justice: The History of the United States District Court for the Southern District of California.* San Francisco: Grabhorn Press, 1948.

Crenson, Matthew. *The Federal Machine: Beginnings of Bureaucracy in Jacksonian America.* Baltimore: Johns Hopkins University Press, 1975.

Crippen, Lee F. *Simon Cameron, Antebellum Years.* Oxford, O.: Mississippi Valley Press, 1942.

Cummings, Homer, and McFarland, Carl. *Federal Justice.* New York: Macmillan Co., 1937.

Curtis, James C. *The Fox at Bay: Martin Van Buren and the Presidency, 1837–1841.* Lexington: University of Kentucky Press, 1970.

Dahrendorf, Ralph. *Class Conflict in Industrial Society.* New York: McGraw-Hill, 1959.

Dargo, George. *Jefferson's Louisiana: Politics and the Clash of Legal Traditions.* Cambridge: Harvard University Press, 1975.

Doherty, Herbert J., Jr. *Richard Keith Call: Southern Unionist.* Gainesville: University of Florida Press, 1961.

———. *The Whigs of Florida, 1845–1854.* Gainesville: University of Florida Press, 1959.

Doyle, Joseph B. *Twentieth Century History of Steubenville and Jefferson County, Ohio.* Chicago: Lewis Historical Publishing Co., 1910.

Dyer, Brainerd. *Zachary Taylor.* Baton Rouge: Louisiana State University Press, 1946.

Elkins, Stanley, and McKitrick, Eric, eds. *The Hofstadter Aegis: A Memorial.* New York: Alfred A. Knopf, 1974.

Ellison, William Henry. *A Self-Governing Dominion: California, 1848–1860.* Berkeley: University of California Press, 1950.

Esarey, Logan. *A History of Indiana.* 2 vols. 2nd ed. Indianapolis: W. K. Stewart Co., 1918.

Fish, Carl Russell. *Removals of Officials by the Presidents of the United States.* Washington, D.C.: American Historical Association, 1899.

Fish, Peter Graham. *The Politics of Federal Judicial Administration.* Princeton: Princeton University Press, 1973.

Formisano, Ronald P. *The Birth of Mass Political Parties: Michigan, 1827–1861.* Princeton: Princeton University Press, 1971.

Fossier, Albert E. *New Orleans: The Glamour Period 1800–1840.* New Orleans: Pelican Press, 1957.

Frank, John P. *Justice Daniel Dissenting: A Biography of Peter V. Daniel, 1784–1860.* Cambridge: Harvard University Press, 1964.

Frankfurter, Felix, and Landis, James M. *The Business of the Supreme Court: A Study in the Federal Judicial System.* New York: Macmillan Co., 1928.

Freehling, William W. *Prelude to Civil War: The Nullification Controversy in South Carolina, 1816–1836.* New York: Harper & Row, 1966.

Freund, Paul A., gen. ed. *The Oliver Wendell Holmes Devise History of the Supreme Court of the United States.* 11 vols. New York: Macmillan Co., 1970–. Vol. 1, *Antecedents and Beginnings to 1801*, by Julius Goebel, Jr., 1970. Vol. 5, *The Taney Period 1836–64*, by Carl B. Swisher, 1974.

Fuess, Claude. *Daniel Webster.* 2 vols. Boston: Little, Brown & Co., 1930.

Furniss, Norman F. *The Mormon Conflict, 1850–1859.* New Haven: Yale University Press, 1960.

Ganaway, Loomis Morton. *New Mexico and the Sectional Controversy, 1846–1861.* Albuquerque: University of New Mexico Press, 1944.

Haines, Charles G., and Sherwood, Foster F. *The American Supreme Court, 1835–1864.* Berkeley: University of California Press, 1959.

Hall, Claude H. *Abel Parker Upshur, Conservative Virginian, 1790–1844.* Madison: Wisconsin Historical Society, 1962.

Hallum, John. *Biographical and Political History of Arkansas.* 2 vols. Albany: Weed, Parsons and Co., 1887.

Hamilton, Holman. *Prologue to Conflict: The Crisis and Compromise of 1850.* Lexington: University of Kentucky Press, 1964.

———. *Zachary Taylor: Soldier in the White House.* 2 vols. Indianapolis: Bobbs-Merrill Co., 1951.

Harper, Clio. *Prominent Members of the Early Arkansas Bar.* Little Rock: Works Progress Administration, 1940.

Hawkins, Wallace. *The Case of John C. Watrous, United States Judge for Texas: A Political History of High Crimes and Misdemeanors.* Dallas: University Press of Dallas, 1950.

Haynes, Evan. *The Selection and Tenure of Judges.* Newark: National Conference of Judicial Councils, 1944.

Heiskell, Samuel G. *Andrew Jackson and Early Tennessee History.* 3 vols. Nashville: Ambrose Printing Co., 1920–21.

Henderickson, James E. *Joe Lane of Oregon: Machine Politics and the Sectional Crisis, 1849–1861.* New Haven: Yale University Press, 1967.

Henderson, Dwight. *Courts for a New Nation.* Washington, D.C.: Public Affairs Press, 1971.

Huntington, Samuel P. *Political Order in Changing Societies.* New Haven: Yale University Press, 1968.

Hyde, William, and Conrad, Howard L., eds. *Encyclopedia of the History of St. Louis.* 2 vols. New York: Southern History Co., 1899.

Jahnige, Thomas P. *The Federal Courts as a Political System.* New York: Harper & Row, 1971.

Johannsen, Robert W. *Stephen A. Douglas.* New York: Oxford University Press, 1973.

Keller, William F. *The Nation's Advocate: Henry Marie Brackenridge and Young America.* Pittsburgh: University of Pittsburgh Press, 1956.

Kirwan, Albert D. *John J. Crittenden: The Struggle for the Union.* Lexington: University of Kentucky Press, 1962.

Klein, Philip S. *Pennsylvania Politics, 1817–1832: A Game Without Rules.* Philadelphia: University of Pensylvania Press, 1940.

———. *President James Buchanan: A Biography.* University Park: State University of Pennsylvania Press, 1962.

Kurland, Phillip B., ed. *The Supreme Court Review: 1967.* Chicago: University of Chicago Press, 1967.

Lipset, Seymour Martin, and Solari, Aldo, eds. *Elites in Latin America.* New York: Oxford University Press, 1967.

McCormac, Eugene I. *James K. Polk: A Political Biography.* Berkeley: University of California Press, 1922.

McCormick, Richard P. *The Second American Party System: Party Formation in the Jacksonian Era.* Chapel Hill: University of North Carolina Press, 1966.

McCoy, Charles A. *Polk and the Presidency.* Austin: University of Texas Press, 1960.

Meyer, Leland W. *The Life and Times of Col. Richard M. Johnson of Kentucky.* New York: Columbia University Press, 1932.

Miles, Edwin. *Jacksonian Democracy in Mississippi.* Chapel Hill: University of North Carolina Press, 1960.

Monks, Leander J. *Courts and Lawyers of Indiana.* 3 vols. Indianapolis: Federal Publishing Co., 1916.

Morgan, Robert J. *A Whig Embattled: The Presidency under John Tyler.* Lincoln: University of Nebraska Press, 1954.

Mueller, Henry R. *The Whig Party in Pennsylvania.* New York: Longmans, Green & Co., 1922.

Nevins, Allan. *The Emergence of Lincoln.* Vol. 1. *Douglas, Buchanan and Party Chaos.* New York: Charles Scribner's Sons, 1950.

———. *Ordeal of the Union.* 2 vols. New York: Charles Scribner's Sons, 1947.

Newmyer, R. Kent. *The Supreme Court under Marshall and Taney.* New York: Thomas Y. Crowell Co., 1970.

Nichols, Roy F. *The Democratic Machine, 1850–1854.* New York: Macmillan Co., 1923.

———. *Franklin Pierce: Young Hickory of the Granite Hills.* Philadelphia: University of Pennsylvania Press, 1958.

Owen, Thomas M. *History of Alabama and Dictionary of Alabama Biography.* 4 vols. Chicago: S. J. Clarke Co., 1921.

Parks, Joseph H. *John Bell of Tennessee.* Baton Rouge: Louisiana State University Press, 1950.

Paul, James C. N. *Rift in the Democracy.* Philadelphia: University of Pennsylvania Press, 1951.

Pessen, Edward. *Jacksonian America: Society, Personality and Politics.* Homewood: Dorsey Press, 1969.

———. *Riches, Class and Power Before the Civil War.* Lexington: D. C. Heath & Co., 1973.

Poldervaart, Arrie W. *Black-Robed Justice: A History of the Administration of Justice in New Mexico from the American Occupation in 1846 until Statehood in 1912.* Sante Fe: Historical Society of New Mexico, 1948.

Rawley, James A. *Race and Politics: "Bleeding Kansas" and the Coming of the Civil War.* Philadelphia: J. B. Lippincott Co., 1969.

Rayback, Robert J. *Millard Fillmore: Biography of a President.* Buffalo: Henry Stewart, 1959.

Remini, Robert. *Martin Van Buren and the Making of the Democratic Party.* New York: Columbia University Press, 1959.

Schlesinger, Arthur M., Jr. *The Age of Jackson.* Boston: Little, Brown & Co., 1945.

Seager, Robert. *And Tyler Too: A Biography of John and Julia Gardiner Tyler.* New York: McGraw-Hill, 1963.

Sellers, Charles G., Jr. *James K. Polk, Continentalist: 1843–1846.* Princeton: Princeton University Press, 1957.

Simms, Henry H. *Life of Robert M. T. Hunter: A Study in Sectionalism and Secession.* Richmond: William Byrd Press, 1935.

———. *The Rise of the Whigs in Virginia, 1824–1840.* Richmond: William Byrd Press, 1929.

Smith, Alice. *James Duane Doty, Frontier Promoter.* Madison: Wisconsin Historical Society, 1954.

Smurr, John W. *Territorial Jurisprudence.* 2 vols. Ann Arbor: Xerox University Microfilms, 1971.

Snyder, Charles McCool. *The Jacksonian Heritage: Pennsylvania Politics, 1833–1848.* Harrisburgh: Pennsylvania Historical Society, 1954.

Soltow, Lee. *Men and Wealth in the United States, 1850–1870.* New Haven: Yale University Press, 1975.

———, ed. *Six Papers on the Size Distribution of Wealth and Income.* Athens: Ohio University Press, 1969.

Steele, Robert V. P. *Between Two Empires: The Life Story of California's First Senator, William McKendree Gwin.* Boston: Houghton Mifflin Co., 1969.

Streeter, Floyd B. *Political Parties in Michigan, 1837–1860.* Lansing: Michigan Historical Commission, 1918.

Thernstrom, Stephen. *Poverty and Progress: Social Mobility in a Nineteenth-Century City.* Cambridge: Harvard University Press, 1969.

Thompson, Arthur W. *Jacksonian Democracy on the Florida Frontier.* Gainesville: University of Florida Press, 1961.

Thornbrough, Emma Lou. *The Negro in Indiana.* Indianapolis: Bobbs-Merrill Co., 1957.

Train, Arthur. *Puritan's Progress.* New York: Charles Scribner's Sons, 1931.

Tyler, Lyon G. *Parties and Patronage in the United States.* New York: G. P. Putnam's Sons, 1891.

Van Deusen, Glyndon G. *The Jacksonian Era, 1828–1848.* New York: Harper & Row, 1959.

Victor, Frances F. *The River of the West.* San Francisco: R. J. Trumbull & Co., 1870.

Warren, Charles. *The Supreme Court in United States History.* 3 vols. Boston: Little, Brown & Co., 1923.

White, Leonard D. *The Jacksonians: A Study in Administrative History, 1829–1861.* New York: Macmillan Co., 1954.

White, Lonnie J. *Politics on the Southwestern Frontier: Arkansas Territory, 1819–1836.* Memphis State University Press, 1964.

Williams, David A. *David C. Broderick: A Political Portrait.* San Marino, Calif.: Huntington Library, 1969.

Wittke, Carl, ed. *The History of the State of Ohio.* 6 vols. Columbus: Ohio Historical Society, 1941. Vol. 3, *The Passing of the Frontier: 1825–1850,* by Francis P. Weisenburger. Vol. 4, *The Civil War Era, 1850–1873,* by Eugene H. Roseboom.

Woodford, Frank B. *Lewis Cass: Last Jacksonian.* New Brunswick: Rutgers University Press, 1950.

Woollen, William Wesley. *Biographical and Historical Sketches of Early Indiana.* Indianapolis: Hammond & Co., 1883.

Young, James Sterling. *The Washington Community, 1800–1828.* New York: Harcourt Brace Jovanovich, 1966.

7. ARTICLES

Barnard, Job. "Early Days of the Supreme Court of the District of Columbia." *Records of the Columbia Historical Society* 22 (1919):1–22.

Bestor, Arthur. "State Sovereignty and Slavery: A Reinterpretation of Pro-slavery Constitutional Doctrine, 1846–1860." *Journal of the Illinois State Historical Society* 54 (Summer 1961):117–80.

Blake, I. George. "Jesse Lynch Holman, Hoosier Pioneer." *Indiana Magazine of History* 39 (March 1943):22–51.

Bowers, Douglas. "Ideology and Political Parties in Maryland, 1851–1856." *Maryland Historical Magazine* 64 (Fall 1969):197–217.

Bradley, Marie M. "Political Beginnings in Oregon: The Period of Provisional Government, 1839–1849." *Quarterly of the Oregon Historical Society* 9 (March 1908): 48–72.

Braverman, Howard. "The Economic and Political Background of the Conservative Revolt in Virginia." *Virginia Magazine of History and Biography* 60 (April 1922):267–87.

Brown, Robert M. "A Territorial Delegate in Action." *Minnesota History* 31 (September 1950):172–78.

Campbell, Randolph. "The Whig Party of Texas in the Election of 1848 and 1852." *Southwestern Historical Quarterly* 73 (July 1969):17–34.

Cooper, J. Willie. "A History of Federal Judges in Mississippi." Federal Records Center. East Point, Georgia.

Cosgrave, George. "James McHall Jones." *California Historical Society Quarterly* 20 (January 1941):97–116.

Curry, Roy M. "James H. Seddon, A Southern Prototype." *Virginia Magazine of History and Biography* 63 (April 1955):126–50.

Davis, Charles B. "Judge James Hawkins Peck." *Missouri Historical Review* 27 (October 1932):3–20.

Doherty, Herbert J., Jr. "Political Factions in Territorial Florida." *Florida Historical Quarterly* 28 (October 1949):131–42.

Ellison, William H. "Memoirs of the Honorable William M. Gwin." *California Historical Society Quarterly* 19 (March, June, September 1940):1–26, 157–84, 256–78.

Eriksson, Erik McKinley. "The Federal Civil Service under President Jackson." *Mississippi Valley Historical Review* 12 (March 1927):517–40.

Fabricant, Solomon. "The Changing Industrial Distribution of Gainful Workers: Comments on the Decennial Censuses, 1820–1840," *Studies in Income and Wealth* 11 (1949):1–35.

Farris, Charles D. "The Courts of Territorial Florida." *Florida Historical Quarterly* 19 (April 1941):346–67.

Folsom, Burton W. "The Collective Biography as a Research Tool." *Mid-America* 54 (October 1972):108–20.

Formisano, Ronald P. "Political Character, Antipartyism and the Second Party System." *American Quarterly* 21 (Winter 1969):683–709.

Fowler, Dorothy. "Congressional Dictation of Local Appointments." *Journal of Politics* 7 (February 1945):25–41.

Freehling, William W. "Spoilsmen and Interests in the Thought and Career of John C. Calhoun." *Journal of American History* 52 (June 1965):25–42.

Gates, Paul Wallace. "A Fragment of Kansas Land History: The Disposal of the Christian Indian Tract." *Kansas Historical Quarterly* 6 (August 1937):230–37.

Goff, John S. "The Last Leaf: George Mortimer Bibb." *Register of the Kentucky Historical Society* 59 (October 1961):331–42.

Goldman, Sheldon. "Characteristics of Eisenhower and Kentucky Appointees to the Lower Federal Courts." *Western Political Quarterly* 18 (December 1965):755–62.

———. "Johnson and Nixon Appointees to the Lower Federal Courts: Some Socio-Political Perspectives." *Journal of Politics* 34 (August 1972):434–42.

———. "Judicial Backgrounds, Recruitment, and the Party Variable: The Case of the Johnson and Nixon Appointees to the United States District and Appeals Courts." *Arizona State Law Review* (1974):211–22.

Graebner, Norman A. "James K. Polk: A Study in Federal Patronage." *Mississippi Valley Historical Review* 30 (March 1952):613–32.

Gruss, Louis. "Judah Philip Benjamin." *Louisiana Historical Quarterly* 19 (October 1936):970–80.

Hall, Kermit L. "Proslavery Constitutional Theory and Federal Judicial Reform: A Retrospect on the Butler Bill." *American Journal of Legal History* 17 (April 1973):166–84.

———. "240 Men: The Antebellum Lower Federal Judiciary, 1829–1861." *Vanderbilt Law Review* 29 (Ocober 1976):1089–1129.

Hamilton, Holman. "Zachary Taylor and Minnesota." *Minnesota History* 30 (June 1949):97–110.

Hansen, William A. "Thomas Hart Benton and the Oregon Question." *Missouri Historical Review* 63 (July 1969):489–97.

Harrison, Joseph H., Jr. "Martin Van Buren and His Southern Supporters." *Journal of Southern History* 22 (November 1956):438–58.

———. "Oligarchs and Democrats—The Richmond Junto." *Virginia Magazine of History and Biography* 78 (April 1970):184–98.

Johannsen, Robert W. "The Lecompton Constitutional Convention: An Analysis of Its Membership." *Kansas Historical Quarterly* 28 (Autumn 1957):225–43.

Jones, Alice Hansen. "Wealth Estimates for the American Middle Colonies, 1774." *Economic Development and Cultural Change* 18 (1970):1–172.

Jordan, Philip D. "The U. S. Marshal on Iowa's Frontier." *Palimpsest* 54 (March–April 1973):2–17.

Jorstad, Erling. "Minnesota's Role in the Democratic Rift of 1860." *Minnesota History* 37 (June 1960):45–51.

———. "Personal Politics in the Origin of Minnesota's Democratic Party." *Minnesota History* 36 (September 1959):259–71.

Kendall, John Smith. "The Chronicles of a Southern Family." *Louisiana Historical Quarterly* 29 (April 1946):277–95.

Lecompte, Samuel D. "A Defense by Samuel D. Lecompte." *Kansas State Historical Society Collections* 8 (1903–1904):384–405.

Leonard, Adam A. "Personal Politics in Indiana." *Indiana Magazine of History* 14 (March, June, September 1923):1–56, 132–68, 241–81.

Lillard, T. M. "Beginnings of the Kansas Judiciary." *Kansas Historical Quarterly* 5 (February 1941):91–95.

Longaker, Richard P. "Andrew Jackson and the Judiciary." *Political Science Quarterly* 71 (September 1956):341–64.

Lythgoe, Dennis L. "Negro Slavery in Utah." *Utah Historical Quarterly* 39 (Winter 1971):48–59.

McCormick, Richard P. "New Perspectives on Jacksonian Politics." *American Historical Review* 65 (January 1960):288–301.

———. "Party Formation in New Jersey in the Jacksonian Era." *Proceedings of the New Jersey Historical Society* 83 (July 1965):161–73.

McLaughlin, William M. "Judge Joseph Williams." *Annals of Iowa* 25 (October 1943):87–98.

Mahan, Bruce E. "Judge Joseph Williams." *Palimpsest* 5 (March 1924):85–101.

Marshall, Lynn L. "The Strange Stillbirth of the Whig Party." *American Historical Review* 72 (January 1967):445–68.

Martin, John. "Biographical Sketch of Judge Rush Elmore." *Kansas State Historical Society Collections* 8 (1903–1904):435–36.

Mendelson, Wallace. "Dred Scott's Case—Reconsidered." *Minneota Law Review* 38 (December 1953):16–28.

Mintz, Max. "The Political Ideas of Martin Van Buren." *New York History* 30 (December 1949):422–48.

Mott, Rodney L.; Albright, Spencer D.; and Semmerling, Helen R. "Judicial Personnel." *Annals of the American Academy of Political and Social Science* 167 (May 1933):143–55.

Nash, Gary B. "The Philadelphia Bench and Bar, 1800–1861." *Comparative Studies in Society and History* 7 (January 1965):203–20.

Nettels, Curtis P. "The Mississippi Valley and the Federal Judiciary, 1807–1837." *Mississippi Valley Historical Review* 12 (September 1925):202–26.

Newmyer, R. Kent. "Justice Joseph Story on Circuit and a Neglected Phase of American Legal History." *American Journal of Legal History* 14 (April 1970):112–35.

Parvin, T. S. "Hon. Joseph Williams." *Iowa Historical Record* 12 (January 1896):387–92.

Pelzer, Louis. "The History and Principles of the Democratic Party of the Territory of Iowa." *Iowa Journal of History and Politics* 6 (January 1908):3–54.

———. "The History and Principles of the Whigs of the Territory of Iowa." *Iowa Journal of History and Politics* 5 (January 1907):46–90.

Pomeroy, Earl. "California, 1846–1860: Politics of a Representative Frontier State." *California Historical Society Quarterly* 32 (December 1953):291–302.

Rosenberg, Maurice. "The Qualities of Justice—Are They Strainable?" *Texas Law Review* 44 (June 1966):1063–80.

Schmidt, Louis B. "The Miller-Thompson Election Contest." *Iowa Journal of History and Politics* 12 (January 1914):34–127.

Sellers, Charles G., Jr. "Andrew Jackson versus the Historians." *Mississippi Valley Historical Review* 44 (March 1958):615–34.

———. "Who Were the Southern Whigs?" *American Historical Review* 69 (January 1954):335–46.

Shapiro, Samuel. "The Rendition of Anthony Burns." *Journal of Negro History* 44 (June 1959):34–51.

Stone, Lawrence. "Prosopography." *Daedalus* 100 (Winter 1971):46–79.

Surrency, Erwin C. "A History of Federal Courts." *Missouri Law Review* 28 (1963):214–44.

Swisher, Jacob A. "The Judiciary of the Territory of Iowa." *Iowa Journal of History and Politics* 20 (April 1922):224–75.

Teiser, Sidney. "First Associate Justice of Oregon Territory: O. C. Pratt." *Oregon Historical Quarterly* 49 (September 1948):171–91.

———. "The First Chief Justice of Oregon Territory: William P. Bryant." *Oregon Historical Quarterly* 48 (June 1947):45–53.

———. "Obadiah B. McFadden, Oregon and Washington Territorial Judge." *Oregon Historical Quarterly* 66 (March 1965):25–37.

———. "A Pioneer Judge of Oregon: Matthew P. Deady." *Oregon Historical Quarterly* 44 (March 1943):61–81.

———. "The Second Chief Justice of Oregon Territory: Thomas Nelson." *Oregon Historical Quarterly* 48 (September 1947):214–24.

Thompson, Arthur W. "The Railroad Background of the Florida Senatorial Election of 1851." *Florida Historical Quarterly* 31 (January 1953):181–95.

Tobie, H. E. "Joseph L. Meek, A Conspicuous Personality." *Oregon Historical Quarterly* 39 (1938):123–46, 286–306, 410–24.

Van Bolt, Roger H. "The Hoosier Politician of the 1840s." *Indiana Magazine of History* 48 (March 1952):26–31.

———. "Some Sectional Aspects of Expansion, 1844–1848." *Indiana Magazine of History* 48 (June 1952):23–36.

Walton, Brian G. "The Second Party System in Arkansas." *Arkansas Historical Quarterly* 28 (Summer 1969):120–55.

Warren, Charles. "New Light on the History of the Judiciary Act of 1789." *Harvard Law Review* 37 (November 1923):49–132.

Westoff, Charles F.; Bressler, Marvin; and Sagi, Philip C. "The Concept of Social Mobility: An Empirical Inquiry." *American Sociological Review* 25 (June 1960):375–85.

Whelpton, P. K. "Occupational Groups in the United States, 1820–1920." *Journal of the American Statistical Association* 21 (September 1926):328–42.

Wimmer, Larry, and Pope, Clane L. "The Genealogical Society Library of Salt Lake City: A Source of Data for Economic and Social Historians." *Historical Methods Newsletter* 8 (April 1975):51–59.

Woodward, W. C. "The Rise and Early History of Political Parties in Oregon." *Quarterly of the Oregon Historical Society* 11 (December 1910):323–54; 12 (March, June, September, December 1911):33–86, 123–63, 125–63, 301–50.

8. DISSERTATIONS

Barrett, Gwyn W. "John M. Bernhisel." Ph.D. dissertation, Brigham Young University, 1968.

Beckwith, Robert R. "Mahlon Dickerson of New Jersey." Ph.D. dissertation, Columbia University, 1964.

Bergeron, Paul H. "The Jacksonian Party on Trial: Presidential Politics in Tennessee, 1836–1856." Ph.D. dissertation, Vanderbilt University, 1965.

Gawalt, Gerard W. "Massachusetts Lawyers: A Historical Analysis of the Process of Professionalization, 1760–1840." Ph.D. dissertation, Clark University, 1969.

Goldman, Sheldon. "Politics, Judges and the Administration of Justice." Ph.D. disseration, Harvard University, 1965.

Hall, Kermit L. "The Taney Court in the Second Party System: The Congressional Response to Federal Judicial Reform." Ph.D. dissertation, University of Minnesota, 1972.

Meerse, David. "James Buchanan, the Patronage and the Northern Democratic Party, 1857–1858." Ph.D. dissertation, University of Illinois, 1969.

Tachau, Mary K. B. "The Federal Courts in Kentucky, 1789–1816." Ph.D. dissertation, University of Kentucky, 1972.

Tregle, Joseph G. "Louisiana in the Age of Jackson: A Study in Ego Politics." Ph.D. dissertation, University of Pennsylvania, 1954.

Voight, Robert C. "Defender of the Common Law: Aaron Goodrich, Chief Justice of Minnesota Territory." Ph.D. dissertation, University of Minnesota, 1962.

INDEX